3000 Plus Beautiful Bible Verses and Amazing Christian Quotes

70 Interactive Categories

Living Life Set Free Publishing

All contents copyright C 2012 by Burton Rager and Living Life Set Free. All rights reserved. No part of this document or the related files may be reproduced or transmitted in any form, by any means (electronic, photocopying, recording, or otherwise) without the prior written permission of the publisher.

English Standard Version (ESV)
"Scripture quotations are from The Holy Bible, English Standard Version® (ESV®), copyright © 2001 by Crossway, a publishing ministry of Good News Publishers. Used by permission. All rights reserved."

New International Version (NIV)
THE HOLY BIBLE, NEW INTERNATIONAL VERSION®, NIV® Copyright © 1973, 1978, 1984, 2011 by Biblica, Inc.™ Used by permission. All rights reserved worldwide.

New American Standard (NASB)
"Scripture taken from the NEW AMERICAN STANDARD BIBLE®, Copyright © 1960,1962,1963,1968,1971,1972,1973,1975,1977,1995 by The Lockman Foundation. Used by permission."

King James Version (KJV) Public domain

New Living Translation (NLT)
Scripture quotations marked (NLT) are taken from the Holy Bible, New Living Translation, copyright © 1996, 2004, 2007 by Tyndale House Foundation. Used by permission of Tyndale House Publishers, Inc., Carol Stream, Illinois 60188. All rights reserved.

Printed in United States of America

ISBN-13: 978-1483944449

Bible Verses and Quotes by Category

Addiction....1
Adultery....7
Adversity....13
Anger....19
Anxiety....25
Bad Day....31
Bereavement....35
Blessings....39
Brokenhearted....45
Cancer....49
Change....55
Children....61
Comfort....67
Couples....73
Courage....79
Death....85
Depression....93
Divorce....99
Doubt....105
Encouragement....111
Enemies....115
Faith....121
Fathers....127
Fear....133
Forgiveness....139
Friendship....145
Funerals....151
Generosity....157
Gentleness....161
Gossip....165
Grief....171
Guidance....177
Hard Times....181
Healing....187

Hope....191
Humility....197
Inspirational....203
Integrity....209
Jealousy....215
Joy....221
Judgment....227
Knowledge....235
Life....239
Love....245
Lying....251
Marriage....257
Obedience....265
Pain....271
Parents....275
Patience....281
Peace....287
Perseverance....293
Power of Prayer....299
Pride....303
Prayer...309
Promises of God....315
Respect....319
Rest....325
Serving....331
Sick....337
Sin....343
Strength....347
Stress....353
Temptation....359
Trials....365
Truth....373
Trust....379
Wisdom....385
Women....391
Worry....397

Addiction

Addiction - Bible Verses

1 Corinthians 6:18 NASB
Flee immorality. Every other sin that a man commits is outside the body, but the immoral man sins against his own body.

1 Peter 2:11 ESV
Beloved, I urge you as sojourners and exiles to abstain from the passions of the flesh, which wage war against your soul.

Galatians 5:19-21 ESV
Now the works of the flesh are evident: sexual immorality, impurity, sensuality, idolatry, sorcery, enmity, strife, jealousy, fits of anger, rivalries, dissensions, divisions, envy, drunkenness, orgies, and things like these. I warn you, as I warned you before, that those who do such things will not inherit the kingdom of God.

Isaiah 5:11 NASB
Woe to those who rise early in the morning that they may pursue strong drink. Who stay up late in the evening that wine may inflame them!

Proverbs 20:1 KJV
Wine is a mocker, strong drink is raging: and whosoever is deceived thereby is not wise.

Proverbs 6:27-29 ESV
Can a man carry fire next to his chest and his clothes not be burned? Or can one walk on hot coals and his feet not be scorched? So is he who goes in to his neighbor's wife; none who touches her will go unpunished.

1 John 3:8 ESV
Whoever makes a practice of sinning is of the devil, for the devil has been sinning from the beginning. The reason the Son of God appeared was to destroy the works of the devil.

1 John 2:16 ESV
For all that is in the world—the desires of the flesh and the desires of the eyes and pride in possessions—is not from the Father but is from the world.

1 Corinthians 10:13 NASB
No temptation has overtaken you but such as is common to man; and God is faithful, who will not allow you to be tempted beyond what you are able, but with the temptation will provide the way of escape also, so that you will be able to endure it.

2 Corinthians 5:17 NASB
Therefore if anyone is in Christ, he is a new creature; the old things passed away; behold, new things have come.

1 Peter 5:8 NASB
Be sober-minded; be watchful. Your adversary the devil prowls around like a roaring lion, seeking someone to devour.

Philippians 4:4-7 ESV
Rejoice in the Lord always; again I will say, Rejoice. Let your reasonableness be known to everyone. The Lord is at hand; do not be anxious about anything, but in everything by prayer and supplication with thanksgiving let your requests be made known to God. And the peace of God, which surpasses all understanding, will guard your hearts and your minds in Christ Jesus.

Matthew 6:13 KJV
And lead us not into temptation, but deliver us from evil: For thine is the kingdom, and the power, and the glory, for ever. Amen.

John 8:36 NASB
So if the Son makes you free, you will be free indeed.

Romans 6:16 KJV
Know ye not, that to whom ye yield yourselves servants to obey, his servants ye are to whom ye obey; whether of sin unto death, or of obedience unto righteousness?

Romans 8:5-6 NIV
Those who live according to the flesh have their minds set on what the flesh desires; but those who live in accordance with the Spirit have their minds set on what the Spirit desires. The mind governed by the flesh is death, but the mind governed by the Spirit is life and peace.

1 Peter 5:10 NIV
And the God of all grace, who called you to his eternal glory in Christ, after you have suffered a little while, will himself restore you and make you strong, firm and steadfast.

Ephesians 5:18-20 NIV
Do not get drunk on wine, which leads to debauchery. Instead, be filled with the Spirit, speaking to one another with psalms, hymns, and songs from the Spirit. Sing and make music from your heart to the Lord, always giving thanks to God the Father for everything, in the name of our Lord Jesus Christ.

Titus 2:12 NIV
It teaches us to say "No" to ungodliness and worldly passions, and to live self-controlled, upright and godly lives in this present age,

James 1:12-15 KJV
Blessed is the man that endureth temptation: for when he is tried, he shall receive the crown of life, which the Lord hath promised to them that love him. Let no man say when he is tempted, I am tempted of God: for God cannot be tempted with evil, neither tempteth he any man: But every man is tempted, when he is drawn away of his own lust, and enticed. Then when

lust hath conceived, it bringeth forth sin: and sin, when it is finished, bringeth forth death.

James 4:7 KJV
Submit yourselves therefore to God. Resist the devil, and he will flee from you.

Colossians 3:5 KJV
Put to death, therefore, whatever belongs to your earthly nature: sexual immorality, impurity, lust, evil desires and greed, which is idolatry.

Galatians 5:24-25 ESV
And those who belong to Christ Jesus have crucified the flesh with its passions and desires. If we live by the Spirit, let us also walk by the Spirit.

Excellent site for additional Bible translations:
http://www.biblegateway.com/resources/commentaries/

Excellent resource for additional Bible study:
(Be sure to read the instructions on their page)
http://www.blueletterbible.org/commentaries/

Addiction - Christian Quotes

"I am not bound to win, but I am bound to be true. I am not bound to succeed, but I am bound to live up to what light I have."
Abraham Lincoln

"Affliction is one of God's medicines! By it He often teaches lessons which would be learned in no other way. By it He often draws souls away from sin and the world, which would otherwise have perished everlastingly. Health is a great blessing but sanctified disease is a greater. Prosperity and worldly comfort, are what all naturally desire, but losses and crosses are far better for us if they lead us to Christ. Let us beware of murmuring in the time of trouble. Let us settle it firmly in our minds, that there is a meaning, a "needs be", and a message from God in every sorrow that falls upon us. There are no lessons so useful as those learned in the school of affliction. There is no commentary that opens up the Bible so much as sickness and sorrow. The resurrection morning will prove, that many of the losses of God's people were in reality, eternal gains. Thousands at the last day will testify with David, "It is good for me that I have been afflicted" (Psalm. 119:71)!"
J.C. Ryle

If we allow the Bible to reveal the unseen spiritual realities behind addictions, we suddenly realize that addictions are more than self-destructive behaviors. They are violations of God's laws: His laws that call us to avoid drunkenness and immoderate self-indulgence (Rom. 13:13), His law that calls us to love others (1 John 4:7), and His law that calls us to live for Him rather than ourselves (1
. 10:31). This means that addiction is more about someone's relationship with God than it is about biology. It reveals our allegiances: what we want, what we love, whom and what we serve. It brings us to that all-important question, "Will you live for the fulfillment of your desires or for God?
Edward T. Welch
Blame in on the Brain? P&R Publishing, 1998, p. 193.

This [boredom] is why people are so prone to an addictive lifestyle. Many people who fall into sinful addictions are people who were once terminally

bored. The reason why addictions are so powerful is that they tap into that place in our hearts that was made for transcendent communion and spiritual romance. These addictive habits either dull and deaden our yearnings for a satisfaction we fear we'll never find or they provide an alternative counterfeit fulfillment that we think will bring long-term happiness, counterfeits like cocaine, overeating, illicit affairs, busyness, efficiency, image, or obsession with physical beauty. They all find their power in the inescapable yearning of the human heart to be fascinated and pleased and enthralled. Our hearts will invariably lead us either to the fleeting pleasures of addiction or to God.
Sam Storms
The Life-Changing Power of Knowing God by Sam Storms, p. 51.

The Bible has a different view of how we first get involved in addictions. Instead of explaining the overpowering urge for [something] as a disease, the Bible talks about our motivations and desires, forces so powerful that they can take over our lives. The Bible says that we first choose our addictions, and only then do our addictions choose us.
Edward T. Welch
Blame in on the Brain? P&R Publishing, 1998, p. 191.

Adultery

Adultery - Bible Verses

Matthew 5:28 ESV
But I say to you that everyone who looks at a woman with lustful intent has already committed adultery with her in his heart.

Proverbs 6:32 NASB
The one who commits adultery with a woman is lacking sense;
He who would destroy himself does it.

Hebrews 13:4 ESV
Let marriage be held in honor among all, and let the marriage bed be undefiled, for God will judge the sexually immoral and adulterous.

1 Corinthians 6:18 ESV
Flee from sexual immorality. Every other sin a person commits is outside the body, but the sexually immoral person sins against his own body.

Matthew 19:9 NIC
I tell you that anyone who divorces his wife, except for sexual immorality, and marries another woman commits adultery."

1 Corinthians 10:8 ESV
We must not indulge in sexual immorality as some of them did, and twenty-three thousand fell in a single day.

Luke 16:18 ESV
"Everyone who divorces his wife and marries another commits adultery, and he who marries a woman divorced from her husband commits adultery.

Proverbs 6:24-29 NLT

It will keep you from the immoral woman,
   from the smooth tongue of a promiscuous woman.
Don't lust for her beauty.
   Don't let her coy glances seduce you.
For a prostitute will bring you to poverty,
   but sleeping with another man's wife will cost you your life.
Can a man scoop a flame into his lap
   and not have his clothes catch on fire?
Can he walk on hot coals
   and not blister his feet?
So it is with the man who sleeps with another man's wife.
   He who embraces her will not go unpunished.

Deuteronomy 22:22 ESV
"If a man is found lying with the wife of another man, both of them shall die, the man who lay with the woman, and the woman. So you shall purge the evil from Israel.

Exodus 20:14 ESV
"You shall not commit adultery.

Matthew 5:32 ESV
But I say to you that everyone who divorces his wife, except on the ground of sexual immorality, makes her commit adultery, and whoever marries a divorced woman commits adultery.

Revelation 21:8 ESV
But as for the cowardly, the faithless, the detestable, as for murderers, the sexually immoral, sorcerers, idolaters, and all liars, their portion will be in the lake that burns with fire and sulfur, which is the second death."

1 Corinthians 10:13 ESV
No temptation has overtaken you that is not common to man. God is faithful, and he will not let you be tempted beyond your ability, but with the temptation he will also provide the way of escape, that you may be able to endure it.

John 8:4-11 ESV
They said to him, "Teacher, this woman has been caught in the act of adultery. Now in the Law Moses commanded us to stone such women. So what do you say?" This they said to test him, that they might have some charge to bring against him. Jesus bent down and wrote with his finger on the ground. And as they continued to ask him, he stood up and said to them, "Let him who is without sin among you be the first to throw a stone at her." And once more he bent down and wrote on the ground. ...

Revelation 2:20-22 NASB
But I have this against you, that you tolerate the woman Jezebel, who calls herself a prophetess, and she teaches and leads My bond-servants astray so that they commit acts of immorality and eat things sacrificed to idols. 21 I gave her time to repent, and she does not want to repent of her immorality. 22 Behold, I will throw her on a bed of sickness, and those who commit adultery with her into great tribulation, unless they repent of her deeds.

Matthew 5:27-28 NIC
"You have heard that it was said, 'You shall not commit adultery.' 28 But I tell you that anyone who looks at a woman lustfully has already committed adultery with her in his heart.

Romans 7:3 ESV
Accordingly, she will be called an adulteress if she lives with another man while her husband is alive. But if her husband dies, she is free from that law, and if she marries another man she is not an adulteress.

Ephesians 5:5 ESV
For you may be sure of this, that everyone who is sexually immoral or impure, or who is covetous (that is, an idolater), has no inheritance in the kingdom of Christ and God.

Proverbs 23:27 ESV
For a prostitute is a deep pit; an adulteress is a narrow well.

1 Corinthians 6:15-18 NLT

Don't you realize that your bodies are actually parts of Christ? Should a man take his body, which is part of Christ, and join it to a prostitute? Never! And don't you realize that if a man joins himself to a prostitute, he becomes one body with her? For the Scriptures say, "The two are united into one." But the person who is joined to the Lord is one spirit with him.
Run from sexual sin! No other sin so clearly affects the body as this one does. For sexual immorality is a sin against your own body.

Excellent site for additional Bible translations:
http://www.biblegateway.com/resources/commentaries/
Excellent resource for additional Bible study:
(Be sure to read the instructions on their page)
http://www.blueletterbible.org/commentaries/

Adultery - Christian Quotes

Even adultery is not the unforgiveable sin. It is a terrible sin, but God forbid that there should be anyone who feels that he or she has sinned himself or herself outside the love of God or outside His kingdom because of adultery. No; if you truly repent and realize the enormity of your sin and cast yourself upon the boundless love and mercy and grace of God, you can be forgiven and I assure you of pardon. But hear the words of our blessed Lord: "Go and sin no more."
Martyn Lloyd-Jones
Studies in the Sermon on the Mount, 1959, p. 261,

In its most technical sense, committing adultery refers to sexual intercourse between a man and woman when one or both of them is married.
John MacArthur

Recently Leadership Magazine commissioned a poll of a thousand pastors. The pastors indicated that 12 percent of them had committed adultery while in ministry – one out of eight pastors! – and 23 percent had done something they considered sexually inappropriate. Christianity Today surveyed a thousand of its subscribers who were not pastors and found the figure to be nearly double, with 23 percent saying they had had extramarital intercourse and 45 percent indicating they had done something they themselves deemed sexually inappropriate. One in four Christian men are unfaithful, and nearly one half have behaved unbecomingly! Shocking statistics! Especially when we remember that Christianity Today readers tend to be college-educated church leaders, elders, deacons, Sunday school superintendents, and teachers. If this is so for the Church's leadership, how much more for the average member of the congregation? Only God knows!
R. Kent Hughes
Disciplines of a Godly Man, Crossway Books, 1991, p. 21-22.

Adultery is an obvious violation of the rights of another. You are stealing what doesn't belong to you.
Sam Storms
Pleasures Evermore: The Life-Changing Power of Knowing God by Sam Storms, © 2000, p. 231.

The monstrosity of sexual intercourse outside marriage is that those who indulge in it are trying to isolate one kind of union (the sexual) from all others kinds of union which were intended to go along with it and make up the total union [of marriage].
C.S. Lewis

You must completely end the adulterous affair. This other person must be plainly told that the relationship is over. If possible, ask for forgiveness (preferably on a conference call with your spouse or pastor on the line) for your selfishness and deceit. There can be no continuing communication (no secret rendezvous, telephone calls, cards, letters, or e-mails). The other person should be emphatically told not to contact you anymore. You must be willing to amputate from your life anything that will tempt you to reopen this [relationship]... Don't keep any mementos, photographs, keepsakes, or other memorabilia that might tempt you to spend time thinking about (and fueling romantic feelings for) the other person. You may have to change your telephone number, your e-mail address, or the route you take to and from the office... [Now you will have to take the] money, time, thoughts, dreams, affection, initiative, and creative energies [that you spent on] the other person...[and reinvest them] with your spouse.
Lou Priolo
Divorce: Before You Say "I Don't," 2007, P&R, p. 29-30.

It is a morbid and depressing fact that when it comes to adultery, there are too many casualties among pastors. Ministers are just as vulnerable as others. No area, no country, no denomination is immune. The damage done in each case is irreparable: the breakdown, as far as ministry is concerned, final. This is a distasteful subject, but we cannot shirk it. The matter demands faithful treatment. Let him who thinks that he stands take heed lest he fall.
Erroll Hulse
The Preacher and Preaching, ed. Samuel Logan, p. 75-76.

Adversity

Adversity - Bible Verses

Psalm 91:1-2 NASB
He who dwells in the shelter of the Most High will abide in the shadow of the Almighty. I will say to the LORD, "My refuge and my fortress, my God, in whom I trust."

Proverbs 3:5-6 ESV
Trust in the LORD with all your heart, and do not lean on your own understanding. In all your ways acknowledge him, and he will make straight your paths.

Romans 8:38-39 NLT
And I am convinced that nothing can ever separate us from God's love. Neither death nor life, neither angels nor demons, neither our fears for today nor our worries about tomorrow—not even the powers of hell can separate us from God's love. No power in the sky above or in the earth below —indeed, nothing in all creation will ever be able to separate us from the love of God that is revealed in Christ Jesus our Lord.

James 1:2-4 NASB
Consider it all joy, my brethren, when you encounter various trials, knowing that the testing of your faith produces endurance. And let endurance have its perfect result, so that you may be perfect and complete, lacking in nothing.

1 Peter 1:6-9 NASB
In this you greatly rejoice, even though now for a little while, if necessary, you have been distressed by various trials, so that the proof of your faith, being more precious than gold which is perishable, even though tested by fire, may be found to result in praise and glory and honor at the revelation of Jesus Christ; and though you have not seen Him, you love Him, and though you do not see Him now, but believe in Him, you greatly rejoice with joy

inexpressible and full of glory, obtaining as the outcome of your faith the salvation of your souls.

Psalm 85:8 ESV
Let me hear what God the LORD will speak, for he will speak peace to his people, to his saints

Isaiah 26:3-4 ESV
You keep him in perfect peace whose mind is stayed on you, because he trusts in you. Trust in the LORD forever, for the LORD GOD is an everlasting rock.

Matthew 11:28-30 NLT
Then Jesus said, "Come to me, all of you who are weary and carry heavy burdens, and I will give you rest. Take my yoke upon you. Let me teach you, because I am humble and gentle at heart, and you will find rest for your souls. For my yoke is easy to bear, and the burden I give you is light."

John 14:27 ESV
Peace I leave with you; my peace I give to you. Not as the world gives do I give to you. Let not your hearts be troubled, neither let them be afraid.

Philippians 4:6-7 NIV
Do not be anxious about anything, but in every situation, by prayer and petition, with thanksgiving, present your requests to God. And the peace of God, which transcends all understanding, will guard your hearts and your minds in Christ Jesus.

Psalm 27:5-6 ESV
For he will hide me in his shelter in the day of trouble; he will conceal me under the cover of his tent; he will lift me high upon a rock. And now my head shall be lifted up above my enemies all around me, and I will offer in his tent sacrifices with shouts of joy; I will sing and make melody to the LORD.

John 9:1-3 NIV

As he went along, he saw a man blind from birth. His disciples asked him, "Rabbi, who sinned, this man or his parents, that he was born blind?"
"Neither this man nor his parents sinned," said Jesus, "but this happened so that the works of God might be displayed in him.

2 Corinthians 1:8-9 NASB

For we do not want you to be unaware, brethren, of our affliction which came to us in Asia, that we were burdened excessively, beyond our strength, so that we despaired even of life; indeed, we had the sentence of death within ourselves so that we would not trust in ourselves, but in God who raises the dead;

2 Corinthians 1:10-11 KJV

Who delivered us from so great a death, and doth deliver: in whom we trust that he will yet deliver us;
Ye also helping together by prayer for us, that for the gift bestowed upon us by the means of many persons thanks may be given by many on our behalf.

Philippians 1:12-14 NLT

And I want you to know, my dear brothers and sisters, that everything that has happened to me here has helped to spread the Good News. For everyone here, including the whole palace guard, knows that I am in chains because of Christ. And because of my imprisonment, most of the believers here have gained confidence and boldly speak God's message without fear.

Romans 8:18-21 ESV

For I consider that the sufferings of this present time are not worth comparing with the glory that is to be revealed to us. For the creation waits with eager longing for the revealing of the sons of God. For the creation was subjected to futility, not willingly, but because of him who subjected it, in hope that the creation itself will be set free from its bondage to corruption and obtain the freedom of the glory of the children of God.

2 Corinthians 4:16-18 ESV
So we do not lose heart. Though our outer self is wasting away, our inner self is being renewed day by day. For this light momentary affliction is preparing for us an eternal weight of glory beyond all comparison, as we look not to the things that are seen but to the things that are unseen. For the things that are seen are transient, but the things that are unseen are eternal.

2 Corinthians 9:8 ESV
And God is able to make all grace abound to you, so that having all sufficiency in all things at all times, you may abound in every good work.

1 Peter 1:3-5 ESV
Blessed be the God and Father of our Lord Jesus Christ! According to his great mercy, he has caused us to be born again to a living hope through the resurrection of Jesus Christ from the dead, to an inheritance that is imperishable, undefiled, and unfading, kept in heaven for you, who by God's power are being guarded through faith for a salvation ready to be revealed in the last time.

Revelation 21:3-4 ESV
And I heard a loud voice from the throne saying, "Behold, the dwelling place of God is with man. He will dwell with them, and they will be his people, and God himself will be with them as their God. He will wipe away every tear from their eyes, and death shall be no more, neither shall there be mourning, nor crying, nor pain anymore, for the former things have passed away."

Excellent site for additional Bible translations:
http://www.biblegateway.com/resources/commentaries/
Excellent resource for additional Bible study:
(Be sure to read the instructions on their page)
http://www.blueletterbible.org/commentaries/

Adversity - Christian Quotes

"We must face today as children of tomorrow. We must meet the uncertainties of this world with the certainty of the world to come."
A. W. Tozer

"Comfort and prosperity have never enriched the world as much as adversity has."
Billy Graham

"If we cannot believe God when circumstances seem be against us, we do not believe Him at all."
Charles H. Spurgeon

"Christian, remember the good of God in the frost of adversity."
Charles H. Spurgeon

"Adversity is the diamond dust heave polishes its jewels with"
Robert Leighton

"The valley of the shadow of death holds no darkness for the child of God. There must be light, else there could be no

shadow. Jesus is the light. He has overcome death."
Dwight L Moody

"The long, dull, monotonous years of middle-aged prosperity or middle-aged adversity are excellent campaigning weather for the devil."
C.S. Lewis

"God hath divers ways into divers men. Into some he comes at noon, in the sunshine of prosperity; to some in the dark and heavy clouds of adversity. Some he affects with the music of the church; some, with some particular collect or prayer; some, with some passage of a sermon, which takes no hold of him that stands next to him. Watch the ways the Spirit of God into thee."
John Donne

"God has given a Christian such power that he can turn afflictions into mercies, can turn darkness into light. If a man had the power that Christ had, when the water pots were filled, he could by a word turn the water into wine. If you who have nothing but water to drink had the power to turn it into wine, then you might be contented; certainly a Christian has received this power from God, to work thus miraculously. It is the nature of grace to turn water into wine, that is, to turn the water of your affliction, into the wine of heavenly consolation."
Jeremiah Burroughs

"In the greatest difficulties, in the heaviest trials, in the deepest poverty and necessities, He has never failed me; but because I was enabled by His grace to trust Him He has always appeared for my help. I delight in speaking well of His name."
George Muller

Anger

Anger - Bible Verses

Psalm 7:11 KJV
God judgeth the righteous, and God is angry with the wicked every day.

1 Kings 11:9-10 ESV
And the LORD was angry with Solomon, because his heart had turned away from the LORD, the God of Israel, who had appeared to him twice and had commanded him concerning this thing, that he should not go after other gods. But he did not keep what the LORD commanded.

2 Kings 17:18 ESV
Therefore the LORD was very angry with Israel and removed them out of his sight. None was left but the tribe of Judah only.

Mark 3:4-5 NIV
And He said to them, "Is it lawful to do good or to do harm on the Sabbath, to save a life or to kill?" But they kept silent. After looking around at them with anger, grieved at their hardness of heart, He said to the man, "Stretch out your hand." And he stretched it out, and his hand was restored.

John 2:13-16 NASB
The Passover of the Jews was near, and Jesus went up to Jerusalem. And He found in the temple those who were selling oxen and sheep and doves, and the money changers seated at their tables. And He made a scourge of cords, and drove them all out of the temple, with the sheep and the oxen; and He poured out the coins of the money changers and overturned their tables; and to those who were selling the doves He said, "Take these things away; stop making My Father's house a place of business."

Genesis 4:5-8 ESV
but for Cain and his offering he had no regard. So Cain was very angry, and his face fell. The LORD said to Cain, "Why are you angry, and why has your

face fallen? If you do well, will you not be accepted? And if you do not do well, sin is crouching at the door. Its desire is for you, but you must rule over it." Cain spoke to Abel his brother. And when they were in the field, Cain rose up against his brother Abel and killed him.

Psalm 37:8 ESV
Refrain from anger, and forsake wrath! Fret not yourself; it tends only to evil.

Proverbs 15:18 ESV
A hot-tempered man stirs up strife, but he who is slow to anger quiets contention.
Proverbs 29:22 A man of wrath stirs up strife, and one given to anger causes much transgression.

Proverbs 30:33 ESV
For pressing milk produces curds, pressing the nose produces blood, and pressing anger produces strife.
Wisdom & Patience Key to Overcoming Anger

Proverbs 14:16-17 KJV
A wise man feareth, and departeth from evil: but the fool rageth, and is confident. He that is soon angry dealeth foolishly: and a man of wicked devices is hated.

Proverbs 14:29 ESV
Whoever is slow to anger has great understanding, but he who has a hasty temper exalts folly.

Proverbs 19:11 ESV
Good sense makes one slow to anger, and it is his glory to overlook an offense.

Ecclesiastes 7:9 ESV
Be not quick in your spirit to become angry, for anger lodges in the bosom of fools.

James 1:19-20 NASB
This you know, my beloved brethren. But everyone must be quick to hear, slow to speak and slow to anger; for the anger of man does not achieve the righteousness of God.

Matthew 5:21-24 NIV
"You have heard that it was said to the people long ago, 'You shall not murder, and anyone who murders will be subject to judgment.' But I tell you that anyone who is angry with a brother or sister will be subject to judgment. Again, anyone who says to a brother or sister, 'Raca,' is answerable to the court. And anyone who says, 'You fool!' will be in danger of the fire of hell.

"Therefore, if you are offering your gift at the altar and there remember that your brother or sister has something against you, leave your gift there in front of the altar. First go and be reconciled to them; then come and offer your gift.

Galatians 5:19-21 ESV
Now the works of the flesh are evident: sexual immorality, impurity, sensuality, idolatry, sorcery, enmity, strife, jealousy, fits of anger, rivalries, dissensions, divisions, envy, drunkenness, orgies, and things like these. I warn you, as I warned you before, that those who do such things will not inherit the kingdom of God.

Galatians 5:22-25 NIV
But the fruit of the Spirit is love, joy, peace, forbearance, kindness, goodness, faithfulness, gentleness and self-control. Against such things there is no law. Those who belong to Christ Jesus have crucified the flesh with its passions and desires. Since we live by the Spirit, let us keep in step with the Spirit.

Ephesians 4:26-28 NIV
"In your anger do not sin": Do not let the sun go down while you are still angry, and do not give the devil a foothold. Anyone who has been stealing must steal no longer, but must work, doing something useful with their own hands, that they may have something to share with those in need.

Colossians 3:8 ESV
But now you must put them all away: anger, wrath, malice, slander, and obscene talk from your mouth.

Excellent site for additional Bible translations
http://www.biblegateway.com/resources/commentaries/

Excellent resource for additional Bible study:
(Be sure to read the instructions on their page)
http://www.blueletterbible.org/commentaries/

Anger - Christian Quotes

"Is all anger sin? No, but some of it is. Even God Himself has righteous anger against sin, injustice, rebellion and pettiness. Anger sometimes serves a useful purpose, so it isn't necessarily always a sin. Obviously, we're going to have adverse feelings, or God wouldn't have needed to provide the fruit of self-control. Just being tempted to do something is not sin. It's when you don't resist the temptation, but do it anyway, that it becomes sin."
Joyce Meyer

"No matter how just your words may be, you ruin everything when you speak with anger."
John Chrysostom

"A sermon often does a man most good when it makes him most angry. Those people who walk down the aisles and say, "I will never hear that man again," very often have an arrow rankling in their breast."
C.H. Spurgeon

"Wise anger is like the fire from the flint; there is a great ado to bring it out; and when it does come, it is out again immediately."
Matthew Henry

"Is it any merit to abstain from wine if one is intoxicated with anger?"
Augustine

"Be not angry that you cannot make others as you wish them to be, since you cannot make yourself as you wish to be."
Thomas A' Kempis

"Pride is one chief cause of undue anger. It is because men are proud, and exalt themselves in their own hearts, that they are revengeful, and are apt to be excited, and to make great things out of little ones that may be against themselves. Yea, they even treat as vices things that are in themselves virtues, when they think their honor is touched, or when their will is

crossed. And it is pride that makes men so unreasonable and rash in their anger, and raises it to such a high degree, and continues it so long, and often keeps it up in the form of habitual malice... If men sought not chiefly their own private and selfish interests, but the glory of God and the common good, then their spirit would be a great deal more stirred up in God's cause than in their own; and they would not be prone to hasty, rash, inconsiderate, immoderate, and long-continued wrath, with any who might have injured or provoked them; but they would in a great measure forget themselves for God's sake, and from their zeal for the honor of Christ. The end they would aim at, would be, not making themselves great, or getting their own will, but the glory of God and the good of their fellow-beings."
Jonathan Edwards
The Spirit of Love the Opposite of An Angry or Wrathful Spirit

"It is only our bad temper that we put down to being tired or worried or hungry; we put our good temper down to ourselves."
C.S. Lewis

"Anger and bitterness are two noticeable signs of being focused on self and not trusting God's sovereignty in your life. When you believe that God causes all things to work together for good to those who belong to Him and love Him, you can respond to trials with joy instead of anger or bitterness."
John C. Boger

"Our God is not an impotent God with one arm; but as he is slow to anger, so is he great in power."
Abraham Wright

Anxiety

Anxiety - Bible Verses

Isaiah 41:10 ESV
fear not, for I am with you; be not dismayed, for I am your God; I will strengthen you, I will help you, I will uphold you with my righteous right hand.

Proverbs 12:25 ESV
Anxiety in a man's heart weighs him down, but a good word makes him glad.

Proverbs 17:22 ESV
A joyful heart is good medicine, but a crushed spirit dries up the bones.

Psalm 34:4 NASB
I sought the Lord, and he answered me and delivered me from all my fears.

Psalm 37:5 ESV
Commit your way to the Lord; trust in him, and he will act.

Proverbs 3:5-6 NASB
Trust in the Lord with all your heart, and do not lean on your own understanding. 6 In all your ways acknowledge him, and he will make straight your paths.

Philippians 4:6-7 NASB
Do not be anxious about anything, but in every situation, by prayer and petition, with thanksgiving, present your requests to God. And the peace of God, which transcends all understanding, will guard your hearts and your minds in Christ Jesus.

1 Peter 5:6-7 NIV
Humble yourselves, therefore, under God's mighty hand, that he may lift you up in due time. Cast all your anxiety on him because he cares for you.

Hebrews 13:6 ESV
So we can confidently say, "The Lord is my helper; I will not fear; what can man do to me?"

Psalm 94:19 ESV
When the cares of my heart are many, your consolations cheer my soul.

Romans 8:26-28 NASB
In the same way the Spirit also helps our weakness; for we do not know how to pray as we should, but the Spirit Himself intercedes for us with groanings too deep for words; and He who searches the hearts knows what the mind of the Spirit is, because He intercedes for the saints according to the will of God.
And we know that God causes all things to work together for good to those who love God, to those who are called according to His purpose.

2 Corinthians 12:10 ESV
For the sake of Christ, then, I am content with weaknesses, insults, hardships, persecutions, and calamities. For when I am weak, then I am strong.

Philippians 4:13 ESV
I can do all things through him who strengthens me.

Philippians 4:19 ESV
And my God will supply every need of yours according to his riches in glory in Christ Jesus.

Matthew 6:26 ESV
Look at the birds of the air: they neither sow nor reap nor gather into barns, and yet your heavenly Father feeds them. Are you not of more value than they?

Matthew 6:28 ESV
And why are you anxious about clothing? Consider the lilies of the field, how they grow: they neither toil nor spin,

Matthew 6:34 NLT
"So don't worry about tomorrow, for tomorrow will bring its own worries. Today's trouble is enough for today.

Romans 5:2 NLT
Because of our faith, Christ has brought us into this place of undeserved privilege where we now stand, and we confidently and joyfully look forward to sharing God's glory.

2 Corinthians 4:17 NLT
For our present troubles are small and won't last very long. Yet they produce for us a glory that vastly outweighs them and will last forever!

James 5:11 ESV
Behold, we consider those blessed who remained steadfast. You have heard of the steadfastness of Job, and you have seen the purpose of the Lord, how the Lord is compassionate and merciful.

Revelation 21:4 ESV
He will wipe away every tear from their eyes, and death shall be no more, neither shall there be mourning, nor crying, nor pain anymore, for the former things have passed away.

Excellent site for additional Bible translations:
http://www.biblegateway.com/resources/commentaries/
Excellent resource for additional Bible study:
(Be sure to read the instructions on their page)
http://www.blueletterbible.org/commentaries/

Anxiety - Christian Quotes

"Anxiety does not empty tomorrow of its sorrows, but only empties today of its strength."
C.H. Spurgeon

"Our yesterdays present irreparable things to us; it is true that we have lost opportunities which will never return, but God can transform this destructive anxiety into a constructive thoughtfulness for the future. Let the past sleep, but let it sleep on the bosom of Christ. Leave the Irreparable Past in His hands, and step out into the Irresistible Future with Him."
Oswald Chambers

"There is no need for two to care, for God to care and the creature too."
C.H. Spurgeon

"The beginning of anxiety is the end of faith, and the beginning of true faith is the end of anxiety."
George Muller

"We imagine that a little anxiety and worry are an indication of how really wise we are; it is much more an indication of how really wicked we are. Fretting springs from a determination to get our own way. Our Lord never worried and He was never anxious, because He was not "out" to realize His own ideas; He was "out" to realize God's ideas. Fretting is wicked if you are a child of God. Have you been bolstering up that stupid soul of yours with the idea that your circumstances are too much for God? Put all "supposing" on one side and dwell in the shadow of the Almighty. Deliberately tell God that you will not fret about that thing. All our fret and worry is caused by calculating without God."
Oswald Chambers

"The apostle Paul in writing to the Philippians gives them the admonition to be "anxious for nothing," telling them that the cure for anxiety is found on one's knees, that it is the peace of God that calms our spirit and dissipates

anxiety (Phil. 4:6)."
R.C. Sproul

"What does your anxiety do? It does not empty tomorrow of its sorrow, but it does empty today of its strength. It does not make you escape the evil; it makes you unfit to cope with it when it comes. God gives us the power to bear all the sorrow of His making, but He does not guarantee to give us strength to bear the burdens of our own making such as worry induces."
Ian Maclaren

"Every tomorrow has two handles. We can take hold of it with the handle of anxiety or the handle of faith."
Henry Ward Beecher

"Anxiety is the poison of human life; the parent of many sins and of more miseries. In a world where everything is doubtful, and where we may be disappointed, and be blessed in disappointment, why this restless stir and commotion of mind? Can it alter the cause, or unravel the mystery of human events?"
Tryon Edwards

"The great antidote to anxiety is to come to God in prayer. We are to pray about everything. Nothing is too big for Him to handle, and nothing is too small to escape His attention."
Jerry Bridges
The Practice of Godliness, NavPress, 1996, p. 159.

Bad Day

Bad Day - Bible Verses

John 16:33 NLT
I have told you all this so that you may have peace in me. Here on earth you will have many trials and sorrows. But take heart, because I have overcome the world."

2 Thessalonians 3:16 ESV
Now may the Lord of peace himself give you his peace at all times and in every situation. The Lord be with you all.

Zephaniah 3:17 ESV
The LORD your God is in your midst, a mighty one who will save; he will rejoice over you with gladness; he will quiet you by his love; he will exult over you with loud singing.

Jeremiah 29:11-12 NIV
For I know the plans I have for you," declares the Lord, "plans to prosper you and not to harm you, plans to give you hope and a future. Then you will call on me and come and pray to me, and I will listen to you.

1 Peter 5:6-7 NIV
Humble yourselves, therefore, under God's mighty hand, that he may lift you up in due time. Cast all your anxiety on him because he cares for you.

Philippians 4:6-7 NIV
Do not be anxious about anything, but in every situation, by prayer and petition, with thanksgiving, present your requests to God. And the peace of God, which transcends all understanding, will guard your hearts and your minds in Christ Jesus.

Psalm 50:15 ESV

and call upon me in the day of trouble; I will deliver you, and you shall glorify me."

Matthew 7:7 NASB

"Ask, and it will be given to you; seek, and you will find; knock, and it will be opened to you.

1 Thessalonians 5:16-18 ESV

Rejoice always, pray without ceasing, give thanks in all circumstances; for this is the will of God in Christ Jesus for you.

Matthew 11:28-30 NASB

"Come to Me, all who are weary and heavy-laden, and I will give you rest. Take My yoke upon you and learn from Me, for I am gentle and humble in heart, and you will find rest for your souls. For My yoke is easy and My burden is light."

Excellent site for additional Bible translations:

http://www.biblegateway.com/resources/commentaries/

Excellent resource for additional Bible study:

(Be sure to read the instructions on their page)
http://www.blueletterbible.org/commentaries/

Bad Day - Christian Quotes

"No words can express how much the world owes to sorrow. Most of the Psalms were born in the wilderness. Most of the Epistles were written in a prison. The greatest thoughts of the greatest thinkers have all passed through fire. The greatest poets have "learned in suffering what they taught in song." In bonds Bunyan lived the allegory that he afterwards wrote, and we may thank Bedford Jail for the Pilgrim's Progress. Take comfort, afflicted Christian! When God is about to make pre-eminent use of a person, He put them in the fire."
George MacDonald

"Most of the grand truths of God have to be learned by trouble; they must be burned into us with the hot iron of affliction, otherwise we shall not truly receive them."
C.H. Spurgeon

"You must submit to supreme suffering in order to discover the completion of joy."
John Calvin

"That which should distinguish the suffering of believers from unbelievers is the confidence that our suffering is under the control of an all-powerful and all-loving God; our suffering has meaning and purpose in God's eternal plan, and He brings or allows to come into our lives only that which is for His glory and our good."
Jerry Bridges
Trusting God, 1988, p. 32.

"But pain insists upon being attended to. God whispers to us in our pleasures, speaks in our conscience, but shouts in our pains: It is His megaphone to rouse a deaf world."
C.S. Lewis

"What then are we to do about our problems? We must learn to live with them until such time as God delivers us from them. We must pray for grace

to endure them without murmuring. Problems patiently endured will work for our spiritual perfecting. They harm us only when we resist them or endure them unwillingly."
A.W. Tozer

"I am certain that I never did grow in grace one-half so much anywhere as I have upon the bed of pain."
C.H. Spurgeon

"God will not permit any troubles to come upon us, unless He has a specific plan by which great blessing can come out of the difficulty."
Peter Marshall

Bereavement

Bereavement - Bible Verses

Isaiah 66:13 ESV
As one whom his mother comforts, so I will comfort you; you shall be comforted in Jerusalem.

Matthew 5:4 ESV
Blessed are those who mourn, for they shall be comforted.

Psalm 55:22 ESV
Cast your burden on the LORD, and he will sustain you;he will never permit the righteous to be moved.

Psalm 23 KJV
The Lord is my shepherd; I shall not want.
He maketh me to lie down in green pastures: he leadeth me beside the still waters.
He restoreth my soul: he leadeth me in the paths of righteousness for his name's sake.
Yea, though I walk through the valley of the shadow of death, I will fear no evil: for thou art with me; thy rod and thy staff they comfort me.
Thou preparest a table before me in the presence of mine enemies: thou anointest my head with oil; my cup runneth over.
Surely goodness and mercy shall follow me all the days of my life: and I will dwell in the house of the Lord for ever.

John 11:25-26 ESV
Jesus said to her, "I am the resurrection and the life. Whoever believes in me, though he die, yet shall he live, and everyone who lives and believes in me shall never die. Do you believe this?"

John 14:1-3 ESV
Let not your hearts be troubled. Believe in God; believe also in me. In my Father's house are many rooms. If it were not so, would I have told you that

I go to prepare a place for you? And if I go and prepare a place for you, I will come again and will take you to myself, that where I am you may be also.

John 6:35-40 ESV
Jesus said to them, "I am the bread of life; whoever comes to me shall not hunger, and whoever believes in me shall never thirst. But I said to you that you have seen me and yet do not believe. All that the Father gives me will come to me, and whoever comes to me I will never cast out. ForI have come down from heaven, not to do my own will but the will of him who sent me. And this is the will of him who sent me, that I should lose nothing of all that he has given me, but raise it up on the last day. For this is the will of my Father, that everyone who looks on the Son and believes in him should have eternal life, and I will raise him up on the last day."

John 14:27 NLT
Peace I leave with you, my peace I give unto you: not as the world giveth, give I unto you. Let not your heart be troubled, neither let it be afraid.

Matthew 11:28-30 NASB
"Come to Me, all who are weary and heavy-laden, and I will give you rest. Take My yoke upon you and learn from Me, for I am gentle and humble in heart, and you will find rest for your souls. For My yoke is easy and My burden is light."

Philippians 4:6-7 NASB
Be anxious for nothing, but in everything by prayer and supplication with thanksgiving let your requests be made known to God. And the peace of God, which surpasses all comprehension, will guard your hearts and your minds in Christ Jesus.

Excellent site for additional Bible translations:
http://www.biblegateway.com/resources/commentaries/
Excellent resource for additional Bible study:
(Be sure to read the instructions on their page)
http://www.blueletterbible.org/commentaries/

Bereavement - Christian Quotes

"Bereavement is the sharpest challenge to our trust in God; if faith can overcome this, there is no mountain which it cannot remove."
William Ralph Inge

"Too many Christians feel that grief is wrong, that we're supposed to rejoice when a loved one goes to be with the Lord. While we can rejoice in their homegoing, we can also grieve our loss."
Bruce Barton

"No words can express how much the world owes to sorrow. Most of the Psalms were born in the wilderness. Most of the Epistles were written in a prison. The greatest thoughts of the greatest thinkers have all passed through fire. The greatest poets have "learned in suffering what they taught in song." In bonds Bunyan lived the allegory that he afterwards wrote, and we may thank Bedford Jail for the Pilgrim's Progress. Take comfort, afflicted Christian! When God is about to make pre-eminent use of a person, He put them in the fire."
George MacDonald

"We are told that it is perfectly legitimate for believers to suffer grief. Our Lord Himself was a man of sorrows and acquainted with grief. Though grief may reach to the roots of our souls, it must not result in bitterness. Grief is a legitimate emotion, at times even a virtue, but there must be no place in the soul for bitterness."
R.C. Sproul

"The friend who can be silent with us in a moment of despair or confusion, who can stay with us in an hour of grief and bereavement, who can tolerate not knowing... not healing, not curing... that is a friend who cares."
Francis Bacon

"No man who is fit to live need fear to die. To us here, death is the most terrible thing we know. But when we have tasted its reality it will mean to us birth, deliverance, a new creation of ourselves. It will be what health is to

the sick man; what home is to the exile; what the loved one given back is to the bereaved. As we draw near to it a solemn gladness should fill our hearts. It is God's great morning lighting up the sky. Our fears are the terror of children in the night. The night with its terrors, its darkness, its feverish dreams, is passing away; and when we awake it will be into the sunlight of God."
Thomas Fuller

"Oh, when we are journeying through the murky night and the dark woods of affliction and sorrow, it is something to find here and there a spray broken, or a leafy stem bent down with the tread of His foot and the brush of His hand as He passed; and to remember that the path He trod He has hallowed, and thus to find lingering fragrance and hidden strength in the remembrance of Him as "in all points tempted like as we are," bearing grief for us, bearing grief with us, bearing grief like us."
Alexander MacLaren

"This day, my God, I hate sin not because it damns me, but because it has done Thee wrong. To have grieved my God is the worst grief to me. "
Charles Spurgeon

Blessings

Blessings - Bible Verses

2 Corinthians 12:10 ESV
For the sake of Christ, then, I am content with weaknesses, insults, hardships, persecutions, and calamities. For when I am weak, then I am strong.

Romans 5:6-8 ESV
For while we were still weak, at the right time Christ died for the ungodly. For one will scarcely die for a righteous person—though perhaps for a good person one would dare even to die—but God shows his love for us in that while we were still sinners, Christ died for us.

James 1:12 ESV
Blessed is the man who remains steadfast under trial, for when he has stood the test he will receive the crown of life, which God has promised to those who love him.

Revelation 2:10 KJV
Fear none of those things which thou shalt suffer: behold, the devil shall cast some of you into prison, that ye may be tried; and ye shall have tribulation ten days: be thou faithful unto death, and I will give thee a crown of life.

1 Corinthians 9:25-27 KJV
And every man that striveth for the mastery is temperate in all things. Now they do it to obtain a corruptible crown; but we an incorruptible. I therefore so run, not as uncertainly; so fight I, not as one that beateth the air: But I keep under my body, and bring it into subjection: lest that by any means, when I have preached to others, I myself should be a castaway.

1 Peter 5:1-4 NASB
Therefore, I exhort the elders among you, as your fellow elder and witness of the sufferings of Christ, and a partaker also of the glory that is to be

revealed, shepherd the flock of God among you, exercising oversight not under compulsion, but voluntarily, according to the will of God; and not for sordid gain, but with eagerness; nor yet as lording it over those allotted to your charge, but proving to be examples to the flock. And when the Chief Shepherd appears, you will receive the unfading crown of glory.

2 Timothy 4:8 NLT
And now the prize awaits me—the crown of righteousness, which the Lord, the righteous Judge, will give me on the day of his return. And the prize is not just for me but for all who eagerly look forward to his appearing.

1 Thessalonians 2:19-20 NASB
For who is our hope or joy or crown of exultation? Is it not even you, in the presence of our Lord Jesus at His coming? For you are our glory and joy.

Deuteronomy 7:13 ESV
He will love you, bless you, and multiply you. He will also bless the fruit of your womb and the fruit of your ground, your grain and your wine and your oil, the increase of your herds and the young of your flock, in the land that he swore to your fathers to give you.

Jeremiah 7:5-7 ESV
"For if you truly amend your ways and your deeds, if you truly execute justice one with another, if you do not oppress the sojourner, the father-less, or the widow, or shed innocent blood in this place, and if you do not go after other gods to your own harm, then I will let you dwell in this place, in the land that I gave of old to your fathers forever..."

Zechariah 3:7-9 ESV
Thus says the LORD of hosts: If you will walk in my ways and keep my charge, then you shall rule my house and have charge of my courts, and I will give you the right of access among those who are standing here. Hear now, O Joshua the high priest, you and your friends who sit before you, for they are men who are a sign: behold, I will bring my servant the Branch. For behold, on the stone that I have set before Joshua, on a single

stone with seven eyes, I will engrave its inscription, declares the LORD of hosts, and I will remove the iniquity of this land in a single day."

Esther 4:14 ESV
For if you keep silent at this time, relief and deliverance will rise for the Jews from another place, but you and your father's house will perish. And who knows whether you have not come to the kingdom for such a time as this?

Matthew 10:21-22 NIV
"Brother will betray brother to death, and a father his child; children will rebel against their parents and have them put to death. You will be hated by everyone because of me, but the one who stands firm to the end will be saved.

James 1:2-4 ESV
Count it all joy, my brothers, when you meet trials of various kinds, for you know that the testing of your faith produces steadfastness. And let steadfastness have its full effect, that you may be perfect and complete, lacking in nothing.

Genesis 50:18-20 ESV
His brothers also came and fell down before him and said, "Behold, we are your servants." But Joseph said to them, "Do not fear, for am I in the place of God? As for you, you meant evil against me, but God meant it for good, to bring it about that many people should be kept alive, as they are today.

2 Chronicles 1:11-12 ESV
God answered Solomon, "Because this was in your heart, and you have not asked possessions, wealth, honor, or the life of those who hate you, and have not even asked long life, but have asked wisdom and knowledge for yourself that you may govern my people over whom I have made you king, and knowledge are granted to you. I will also give you riches, possessions, and honor, such as none of the kings had who were before you, and none after you shall have the like."

Luke 24:30-34 NIV

When he was at the table with them, he took bread, gave thanks, broke it and began to give it to them. Then their eyes were opened and they recognized him, and he disappeared from their sight. They asked each other, "Were not our hearts burning within us while he talked with us on the road and opened the Scriptures to us?"

They got up and returned at once to Jerusalem. There they found the Eleven and those with them, assembled together and saying, "It is true! The Lord has risen and has appeared to Simon."

Acts 9:17-19 NIV

Then Ananias went to the house and entered it. Placing his hands on Saul, he said, "Brother Saul, the Lord—Jesus, who appeared to you on the road as you were coming here—has sent me so that you may see again and be filled with the Holy Spirit." Immediately, something like scales fell from Saul's eyes, and he could see again. He got up and was baptized, and after taking some food, he regained his strength.

Excellent site for additional Bible translations

http://www.biblegateway.com/resources/commentaries/

Excellent resource for additional Bible study:

(Be sure to read the instructions on their page)
http://www.blueletterbible.org/commentaries/

Blessings - Christian Quotes

"The riches of His free grace cause me to daily triumph over all the temptations of the wicked one, who is very vigilant, and seeks all occasions to disturb me."
George Whitefield

"Did you ever run for shelter in a storm, and find fruit which you expected not? Did you never go to God for safeguard, driven by outward storms, and there find unexpected fruit?"
John Owen

"There is more healing joy in five minutes of worship than there is in five nights of revelry."
A. W. Tozer

"God forgives, then He gives; till He be merciful to pardon our sins through Christ, He cannot bless or look kindly upon us sinners. All our enjoyments are but blessings in bullion, till Gospel grace and pardoning mercy stamp and make them current."
William Gurnall

"Temporal blessings are not definite marks of divine favor, since God gives them to the unworthy, and to the wicked, as well as to the righteous"
C. H. Spurgeon

To bless God for mercies is the way to increase them; to bless Him for miseries is the way to remove them."
William Dyer

Brokenhearted

Brokenhearted - Bible Verses

Psalm 73:26 ESV
My flesh and my heart may fail, but God is the strength of my heart and my portion forever.

Isaiah 41:10 NIV
fear not, for I am with you; be not dismayed, for I am your God; I will strengthen you, I will help you, I will uphold you with my righteous right hand.

Matthew 11:28-30 NIV
"Come to me, all you who are weary and burdened, and I will give you rest. Take my yoke upon you and learn from me, for I am gentle and humble in heart, and you will find rest for your souls. For my yoke is easy and my burden is light."

John 14:27 ESV
Peace I leave with you; my peace I give to you. Not as the world gives do I give to you. Let not your hearts be troubled, neither let them be afraid.

2 Corinthians 12:9 ESV
But he said to me, "My grace is sufficient for you, for my power is made perfect in weakness." Therefore I will boast all the more gladly about my weaknesses, so that Christ's power may rest on me.

Psalm 55:22 NLT
Give your burdens to the Lord,
    and he will take care of you.
    He will not permit the godly to slip and fall.

Psalm 107:20 NLT
He sent out his word and healed them,
   snatching them from the door of death.

Psalm 147:3 NASB
He heals the brokenhearted. And binds up their wounds.

Proverbs 3:5-6 NASB
Trust in the Lord with all your heart
And do not lean on your own understanding.
In all your ways acknowledge Him,
And He will make your paths straight.

1 Peter 4:19 ESV
Therefore let those who suffer according to God's will entrust their souls to a faithful Creator while doing good.

Isaiah 43:18 ESV
Remember not the former things, nor consider the things of old.

Mark 11:23 ESV
Truly, I say to you, whoever says to this mountain, 'Be taken up and thrown into the sea,' and does not doubt in his heart, but believes that what he says will come to pass, it will be done for him.

Romans 5:1-2 NASB
Therefore, having been justified by faith, we have peace with God through our Lord Jesus Christ, through whom also we have obtained our introduction by faith into this grace in which we stand; and we exult in hope of the glory of God.

Romans 8:28 ESV
And we know that for those who love God all things work together for good, for those who are called according to his purpose.

1 Corinthians 13:7 ESV
Love bears all things, believes all things, hopes all things, endures all things.

2 Corinthians 5:6-7 NLT
So we are always confident, even though we know that as long as we live in these bodies we are not at home with the Lord. 7 For we live by believing and not by seeing.

Philippians 3:13-14 NIV
Brothers and sisters, I do not consider myself yet to have taken hold of it. But one thing I do: Forgetting what is behind and straining toward what is ahead, I press on toward the goal to win the prize for which God has called me heavenward in Christ Jesus.

Hebrews 11:1 KJV
Now faith is the substance of things hoped for, the evidence of things not seen.

Revelation 21:3-4 NIV
And I heard a loud voice from the throne saying, "Look! God's dwelling place is now among the people, and he will dwell with them. They will be his people, and God himself will be with them and be their God. 'He will wipe every tear from their eyes. There will be no more death' or mourning or crying or pain, for the old order of things has passed away."

Excellent site for additional Bible translations:
http://www.biblegateway.com/resources/commentaries/
Excellent resource for additional Bible study:
(Be sure to read the instructions on their page)
http://www.blueletterbible.org/commentaries/

Brokenhearted - Christian Quotes

"My grand point in preaching is to break the hard heart, and to heal the broken one."
John Newton

"Leave the broken, irreversible past in God's hands, and step out into the invincible future with Him."
Oswald Chambers

"We want to avoid suffering, death, sin, ashes. But we live in a world crushed and broken and torn, a world God Himself visited to redeem. We receive his poured-out life, and being allowed the high privilege of suffering with Him, may then pour ourselves out for others."
Elisabeth Elliot

"The church is not a select circle of the immaculate, but a home where the outcast may come in. It is not a palace with gate attendants and challenging sentinels along the entrance-ways holding off at arm's-length the stranger, but rather a hospital where the broken-hearted may be healed, and where all the weary and troubled may find rest and take counsel together."
James H. Aughey

"Your most profound and intimate experiences of worship will likely be in your darkest days – when your heart is broken, when you feel abandoned, when your out of options, when the pain is great – and you turn to God alone."
Rick Warren

Cancer

Deuteronomy 31:6 ESV
"Be strong and courageous. Do not fear or be in dread of them, for it is the Lord your God who goes with you. He will not leave you or forsake you."

Psalm 138:3 ESV
On the day I called, you answered me; my strength of soul you increased.

Proverbs 3:5-6 ESV
Trust in the LORD with all your heart, and do not lean on your own understanding. In all your ways acknowledge him, and he will make straight your paths.

Matthew 11:28-29 NASB
"Come to Me, all who are weary and heavy-laden, and I will give you rest. Take My yoke upon you and learn from Me, for I am gentle and humble in heart, and you will find rest for your souls.

2 Corinthians 1:3-4 KJV
Blessed be God, even the Father of our Lord Jesus Christ, the Father of mercies, and the God of all comfort; Who comforteth us in all our tribulation, that we may be able to comfort them which are in any trouble, by the comfort wherewith we ourselves are comforted of God.

Psalm 18:6 ESV
In my distress I called upon the Lord; to my God I cried for help. From his temple he heard my voice, and my cry to him reached his ears.

Psalm 33:20-22 NLT
We put our hope in the Lord.
   He is our help and our shield.
In him our hearts rejoice,
   for we trust in his holy name.
Let your unfailing love surround us, Lord,
   for our hope is in you alone.

Philippians 1:6 ESV
And I am sure of this, that he who began a good work in you will bring it to completion at the day of Jesus Christ.

Philippians 4:6-7 NASB
Be anxious for nothing, but in everything by prayer and supplication with thanksgiving let your requests be made known to God. And the peace of God, which surpasses all comprehension, will guard your hearts and your minds in Christ Jesus.

1 Peter 5:6-7 KJV
Humble yourselves therefore under the mighty hand of God, that he may exalt you in due time: Casting all your care upon him; for he careth for you.

Ecclesiastes 3:1 ESV
For everything there is a season, and a time for every matter under heaven:

Jeremiah 29:11 ESV
For I know the plans I have for you, declares the LORD, plans for welfare and not for evil, to give you a future and a hope.

John 14:1-3 NIV
"Do not let your hearts be troubled. You believe in God; believe also in me. My Father's house has many rooms; if that were not so, would I have told you that I am going there to prepare a place for you? And if I go and prepare a place for you, I will come back and take you to be with me that you also may be where I am.

Romans 8:16-17 NIV
The Spirit himself testifies with our spirit that we are God's children. Now if we are children, then we are heirs—heirs of God and co-heirs with Christ, if indeed we share in his sufferings in order that we may also share in his glory.

Romans 8:24-25 ESV
For in this hope we were saved. Now hope that is seen is not hope. For who hopes for what he sees? But if we hope for what we do not see, we wait for it with patience.

Romans 8:38-39 NLT
And I am convinced that nothing can ever separate us from God's love. Neither death nor life, neither angels nor demons, neither our fears for today nor our worries about tomorrow—not even the powers of hell can separate us from God's love. No power in the sky above or in the earth below —indeed, nothing in all creation will ever be able to separate us from the love of God that is revealed in Christ Jesus our Lord.

1 Peter 1:3-5 NLT
BAll praise to God, the Father of our Lord Jesus Christ. It is by his great mercy that we have been born again, because God raised Jesus Christ from the dead. Now we live with great expectation, and we have a priceless inheritance—an inheritance that is kept in heaven for you, pure and undefiled, beyond the reach of change and decay. And through your faith, God is protecting you by his power until you receive this salvation, which is ready to be revealed on the last day for all to see.

Excellent site for additional Bible translations:
http://www.biblegateway.com/resources/commentaries/
Excellent resource for additional Bible study:
(Be sure to read the instructions on their page)
http://www.blueletterbible.org/commentaries/

Cancer - Christian Quotes

"I venture to say that the greatest earthly blessing that God can give to any of us is health, with the exception of sickness. Sickness has frequently been of more use to the saints of God than health has."
C.H. Spurgeon

"The storms of winter often bring out the defects in a man's dwelling, and sickness often exposes the gracelessness of a man's soul. Surely anything that makes us find out the real character of our faith is a good."
J.C. Ryle

"Sickness helps to remind men of death.
Sickness helps to make men think seriously of God, and their souls, and the world to come.
Sickness helps to soften men's hearts, and teach them wisdom.
Sickness helps to level and humble us.
Sickness helps to try men's religion, of what sort it is."
J.C. Ryle

"We must leave room for mystery in God's ways. Some things will always remain unexplained. Why God does or does not choose to heal is ultimately subject to his wisdom and sovereign purposes. Why God chooses to heal in part or in whole, now or later, this person but not that one, is often beyond our capacity to understand. Resist the tendency to replace divine mystery with human formulas."
Sam Storms

"In...the instances where faith is mentioned (in Matthew 9), the object of faith was in Jesus' ability to heal, not His will to heal. Today as we pray for the healing of our friends or loved ones who suffer severe illness or disease, we too should believe that God is able to heal, either directly or through conventional means. To say I have faith that God will heal is presumptuous since we do not know the mind of God, but to say God is able to heal is to exercise faith."
Jerry Bridges

"We have no right to expect that all our illnesses will be healed in this present age, only in the eternal state will Christ's work be fully applied and all disease gone. Still, we should pray for the sick knowing that our God may bring healing if we ask in faith and trust in His good purposes."
Author Unknown

Change

Change - Bible Verses

Genesis 46:3-4 KJV
And he said, I am God, the God of thy father: fear not to go down into Egypt; for I will there make of thee a great nation:
I will go down with thee into Egypt; and I will also surely bring thee up again: and Joseph shall put his hand upon thine eyes.

Exodus 12:40-42 KJV
Now the sojourning of the children of Israel, who dwelt in Egypt, was four hundred and thirty years.
And it came to pass at the end of the four hundred and thirty years, even the selfsame day it came to pass, that all the hosts of the Lord went out from the land of Egypt.
It is a night to be much observed unto the Lord for bringing them out from the land of Egypt: this is that night of the Lord to be observed of all the children of Israel in their generations.

Ezekiel 12:3 ESV
As for you, son of man, prepare for yourself an exile's baggage, and go into exile by day in their sight. You shall go like an exile from your place to another place in their sight. Perhaps they will understand, though they are a rebellious house.

Acts 8:26 NASB
But an angel of the Lord spoke to Philip saying, "Get up and go south to the road that descends from Jerusalem to Gaza."

Genesis 17:5 NASB
"No longer shall your name be called Abram,
But your name shall be Abraham;
For I have made you the father of a multitude of nations.

Genesis 17:15 NASB
Then God said to Abraham, "As for Sarai your wife, you shall not call her name Sarai, but Sarah shall be her name.

Genesis 32:28 ESV
Then he said, "Your name shall no longer be called Jacob, but Israel, for you have striven with God and with men, and have prevailed."

Genesis 41:45 NASB
Then Pharaoh named Joseph Zaphenath-paneah; and he gave him Asenath, the daughter of Potiphera priest of On, as his wife. And Joseph went forth over the land of Egypt.

Isaiah 62:2 NASB
The nations shall see your righteousness, and all the kings your glory, and you shall be called by a new name that the mouth of the LORD will give.

Genesis 12:1-3 KJV
Now the Lord had said unto Abram, Get thee out of thy country, and from thy kindred, and from thy father's house, unto a land that I will shew thee:
And I will make of thee a great nation, and I will bless thee, and make thy name great; and thou shalt be a blessing:
And I will bless them that bless thee, and curse him that curseth thee: and in thee shall all families of the earth be blessed.

Psalm 7:11-13 ESV
God is a righteous judge, and a God who feels indignation every day. If a man does not repent, God will whet his sword; he has bent and readied his bow; he has prepared for him his deadly weapons, making his arrows fiery shafts.

Mark 1:14-15 NASB
Now after John had been taken into custody, Jesus came into Galilee, preaching the gospel of God, and saying, "The time is fulfilled, and the kingdom of God is at hand; repent and believe in the gospel."

Acts 17:29-31 NIV

"Therefore since we are God's offspring, we should not think that the divine being is like gold or silver or stone—an image made by human design and skill. In the past God overlooked such ignorance, but now he commands all people everywhere to repent. For he has set a day when he will judge the world with justice by the man he has appointed. He has given proof of this to everyone by raising him from the dead."

2 Peter 3:9 NIV
The Lord is not slow in keeping his promise, as some understand slowness. Instead he is patient with you, not wanting anyone to perish, but everyone to come to repentance.

2 Chronicles 6:38-39 NASB
if they return to You with all their heart and with all their soul in the land of their captivity, where they have been taken captive, and pray toward their land which You have given to their fathers and the city which You have chosen, and toward the house which I have built for Your name, then hear from heaven, from Your dwelling place, their prayer and supplications, and maintain their cause and forgive Your people who have sinned against You.

Deuteronomy 32:4 NLT
He is the Rock; his deeds are perfect.
    Everything he does is just and fair.
He is a faithful God who does no wrong;
    how just and upright he is!

Numbers 23:19 ESV
God is not man, that he should lie, or a son of man, that he should change his mind. Has he said, and will he not do it? Or has he spoken, and will he not fulfill it?

Psalm 18:2 KJV
The Lord is my rock, and my fortress, and my deliverer; my God, my strength, in whom I will trust; my buckler, and the horn of my salvation, and my high tower.

James 1:17 ESV

Every good gift and every perfect gift is from above, coming down from the Father of lights with whom there is no variation or shadow due to change.

Excellent site for additional Bible translations:
http://www.biblegateway.com/resources/commentaries/
Excellent resource for additional Bible study:
(Be sure to read the instructions on their page)
http://www.blueletterbible.org/commentaries/

Change - Christian Quotes

"He is intangible and invisible. But His work is more powerful than the most ferocious wind. The Spirit brings order out of chaos and beauty out of ugliness. He can transform a sin-blistered man into a paragon of virtue. The Spirit changes people. The Author of life is also the Transformer of life."
R. C. Sproul

"Often times God demonstrates His faithfulness in adversity by providing for us what we need to survive. He does not change our painful circumstances. He sustains us through them."
Charles Stanley

"God cannot change for the better, for He is already perfect; and being perfect, He cannot change for the worse."
A. W. Pink

"There is need of a great revival of spiritual life, of truly fervent devotion to our Lord Jesus, of entire consecration to His service. It is only in a church in which this spirit of revival has at least begun, that there is any hope of radical change in the

relation of the majority of our Christian people to mission work."
Andrew Murray

"He who shall introduce into public affairs the principles of primitive Christianity will change the face of the world."
Benjamin Franklin

"It is well for us that, amidst all the variableness of life, there is One whom change cannot affect; One whose heart can never alter, and on whose brow mutability can make no furrows."
Charles Spurgeon

Children

Children - Bible Verses

Psalm 127:3-5 ESV
Behold, children are a heritage from the LORD, the fruit of the womb a reward. Like arrows in the hand of a warrior are the children of one's youth. Blessed is the man who fills his quiver with them! He shall not be put to shame when he speaks with his enemies in the gate.

Proverbs 22:6 ESV
Train up a child in the way he should go; even when he is old he will not depart from it.

Isaiah 54:13 KJV
And all thy children shall be taught of the Lord; and great shall be the peace of thy children.

Genesis 18:19 ESV
For I have chosen him, that he may command his children and his household after him to keep the way of the LORD by doing righteousness and justice, so that the LORD may bring to Abraham what he has promised him."

2 Timothy 3:16-17 NIV
All Scripture is God-breathed and is useful for teaching, rebuking, correcting and training in righteousness, so that the servant of God may be thoroughly equipped for every good work.

Deuteronomy 4:9 ESV
"Only take care, and keep your soul diligently, lest you forget the things that your eyes have seen, and lest they depart from your heart all the days of your life. Make them known to your children and your children's children.

Colossians 3:21 ESV
Fathers, do not provoke your children, lest they become discouraged.

Deuteronomy 6:6-9 NIV
These commandments that I give you today are to be on your hearts. Impress them on your children. Talk about them when you sit at home and when you walk along the road, when you lie down and when you get up. Tie them as symbols on your hands and bind them on your foreheads. Write them on the doorframes of your houses and on your gates.

Isaiah 38:19 KJV
The living, the living, he shall praise thee, as I do this day: the father to the children shall make known thy truth.

Matthew 7:12 NASB
So in everything, do to others what you would have them do to you, for this sums up the Law and the Prophets.

2 Timothy 1:5 ESV
I am reminded of your sincere faith, a faith that dwelt first in your grandmother Lois and your mother Eunice and now, I am sure, dwells in you as well.

Proverbs 13:24 ESV
Whoever spares the rod hates his son, but he who loves him is diligent to discipline him.

Proverbs 23:13-14 ESV
Do not withhold discipline from a child; if you strike him with a rod, he will not die. If you strike him with the rod, you will save his soul from Sheol.

2 Timothy 3:14-15 NLT
But you must remain faithful to the things you have been taught. You know they are true, for you know you can trust those who taught you. 15 You have been taught the holy Scriptures from childhood, and they have given you the wisdom to receive the salvation that comes by trusting in Christ Jesus.

Proverbs 29:15 ESV
The rod and reproof give wisdom, but a child left to himself brings shame to his mother

Proverbs 29:17 ESV
Discipline your son, and he will give you rest; he will give delight to your heart.

Ephesians 6:4 ESV
Fathers, do not provoke your children to anger, but bring them up in the discipline and instruction of the Lord.

Psalm 113:9 ESV
He gives the barren woman a home, making her the joyous mother of children.Praise the LORD!

Psalm 139:13-16 NLT
You made all the delicate, inner parts of my body
    and knit me together in my mother's womb.
Thank you for making me so wonderfully complex!
    Your workmanship is marvelous—how well I know it.
You watched me as I was being formed in utter seclusion,
    as I was woven together in the dark of the womb.
You saw me before I was born.
    Every day of my life was recorded in your book.
Every moment was laid out
    before a single day had passed.

John 16:21 NASB
Whenever a woman is in labor she has pain, because her hour has come; but when she gives birth to the child, she no longer remembers the anguish because of the joy that a child has been born into the world.

James 1:17 NASB

Every good thing given and every perfect gift is from above, coming down from the Father of lights, with whom there is no variation or shifting shadow.

Excellent site for additional Bible translations

http://www.biblegateway.com/resources/commentaries/

Excellent resource for additional Bible study:

(Be sure to read the instructions on their page)
http://www.blueletterbible.org/commentaries/

Children - Christian Quotes

"A child needs both to be hugged and unhugged. The hug lets her know she is valuable. The unhug lets her know that she is viable. If you're always shoving your child away, they will cling to you for love. If you're always holding them closer, they will cling to you for fear."
Billy Graham

"The happiest and holiest children in the world are the children whose fathers succeed in winning both their tender affection and their reverential and loving fear. And they are the children who will come to understand most easily the mystery of the fatherhood of God."
John Piper
Sermon: Malachi 1:6-14, October 25, 1987

"Remember children are born with a decided bias toward evil, and therefore if you let them choose for themselves, they are certain to choose wrong. The mother cannot tell what her tender infant may grow up to be - tall or short, weak or strong, wise or foolish; he may or may not be any of these it is all uncertain. But one thing the mother can say with certainty: he will have a corrupt and sinful heart. It is natural for us to do

wrong... Our hearts are like the earth on which we tread; let it alone, and it is sure to bear weeds."
J. C. Ryle

"Children, obey. Why does the apostle use the word obey instead of honor, which has a greater extent of meaning? It is because obedience is the evidence of that honor which children owe to their parents, and it therefore more earnestly enforced. It is likewise more difficult; for the human mind recoils from the idea of subjection, and with difficulty allows itself to be placed under the control of another."
John Calvin

"As the flower in the garden stretches toward the light of the sun, so there is in the child a mysterious inclination toward the eternal light. Have you ever

noticed this mysterious thing that when you tell the smallest child about God, [he or she] never asks with strangeness and wonder, "What or who is God – I have never seen Him," but listens with shining face to the words as though they soft loving sounds from the land of home. Or when you teach a child to fold [his or her] little hands in prayer that [he or she] does this as though it were a matter of course, as though [it was] opening for [the child] that world of which [he or she] had been dreaming with longing and anticipation. Or tell them, these little ones, the stories of the Savior, show them the pictures with scenes and personages of the Bible – how their pure eyes shine, how their little hearts beat."
R.C.H. Lenski
From Interpretation of Saint Matthews Gospel by Richard C. Lenski, © 1932, Augsburg Publishing House, p. 743.

"Rejection of parental authority is a rejection of God's authority. And the rejection of God's authority is, in fact, claiming his authority as my own. It is an attempt to be God."
Paul David Tripp
Age of Opportunity, P&R Publishing, 1997, p. 120,

"What a mercy was it to us to have parents that prayed for us before they had us, as well as in our infancy when we could not pray for ourselves!"
John Flavel

Comfort

Comfort - Bible Verses

Psalm 27:4-5 ESV
One thing have I asked of the LORD, that will I seek after: that I may dwell in the house of the LORD all the days of my life, to gaze upon the beauty of the LORD and to inquire in his temple. For he will hide me in his shelter in the day of trouble; he will conceal me under the cover of his tent; he will lift me high upon a rock.

Psalm 46:1 ESV
God is our refuge and strength, a very present help in trouble.

1 Peter 5:6-7 KJV
Humble yourselves therefore under the mighty hand of God, that he may exalt you in due time: Casting all your care upon him; for he careth for you.

Psalm 22:24 ESV
For he has not despised or abhorred the affliction of the afflicted, and he has not hidden his face from him, but has heard, when he cried to him.

Psalm 56:8 ESV
You have kept count of my tossings; put my tears in your bottle. Are they not in your book?

Psalm 116:1-2 ESV
I love the LORD, because he has heard my voice and my pleas for mercy. Because he inclined his ear to me, therefore I will call on him as long as I live.

Jeremiah 29:11 KJV
For I know the thoughts that I think toward you, saith the LORD, thoughts of peace, and not of evil, to give you an expected end.

Psalm 55:22 ESV
Cast your burden on the LORD, and he will sustain you; he will never permit the righteous to be moved.

Nahum 1:7 ESV
The LORD is good, a stronghold in the day of trouble; he knows those who take refuge in him.

Psalm 119:48-52 NLT
I honor and love your commands.
  I meditate on your decrees.
Remember your promise to me;
  it is my only hope.
Your promise revives me;
  it comforts me in all my troubles.
The proud hold me in utter contempt,
  but I do not turn away from your instructions.
I meditate on your age-old regulations;
  O Lord, they comfort me.

Lamentations 3:31-32 NLT
For no one is abandoned
  by the Lord forever.
Though he brings grief, he also shows compassion
  because of the greatness of his unfailing love.

John 14:16-18 NASB
I will ask the Father, and He will give you another Helper, that He may be with you forever; that is the Spirit of truth, whom the world cannot receive, because it does not see Him or know Him, but you know Him because He abides with you and will be in you.
"I will not leave you as orphans; I will come to you.

John 14:26-27 NASB
But the Helper, the Holy Spirit, whom the Father will send in My name, He will teach you all things, and bring to your remembrance all that I said to

you. Peace I leave with you; My peace I give to you; not as the world gives do I give to you. Do not let your heart be troubled, nor let it be fearful.

Lamentations 3:22-23 KJV
It is of the LORD's mercies that we are not consumed, because his compassions fail not. They are new every morning: great is thy faithfulness.

Psalm 9:9 ESV
The LORD is a stronghold for the oppressed, a stronghold in times of trouble.

Psalm 30:5 NLT
For his anger lasts only a moment,
   but his favor lasts a lifetime!
Weeping may last through the night,
   but joy comes with the morning.

Psalm 71:20-21 ESV
You who have made me see many troubles and calamities will revive me again; from the depths of the earth you will bring me up again. You will increase my greatness and comfort me again.

John 16:22 NASB
Therefore you too have grief now; but I will see you again, and your heart will rejoice, and no one will take your joy away from you.

2 Corinthians 5:17 NIV
Therefore, if anyone is in Christ, the new creation has come: The old has gone, the new is here!

Revelation 21:5 NIV
He who was seated on the throne said, "I am making everything new!" Then he said, "Write this down, for these words are trustworthy and true."

Excellent site for additional Bible translations:
http://www.biblegateway.com/resources/commentaries/

Excellent resource for additional Bible study:
(Be sure to read the instructions on their page)
http://www.blueletterbible.org/commentaries/

Comfort - Christian Quotes

"Thanks be to God, not—only for 'rivers of endless joys above, but for 'rills of comfort here below.' "
Adoniram Judson

"We find thus by experience that there is no good applying to heaven for earthly comfort. Heaven can give heavenly comfort; no other kind. Earth cannot give earthly comfort either, as there is no earthly comfort in the long run."
C.S. Lewis

"Comfort and prosperity have never enriched the world as much as adversity has."
Billy Graham

"If you look for truth, you may find comfort in the end; if you look for comfort you will not get either comfort or truth only soft soap and wishful thinking to begin, and in the end, despair."
C. S. Lewis

"We act as though comfort and luxury were the chief requirements of life, when all that we need to make us really

happy is something to be enthusiastic about."
Charles Kingsley

"Multitudes who come to church for comfort need to be severely discomfited and awakened out of their lethal slumbering."
Richard Owen Roberts
Preaching that Hinders Revival, Revival Commentary, v. 2, n. 2.

"He has held me when I have had no more strength and have wondered how I would ever make it. He has held me when I have felt defeated by all that I had to do. When I have run to my El Shaddai, I have never come away wanting. He is my all-sufficient One. O Beloved, do you understand? Have

you experienced Him as your El Shaddai? If not, He is waiting - arms opened wide - for you."
Kay Arthur

"The whole world appears to me like a huge vacuum, a vast empty space, whence nothing desirable, or at least satisfactory, can possibly be derived; and I long daily to die more and more to it; even though I obtain not that comfort from spiritual things which I earnestly desire."
David Brainerd

"We're too comfortable to be spiritual. ...We think we will be able to pursue God better without danger or hardship. And yet it works in just the opposite way. Nothing is more difficult than to grow spiritually when comfortable."
Tim Bascom
The Comfort Trap: Spiritual Dangers in the Convenience Culture, Intervarsity, 1993.

"Snuggle in God's arms. When you are hurting, when you feel lonely, left out. let Him cradle you, comfort you, reassure you of His all-sufficient power and love."
Kay Arthur

"God of our life, there are days when the burdens we carry chafe our shoulders and weigh us down; when the road seems dreary and endless, the skies grey and threatening; when our lives have no music in them, and our hearts are lonely, and our souls have lost their courage. Flood the path with light, run our eyes to where the skies are full of promise; tune our hearts to brave music; give us the sense of comradeship with heroes and saints of every age; and so quicken our spirits that we may be able to encourage the souls of all who journey with us on the road of life, to Your honour and glory."
Augustine

Couples

Couples - Bible Verses

Deuteronomy 24:5 ESV
"When a man is newly married, he shall not go out with the army or be liable for any other public duty. He shall be free at home one year to be happy with his wife whom he has taken."

Ephesians 5:31-32 NIV
"For this reason a man will leave his father and mother and be united to his wife, and the two will become one flesh." This is a profound mystery—but I am talking about Christ and the church.

Proverbs 24:29 ESV
Do not say, "I will do to him as he has done to me; I will pay the man back for what he has done."

Malachi 2:14-15 ESV
But you say, "Why does he not?" Because the LORD was witness between you and the wife of your youth, to whom you have been faithless, though she is your companion and your wife by covenant. Did he not make them one, with a portion of the Spirit in their union? And what was the one God seeking? Godly offspring. So guard yourselves in your spirit, and let none of you be faithless to the wife of your youth.

Romans 12:17 NLT
Never pay back evil with more evil. Do things in such a way that everyone can see you are honorable.

Genesis 1:26-28 NASB
Then God said, "Let Us make man in Our image, according to Our likeness; and let them rule over the fish of the sea and over the birds of the sky and over the cattle and over all the earth, and over every creeping thing that creeps on the earth." God created man in His own image, in the image of

God He created him; male and female He created them. God blessed them; and God said to them, "Be fruitful and multiply, and fill the earth, and subdue it; and rule over the fish of the sea and over the birds of the sky and over every living thing that moves on the earth."

Genesis 2:18 ESV
Then the Lord God said, "It is not good for the man to be alone; I will make him a helper suitable for him."

Ephesians 4:1-3 NIV
As a prisoner for the Lord, then, I urge you to live a life worthy of the calling you have received. Be completely humble and gentle; be patient, bearing with one another in love. Make every effort to keep the unity of the Spirit through the bond of peace.

Ephesians 4:31-32 NIV
Get rid of all bitterness, rage and anger, brawling and slander, along with every form of malice. Be kind and compassionate to one another, forgiving each other, just as in Christ God forgave you.

Matthew 19:5-6 NIV
and said, 'For this reason a man shall leave his father and mother and be joined to his wife, and the two shall become one flesh'? So they are no longer two, but one flesh. What therefore God has joined together, let no man separate."

Mark 10:9 ESV
"What therefore God has joined together, let not man separate."

Philippians 2:2 ESV
complete my joy by being of the same mind, having the same love, being in full accord and of one mind.

Colossians 3:12-14 NIV
Therefore, as God's chosen people, holy and dearly loved, clothe yourselves with compassion, kindness, humility, gentleness and patience. Bear with

each other and forgive one another if any of you has a grievance against someone. Forgive as the Lord forgave you. And over all these virtues put on love, which binds them all together in perfect unity.

Philippians 1:9-10 NASB
And this I pray, that your love may abound still more and more in real knowledge and all discernment, so that you may approve the things that are excellent, in order to be sincere and blameless until the day of Christ;

Hebrews 13:4 ESV
Let marriage be held in honor among all, and let the marriage bed be undefiled, for God will judge the sexually immoral and adulterous.

1 Peter 1:22 ESV
Having purified your souls by your obedience to the truth for a sincere brotherly love, love one another earnestly from a pure heart

1 Peter 3:7 ESV
Likewise, husbands, live with your wives in an understanding way, showing honor to the woman as the weaker vessel, since they are heirs with you of the grace of life, so that your prayers may not be hindered.

Proverbs 19:14 ESV
House and wealth are inherited from fathers, but a prudent wife is from the LORD.

Ecclesiastes 4:11-12 NASB
Furthermore, if two lie down together they keep warm, but how can one be warm alone? And if one can overpower him who is alone, two can resist him. A cord of three strands is not quickly torn apart.

Ecclesiastes 9:9 NASB
Enjoy life with the woman whom you love all the days of your fleeting life which He has given to you under the sun; for this is your reward in life and in your toil in which you have labored under the sun.

Excellent site for additional Bible translations:
http://www.biblegateway.com/resources/commentaries/
Excellent resource for additional Bible study:
(Be sure to read the instructions on their page)
http://www.blueletterbible.org/commentaries/

Couples - Christian Quotes

"Marriage is not a mere civil thing, but is partly spiritual and Divine, and therefore God alone has the power to appoint the beginning, the continuance, and the end thereof."
A.W. Pink
An Exposition of the Sermon on the Mount, Chapter 13.

"The man and his wife become one flesh (Gen 2:24). Together they form one complete unit. As they come together physically, intellectually, emotionally, there is a wholeness that did not exist before. They are fused into one."
Jay E. Adams
Christian Living in the Home, P&R Publishing, 1972, p. 48,

"In marriage a man and woman are so closely joined that they become "one flesh," which involves spiritual as well as physical oneness. In marriage God brings a husband and wife together in a unique physical and spiritual bond that reaches to the very depths of their souls. As God designed it, marriage is to be the welding of two people together into one unit, the blending of two minds, two wills, two sets of emotions, two spirits. It is a bond the Lord intends to be indissoluble as long as both partners are alive. The Lord created sex and procreation to be the fullest expression of that oneness, and the intimacies of marriage are not to be shared with any other human being."
John MacArthur
Matthew 1-7, Moody, 1985, p. 311.

"When a couple speaks their vows, it is not a man or a woman or a pastor or parent who is the main actor – the main doer. God is. God joins a husband and a wife into a one-flesh union. God does that. The world does not know this. Which is one of the reasons why marriage is treated so casually. And Christians often act like they don't know it, which is one of the reasons marriage in the church is not seen as the wonder it is. Marriage is God's doing because it is a one-flesh union that God Himself performs."
John Piper
This Momentary Marriage – A Parable of Permanence, Desiring God Foundation, 2008, p. 23,

The first negative judgment we find in Holy Writ is a judgment on loneliness. God said, "It is not good for man to be alone."
R.C. Sproul
The Intimate Marriage, P&R Publishing, 1975, p. 43

"One of the most difficult things to admit or to understand is that there is probably nothing that a man wants more from his wife than her admiration. There is probably nothing that a woman wants more from her husband than his attention, taking her seriously and treating her with the greatest dignity. Here what we are getting at is the question of respect. If I exercise my headship over my wife in a tyrannical way, I am not respecting my wife. If my wife gives slavish obedience to me without any love, she is not respecting me. The whole basis of the relationship is built upon love, cherishing and respecting one another."
R.C. Sproul
The Purpose of God, An Exposition of Ephesians, Christian Focus Publications, 1994, p. 139.

"Man and woman are one in essence. That is to say, Adam and Eve are equal in dignity, value, and glory. In essential unity there is absolutely no room for inferiority of person. The man and woman are equal in every respect except one – authority. Two different tasks are given to people of equal value and dignity. In the economy of marriage, only the job descriptions are different."
R.C. Sproul
The Intimate Marriage, P&R Publishing, 1975, p. 44.

"Let the wife make her husband glad to come home and let him make her sorry to see him leave."
Martin Luther

"To have peace and love in a marriage is a gift that is next to the knowledge of the gospel."
Martin Luther

Courage

Courage - Bible Verses

Psalm 31:24 NASB
Be strong and let your heart take courage,
All you who hope in the Lord.

Isaiah 41:10-13 KJV
"Fear thou not; for I am with thee: be not dismayed; for I am thy God: I will strengthen thee; yea, I will help thee; yea, I will uphold thee with the right hand of my righteousness.Behold, all they that were incensed against thee shall be ashamed and confounded: they shall be as nothing; and they that strive with thee shall perish. Thou shalt seek them, and shalt not find them, even them that contended with thee: they that war against thee shall be as nothing, and as a thing of nought. For I the LORD thy God will hold thy right hand, saying unto thee, Fear not; I will help thee."

1 Corinthians 15:58 KJV
"Therefore, my beloved brethren, be ye stedfast, unmoveable, always abounding in the work of the Lord, forasmuch as ye know that your labour is not in vain in the Lord."

1 Corinthians 16:13 NASB
Be on the alert, stand firm in the faith, act like men, be strong.

Psalm 23:4 KJV
"Yea, though I walk through the valley of the shadow of death, I will fear no evil: for thou art with me; thy rod and thy staff they comfort me."

Joshua 1:7-9 KJV
"Only be thou strong and very courageous, that thou mayest observe to do according to all the law, which Moses my servant commanded thee: turn not from it to the right hand or to the left, that thou mayest prosper withersoever thou goest. This book of the law shall not depart out of thy

mouth; but thou shalt meditate therein day and night, that thou mayest observe to do according to all that is written therein: for then thou shalt make thy way prosperous, and then thou shalt have good success. Have not I commanded thee? Be strong and of a good courage; be not afraid, neither be thou dismayed: for the LORD thy God is with thee whithersoever thou goest."

1 Chronicles 28:20 KJV
"And David said to Solomon his son, Be strong and of good courage, and do it: fear not, nor be dismayed: for the LORD God, even my God, will be with thee; he will not fail thee, nor forsake thee, until thou hast finished all the work for the service of the house of the LORD."

Psalm 27:1 NLT
The Lord is my light and my salvation—
    so why should I be afraid?
The Lord is my fortress, protecting me from danger,
    so why should I tremble?

Psalm 56:3-4 KJV
"What time I am afraid, I will trust in thee. In God I will praise his word, in God I have put my trust; I will not fear what flesh can do unto me."

Deuteronomy 31:6 KJV
Be strong and courageous. Do not be afraid or terrified because of them, for the Lord your God goes with you; he will never leave you nor forsake you."

Isaiah 54:4 NLT
"Fear not; you will no longer live in shame.
    Don't be afraid; there is no more disgrace for you.
You will no longer remember the shame of your youth
    and the sorrows of widowhood.

Matthew 10:28 KJV
"And fear not them which kill the body, but are not able to kill the soul: but rather fear him which is able to destroy both soul and body in hell."

2 Timothy 1:7 KJV
"For God hath not given us the spirit of fear; but of power, and of love, and of a sound mind."

Hebrews 13:5-6 NLT
Don't love money; be satisfied with what you have. For God has said,
"I will never fail you.
   I will never abandon you."
So we can say with confidence,
"The Lord is my helper,
   so I will have no fear.
   What can mere people do to me?"

1 John 4:18 KJV
"There is no fear in love; but perfect love casteth out fear: because fear hath torment. He that feareth is not made perfect in love."

John 14:27 KJV
"Peace I leave with you, my peace I give unto you: not as the world giveth, give I unto you. Let not your heart be troubled, neither let it be afraid."

Romans 8:15 NASB
For you have not received a spirit of slavery leading to fear again, but you have received a spirit of adoption as sons by which we cry out, "Abba! Father!"

Philippians 1:12-14 KJV
"But I would ye should understand, brethren, that the things which happened unto me have fallen out rather unto the furtherance of the gospel; So that my bonds in Christ are manifest in all the palace, and in all other places; And many of the brethren in the Lord, waxing confident by my bonds, are much more bold to speak the word without fear."

1 Peter 3:14-16 NLT
But even if you suffer for doing what is right, God will reward you for it. So don't worry or be afraid of their threats. 15 Instead, you must worship Christ

as Lord of your life. And if someone asks about your Christian hope, always be ready to explain it. 16 But do this in a gentle and respectful way. Keep your conscience clear. Then if people speak against you, they will be ashamed when they see what a good life you live because you belong to Christ.

Excellent site for additional Bible translations:
http://www.biblegateway.com/resources/commentaries/
Excellent resource for additional Bible study:
(Be sure to read the instructions on their page)
http://www.blueletterbible.org/commentaries/

Courage - Christian Quotes

"Have patience with all things, but chiefly have patience with yourself. Do not lose courage in considering your own imperfections but instantly set about remedying them-- every day begin the task anew."
Francis de Sales

"God of our life, there are days when the burdens we carry chafe our shoulders and weigh us down; when the road seems dreary and endless, the skies grey and threatening; when our lives have no music in them, and our hearts are lonely, and our souls have lost their courage. Flood the path with light, run our eyes to where the skies are full of promise; tune our hearts to brave music; give us the sense of comradeship with heroes and saints of every age; and so quicken our spirits that we may be able to encourage the souls of all who journey with us on the road of life, to Your honour and glory."
Augustine

"Have courage for the great sorrows of life and patience for the small ones. And when you have finished your daily task, go to sleep in peace. God is awake."
Victor Hugo

"Down through the centuries in times of trouble and trial God has brought courage to the hearts of those who love Him. The Bible is filled with assurances of God's help and comfort in every kind of trouble which might cause fears to arise in the human heart. You can look ahead with promise, hope, and joy."
Billy Graham

The true follower of Christ will not ask, "If I embrace this truth, what will it cost me?" Rather he will say, "This is truth. God help me to walk in it, let come what may!"
A. W. Tozer

"Even a coward can praise Christ, but it takes a man of courage to follow him."
Anonymous

"Courage is contagious. When a brave man takes a stand, the spines of others are often stiffened."
Billy Graham

"Yet, surely, there must be some who will fling aside the (cowardly) love of peace, and speak out for our Lord, and for His truth. A craven spirit is upon man, and their tongues are paralyzed. Oh, for an outburst of true faith and holy zeal."
C.H. Spurgeon

"Courage we shall need, and for the exercise of it we have as much reason as necessary, if we are soldiers of King Jesus."
C.H. Spurgeon

"Courage is that quality of mind which enables people to encounter danger or difficulty firmly, without fear or discouragement."
Oswald Sanders
Spiritual Leadership, Moody Publishers, 1967, p. 59.

Death

Death- Bible Verses

Romans 8:16-17 NLT
For his Spirit joins with our spirit to affirm that we are God's children. And since we are his children, we are his heirs. In fact, together with Christ we are heirs of God's glory. But if we are to share his glory, we must also share his suffering.

2 Corinthians 5:6-8 NLT
So we are always confident, even though we know that as long as we live in these bodies we are not at home with the Lord. For we live by believing and not by seeing. Yes, we are fully confident, and we would rather be away from these earthly bodies, for then we will be at home with the Lord.

1 Thessalonians 4:16-18 NIV
For the Lord himself will come down from heaven, with a loud command, with the voice of the archangel and with the trumpet call of God, and the dead in Christ will rise first. After that, we who are still alive and are left will be caught up together with them in the clouds to meet the Lord in the air. And so we will be with the Lord forever. Therefore encourage one another with these words.

John 14:1-4 NIV
"Don't let your hearts be troubled. Trust in God, and trust also in me. There is more than enough room in my Father's home. If this were not so, would I have told you that I am going to prepare a place for you? When everything is ready, I will come and get you, so that you will always be with me where I am. And you know the way to where I am going."

1 Thessalonians 5:9-11 NIV
For God did not appoint us to suffer wrath but to receive salvation through our Lord Jesus Christ. He died for us so that, whether we are awake or asleep, we may live together with him. Therefore encourage one another and build each other up, just as in fact you are doing.

John 11:23-26 NIV
Jesus said to her, "Your brother will rise again."
Martha answered, "I know he will rise again in the resurrection at the last day."
Jesus said to her, "I am the resurrection and the life. The one who believes in me will live, even though they die; and whoever lives by believing in me will never die. Do you believe this?"

1 Corinthians 15:54-57 NASB
But when this perishable will have put on the imperishable, and this mortal will have put on immortality, then will come about the saying that is written, "Death is swallowed up in victory. O death, where is your victory? O death, where is your sting?" The sting of death is sin, and the power of sin is the law; but thanks be to God, who gives us the victory through our Lord Jesus Christ.

Philippians 3:20-21 NASB
For our citizenship is in heaven, from which also we eagerly wait for a Savior, the Lord Jesus Christ; who will transform the body of our humble state into conformity with the body of His glory, by the exertion of the power that He has even to subject all things to Himself.

2 Samuel 12:23 ESV
But now he is dead. Why should I fast? Can I bring him back again? I shall go to him, but he will not return to me."

1 Corinthians 15:20-23 NASB
But now Christ has been raised from the dead, the first fruits of those who are asleep. For since by a man came death, by a man also came the resurrection of the dead. For as in Adam all die, so also in Christ all will be

made alive. But each in his own order: Christ the first fruits, after that those who are Christ's at His coming,

Philippians 1:23-24 ESV
I am hard pressed between the two. My desire is to depart and be with Christ, for that is far better. But to remain in the flesh is more necessary on your account.

1 Peter 1:3-5 ESV
Blessed be the God and Father of our Lord Jesus Christ! According to his great mercy, he has caused us to be born again to a living hope through the resurrection of Jesus Christ from the dead, to an inheritance that is imperishable, undefiled, and unfading, kept in heaven for you, who by God's power are being guarded through faith for a salvation ready to be revealed in the last time.

1 John 3:1-2 ESV
See what kind of love the Father has given to us, that we should be called children of God; and so we are. The reason why the world does not know us is that it did not know him. Beloved, we are God's children now, and what we will be has not yet appeared; but we know that when he appears we shall be like him, because we shall see him as he is.

Revelation 21:1-4 NLT
Then I saw a new heaven and a new earth, for the old heaven and the old earth had disappeared. And the sea was also gone. And I saw the holy city, the new Jerusalem, coming down from God out of heaven like a bride beautifully dressed for her husband.
I heard a loud shout from the throne, saying, "Look, God's home is now among his people! He will live with them, and they will be his people. God himself will be with them. He will wipe every tear from their eyes, and there will be no more death or sorrow or crying or pain. All these things are gone forever."

Psalm 23:4 KJV

Yea, though I walk through the valley of the shadow of death, I will fear no evil: for thou art with me; thy rod and thy staff they comfort me.

John 10:27-29 NASB
My sheep hear My voice, and I know them, and they follow Me; and I give eternal life to them, and they will never perish; and no one will snatch them out of My hand. My Father, who has given them to Me, is greater than all; and no one is able to snatch them out of the Father's hand.

Romans 8:38-39 NIV
For I am convinced that neither death nor life, neither angels nor demons, neither the present nor the future, nor any powers, 39 neither height nor depth, nor anything else in all creation, will be able to separate us from the love of God that is in Christ Jesus our Lord.

Romans 14:8 ESV
For if we live, we live to the Lord, and if we die, we die to the Lord. So then, whether we live or whether we die, we are the Lord's.

Revelation 14:13 ESV
And I heard a voice from heaven saying, "Write this: Blessed are the dead who die in the Lord from now on." "Blessed indeed," says the Spirit, "that they may rest from their labors, for their deeds follow them!"

Psalm 116:15 ESV
Precious in the sight of the LORD is the death of his saints.

Excellent site for additional Bible translations:
http://www.biblegateway.com/resources/commentaries/
Excellent resource for additional Bible study:
(Be sure to read the instructions on their page)
http://www.blueletterbible.org/commentaries/

Death- Christian Quotes

"They that love beyond the world cannot be separated by it. Death cannot kill what never dies."
Williams Penn

"When the time comes for you to die, you need not be afraid, because death cannot separate you from God's love."
Charles H. Spurgeon

"Many Christians dread the thought of leaving this world. Why? Because so many have stored up their treasures on earth, not in heaven. Each day brings us closer to death. If your treasures are on earth, that means each day brings you closer to losing your treasures."
Randy Alcorn
Excerpted from The Treasure Principle by Randy Alcorn © 2002 by Eternal Perspective Ministries, p. 40.

Let us consider this settled, that no one has made progress in the school of Christ who does not joyfully await the day of death and final resurrection.
John Calvin

"It is better for me to die in behalf of Jesus Christ, than to reign over all the ends of the earth."
Ignatius of Antioch

"He whose head is in heaven need not fear to put his feet into the grave."
Matthew Henry

"Has this world been so kind to you that you should leave with regret? There are better things ahead than any we leave behind."
C.S. Lewis

"The very happiest persons I have ever met with have been departing believers. The only people for whom I have felt any envy have been dying members of this very church, whose hands I have grasped in their passing

away. Almost without exception I have seen in them holy delight and triumph. And in the exceptions to this exceeding joy I have seen deep peace, exhibited in a calm and deliberate readiness to enter into the presence of their God."
C.H. Spurgeon

"The best moment of a Christian's life is his last one, because it is the one that is nearest heaven. And then it is that he begins to strike the keynote of the song which he shall sing to all eternity. "
C.H. Spurgeon

"Death in its substance has been removed, and only the shadow of it remains… Nobody is afraid of a shadow, for a shadow cannot block a man's pathway for even a moment. The shadow of a dog can't bite; the shadow of a sword can't kill."
C.H. Spurgeon

"We see his smile of love even when others see nothing but the black hand of Death smiting our best beloved."
C.H. Spurgeon

"Depend upon it, your dying hour will be the best hour you have ever known! Your last moment will be your richest moment, better than the day of your birth will be the day of your death. It shall be the beginning of heaven, the rising of a sun that shall go no more down forever!"
C.H. Spurgeon

"This is our comfort. We are "immortal until our work is done;" mortal still, but immortal also. Let us never fear death, then, but rather rejoice at the approach of it, since it comes at our dear Bridegroom's bidding!"
C.H. Spurgeon

"Death is never sudden to a saint; no guest comes unawares to him who keeps a constant table."
George Swinnock

"Let thy hope of heaven master they fear of death. Why shouldst thou be afraid to die, who hopest to live by dying!"
William Gurnall

Depression

Depression - Bible Verses

Deuteronomy 32:10 NLT
He found them in a desert land,
   in an empty, howling wasteland.
He surrounded them and watched over them;
   he guarded them as he would guard his own eyes.

Psalm 34:17 ESV
When the righteous cry for help, the LORD hears and delivers them out of all their troubles.

Psalm 40:1-3 NLT
I waited patiently for the Lord to help me,
   and he turned to me and heard my cry.
He lifted me out of the pit of despair,
   out of the mud and the mire.
He set my feet on solid ground
   and steadied me as I walked along.
He has given me a new song to sing,
   a hymn of praise to our God.
Many will see what he has done and be amazed.
   They will put their trust in the Lord.

Philippians 4:8 ESV
Finally, brothers, whatever is true, whatever is honorable, whatever is just, whatever is pure, whatever is lovely, whatever is commendable, if there is any excellence, if there is anything worthy of praise, think about these things.

Psalm 3:3 ESV
But you, O LORD, are a shield about me, my glory, and the lifter of my head.

Psalm 37:3-4 ESV

Trust in the LORD, and do good; dwell in the land and befriend faithfulness. Delight yourself in the LORD, and he will give you the desires of your heart.

Deuteronomy 31:8 NLT

Do not be afraid or discouraged, for the Lord will personally go ahead of you. He will be with you; he will neither fail you nor abandon you."

Psalm 32:10 ESV

Many are the sorrows of the wicked, but steadfast love surrounds the one who trusts in the LORD.

Psalm 42:11 ESV

Why are you cast down, O my soul, and why are you in turmoil within me? Hope in God; for I shall again praise him, my salvation and my God.

1 Peter 5:6-7 KJV

Humble yourselves therefore under the mighty hand of God, that he may exalt you in due time: Casting all your care upon him; for he careth for you.

Jeremiah 29:11 NIV

For I know the plans I have for you," declares the Lord, "plans to prosper you and not to harm you, plans to give you hope and a future.

Romans 8:38-39 NASB

For I am convinced that neither death nor life, neither angels nor demons, neither the present nor the future, nor any powers, neither height nor depth, nor anything else in all creation, will be able to separate us from the love of God that is in Christ Jesus our Lord.

2 Corinthians 1:3-4 ESV

Blessed be the God and Father of our Lord Jesus Christ, the Father of mercies and God of all comfort, who comforts us in all our affliction so that we will be able to comfort those who are in any affliction with the comfort with which we ourselves are comforted by God.

John 16:33 NIV
"I have told you these things, so that in me you may have peace. In this world you will have trouble. But take heart! I have overcome the world."

1 Peter 4:12-13 NASB
Beloved, do not be surprised at the fiery ordeal among you, which comes upon you for your testing, as though some strange thing were happening to you; but to the degree that you share the sufferings of Christ, keep on rejoicing, so that also at the revelation of His glory you may rejoice with exultation.

Excellent site for additional Bible translations:
http://www.biblegateway.com/resources/commentaries/
Excellent resource for additional Bible study:
(Be sure to read the instructions on their page)
http://www.blueletterbible.org/commentaries/

Depression - Christian Quotes

"I find myself frequently depressed – perhaps more so than any other person here. And I find no better cure for that depression than to trust in the Lord with all my heart, and seek to realize afresh the power of the peace-speaking blood of Jesus, and His infinite love in dying upon the cross to put away all my transgressions."
C.H. Spurgeon

"Before any great achievement, some measure of depression is very usual."
C.H. Spurgeon

"Indeed I can put it, finally like this; the ultimate cause of all spiritual depression is unbelief. For if it were not or unbelief even the devil could do nothing. It is because we listen to the devil instead of listening to God that we go down before him and fall before his attacks."
Martyn Lloyd-Jones

"I know, perhaps as well as anyone, what depression means, and what it is to feel myself sinking lower and lower. Yet at the worst, when I reach the lowest depths, I have an inward peace which no pain or depression can in the least disturb. Trusting in Jesus Christ my Savior, there is still a blessed quietness in the deep caverns of my soul, though upon the surface, a rough tempest may be raging, and there may be little apparent calm."
C.H. Spurgeon

"This depression comes over me whenever the Lord is preparing a larger blessing for my ministry; the cloud is black before it breaks, and overshadows before it yields its deluge of mercy. Depression has now become to me as a prophet in rough clothing, a John the Baptist, heralding the nearer coming of my Lord's richer benison. So have far better men found it. The scouring of the vessel has fitted it for the Master's use. Immersion in suffering has preceded the baptism of the Holy Ghost. Fasting gives an appetite for the banquet. The Lord is revealed in the backside of the desert, while his servant keepeth the sheep and waits in solitary awe. The

wilderness is the way to Canaan. The low valley leads to the towering mountain. Defeat prepares for victory."
C.H. Spurgeon

Divorce

Divorce- Bible Verses

Genesis 2:18 NASB
Then the Lord God said, "It is not good for the man to be alone; I will make him a helper suitable for him."

Deuteronomy 22:29 NIV
he shall pay her father fifty shekels of silver. He must marry the young woman, for he has violated her. He can never divorce her as long as he lives.

Jeremiah 3:1 ESV
"If a man divorces his wife and she goes from him and becomes another man's wife, will he return to her?

Malachi 2:16 ESV
"For the man who does not love his wife but divorces her, says the LORD, the God of Israel, covers his garment with violence, says the LORD of hosts. So guard yourselves in your spirit, and do not be faithless."

Matthew 1:19 NIV
Because Joseph her husband was faithful to the law, and yet did not want to expose her to public disgrace, he had in mind to divorce her quietly.

Deuteronomy 22:19 NASB
and they shall fine him a hundred shekels of silver and give it to the girl's father, because he publicly defamed a virgin of Israel. And she shall remain his wife; he cannot divorce her all his days

Mark 10:2 NIV
Some Pharisees came and tested him by asking, "Is it lawful for a man to divorce his wife?"

1 Corinthians 7:11 NIV
But if she does, she must remain unmarried or else be reconciled to her husband. And a husband must not divorce his wife.

Matthew 5:31 ESV
It was also said, 'Whoever divorces his wife, let him give her a certificate of divorce.'

Deuteronomy 24:1-3 ESV
"When a man takes a wife and marries her, if then she finds no favor in his eyes because he has found some indecency in her, and he writes her a certificate of divorce and puts it in her hand and sends her out of his house, and she departs out of his house, 2 and if she goes and becomes another man's wife, 3 and the latter man hates her and writes her a certificate of divorce and puts it in her hand and sends her out of his house, or if the latter man dies, who took her to be his wife,

Isaiah. 50:1 ESV
Thus says the LORD: "Where is your mother's certificate of divorce, with which I sent her away? Or which of my creditors is it to whom I have sold you? Behold, for your iniquities you were sold, and for your transgressions your mother was sent away.

Jeremiah 3:8 ESV
She saw that for all the adulteries of that faithless one, Israel, I had sent her away with a decree of divorce. Yet her treacherous sister Judah did not fear, but she too went and played the whore.

Matthew 19:7-9 NLT
"Then why did Moses say in the law that a man could give his wife a written notice of divorce and send her away?" they asked.
Jesus replied, "Moses permitted divorce only as a concession to your hard hearts, but it was not what God had originally intended. And I tell you this, whoever divorces his wife and marries someone else commits adultery—unless his wife has been unfaithful."

1 Corinthians 7:12-13 NLT

Now, I will speak to the rest of you, though I do not have a direct command from the Lord. If a Christian man has a wife who is not a believer and she is willing to continue living with him, he must not leave her. And if a Christian woman has a husband who is not a believer and he is willing to continue living with her, she must not leave him.

Romans 7:2 ESV

For a married woman is bound by law to her husband while he lives, but if her husband dies she is released from the law of marriage.

1 Corinthians 7:39 NLT

A wife is bound to her husband as long as he lives. If her husband dies, she is free to marry anyone she wishes, but only if he loves the Lord.

Matthew 5:32 ESV

But I say to you that everyone who divorces his wife, except on the ground of sexual immorality, makes her commit adultery, and whoever marries a divorced woman commits adultery.

Mark 10:11 NLT

He told them, "Whoever divorces his wife and marries someone else commits adultery against her.

Luke 16:18 NLT

"For example, a man who divorces his wife and marries someone else commits adultery. And anyone who marries a woman divorced from her husband commits adultery."

Excellent site for additional Bible translations
http://www.biblegateway.com/resources/commentaries/
Excellent resource for additional Bible study:
(Be sure to read the instructions on their page)
http://www.blueletterbible.org/commentaries/

Divorce- Christian Quotes

"Unbiblical reasons to pursue a divorce:
'My feelings have changed. I've fallen out of love with her' (Pr. 28:26; Mt. 24:12; 1 Cor. 13:5-6; Rev. 2:1-7).
'That man has killed all the love I ever had for him' (Lev. 19:18; Mt. 5:43-48; 22:34-40; Gal. 5:14; Eph. 5:25; Tit. 2:3-5).
'It is not good for the children to have to live in a home with so much conflict, hatred, and disharmony' (Jer. 16:12; Lk. 12:1; Rom. 12:18; 14:19; 1 Cor. 7:12-16; Eph. 4:3; 6:4; 1 Thes. 5:13; 1 Tim. 4:12; Heb. 12:25).
'I'm tired of trying' (1 Sam. 1:24ff; Heb. 10:36; 12:1-11; Jas. 1:2-8).
'I have peace about it' (Jonah 1:5-6; Rom. 14:22-23; Col. 3:15).
'He has lied to me repeatedly. I will never be able to trust him again' (Pr. 3:5-6; 20:6; Lk. 17:3; Ac. 15:36-39; Col. 4:10; 2 Tim. 4:11' 1 Pet. 3:5-6).
'I cannot continue to live in this constant state of confusion that this marriage keeps me in' (2 Cor. 4:8; 1 Cor. 10:13; Phil. 4:13).
'I've lived with her for umpteen years and I know that she will never change' (Psm. 138:8; 1 Cor. 1:8; Eph. 3:20; Phil. 1:6; 2:13; 2 Tim. 1:12; Ju. 24).
'My family and friends are all advising me to get out of this horrible marriage' (Pr. 11:14; 15:22, 24; 24:6; Rom. 14:22-23; 1 Cor. 15:33)."
Lou Priolo

Excerpted from: Divorce: Before You Say "I Don't," 2007, P&R, p. 18-23.

"It is clear that divorce is like a person cutting off an arm or leg because he has a splinter in it. Instead of dealing with whatever trouble arises between a husband and wife, divorce tries to solve the problem by destroying the union. On a deeper level, divorce destroys a union that God Himself has made. That is why Jesus said unequivocally, "What therefore God has joined together, let no man separate" (Matt. 19:6). The union of marriage is one which God, as its Creator, never desires to be broken. Divorce is a denial of His will and a destruction of His work."
John MacArthur

Matthew 1-7, Moody, 1985, p. 312.

"In hard, cold reality, a person rarely seeks divorce for the well-being of the children. What is distressing about this myth is not so much the fallacy of it as its blatant hypocrisy. If people were really concerned for the well-being of their children, I would think they would move heaven and earth to transcend their false dilemma and move in the direction of responsible parenthood. With the use of this myth as a justification for divorce, humankind exposes its capacity for calling good evil and evil good. Here an act of selfishness is painted or portrayed as a noble act of self-sacrifice for the good of the children."
R.C. Sproul

"Marriage is not a mere civil thing, but is partly spiritual and Divine, and therefore God alone has the power to appoint the beginning, the continuance, and the end thereof."
A.W. Pink

"In every marriage that ends in disaster, some stupid decisions were made with respect to God's regulations. If God's regulations were followed scrupulously, not only would there be no divorces; there would be no unhappy marriages. To violate the regulations of God is not only an exercise in disobedience but also an exercise in foolishness. If you want a happy marriage, the most intelligent thing you can do is to submit to God's regulations. They are designed to promote and protect your full happiness."
R.C. Sproul

"All history bears witness to the fact that when vital goodness is at a low ebb, the sacred institution of marriage is held in light esteem. It is both solemn and sad to behold an exemplification of the same in our own times; as the claims of God are less and less regarded by those of high and low estate alike; the holy obligations of wedlock are gradually whittled down and then increasingly disregarded. When a country, avowedly Christian, begins to tamper with the institution of marriage and make more elastic its divorce laws, it is a certain proof of its ethical decadence."
A.W. Pink

"A married person does not live in isolation. He or she has made a promise, a pledge, a vow, to another person. Until that vow is fulfilled and the promise is kept, the individual is in debt to his marriage partner. That is what he owes. "You owe it to yourself" is not a valid excuse for breaking a marriage vow but a creed of selfishness."
R.C. Sproul

"According to the law, adultery is the only sufficient reason for divorce."
A.W. Pink

Doubt

Doubt - Bible Verses

Matthew 21:21 ESV
And Jesus answered them, "Truly, I say to you, if you have faith and do not doubt, you will not only do what has been done to the fig tree, but even if you say to this mountain, 'Be taken up and thrown into the sea,' it will happen.

Jude 1:22 ESV
And have mercy on those who doubt;

Genesis 37:33 NLT
Their father recognized it immediately. "Yes," he said, "it is my son's robe. A wild animal must have eaten him. Joseph has clearly been torn to pieces!"

Deuteronomy 28:66 NASB
So your life shall hang in doubt before you; and you will be in dread night and day, and shall have no assurance of your life.

Acts 28:4 NASB
When the natives saw the creature hanging from his hand, they began saying to one another, "Undoubtedly this man is a murderer, and though he has been saved from the sea, justice has not allowed him to live."

Luke 24:37-38 NASB
But they were startled and frightened and thought that they were seeing a spirit. And He said to them, "Why are you troubled, and why do doubts arise in your hearts?

Romans 14:23 ESV
But whoever has doubts is condemned if he eats, because the eating is not from faith. For whatever does not proceed from faith is sin.

James 1:6 ESV
But let him ask in faith, with no doubting, for the one who doubts is like a wave of the sea that is driven and tossed by the wind.

Mark 9:24 KJV
And straightway the father of the child cried out, and said with tears, Lord, I believe; help thou mine unbelief.

Matthew 13:58 KJV
And he did not many mighty works there because of their unbelief.

Mark 6:6 ESV
And he marveled because of their unbelief. And he went about among the villages teaching.

Mark 16:14 ESV
Afterward he appeared to the eleven themselves as they were reclining at table, and he rebuked them for their unbelief and hardness of heart, because they had not believed those who saw him after he had risen.

Mark 16:16 ESV
Whoever believes and is baptized will be saved, but whoever does not believe will be condemned.

John 20:27 ESV
Then he said to Thomas, "Put your finger here, and see my hands; and put out your hand, and place it in my side. Do not disbelieve, but believe."

Romans 11:20 ESV
That is true. They were broken off because of their unbelief, but you stand fast through faith. So do not become proud, but fear.

Matthew 14:3 NIV
Now Herod had arrested John and bound him and put him in prison because of Herodias, his brother Philip's wife,

Mark 11:23 NIV
"Truly I tell you, if anyone says to this mountain, 'Go, throw yourself into the sea,' and does not doubt in their heart but believes that what they say will happen, it will be done for them.

Hebrews 11:6 ESV
And without faith it is impossible to please him, for whoever would draw near to God must believe that he exists and that he rewards those who seek him.

Mark 4:40 ESV
He said to them, "Why are you so afraid? Have you still no faith?"

Matthew 8:26 NIV
He replied, "You of little faith, why are you so afraid?" Then he got up and rebuked the winds and the waves, and it was completely calm.

Excellent site for additional Bible translations:
http://www.biblegateway.com/resources/commentaries/
Excellent resource for additional Bible study:
(Be sure to read the instructions on their page)
http://www.blueletterbible.org/commentaries/

Doubt - Christian Quotes

"Some of us who have preached the Word for years, and have been the means of working faith in others and of establishing them in the knowledge of the fundamental doctrines of the Bible, have nevertheless been the subjects of the most fearful and violent doubts as to the truth of the very gospel we have preached."
C.H. Spurgeon

"When we dare to depend entirely upon God and do not doubt, the humblest and feeblest agencies will become mighty through God, to the pulling down of strongholds."
A.B. Simpson

"Satan is ever seeking to inject that poison into our hearts to distrust God's goodness - especially in connection with his commandments. That is what really lies behind all evil, lusting and disobedience. A discontent with our position and portion, a craving from something which God has wisely held from us. Reject any suggestion that God is unduly severe with you. Resist with the utmost abhorrence anything that causes you to doubt God's love and his lovingkindness toward you. Allow nothing to make you question the Father's love for his child."
A.W. Pink

"We need a baptism of clear seeing. We desperately need seers who can see through the mist--Christian leaders with prophetic vision. Unless they come soon it will be too late for this generation. And if they do come we will no doubt crucify a few of them in the name of our worldly orthodoxy."
A.W. Tozer

"Now, as always, God discloses Himself to "babes" and hides Himself in thick darkness from the wise and the prudent. We must simplify our approach to Him. We must strip down to essentials (and they will be found to be blessedly few). We must put away all effort to impress, and come with the guileless candor of childhood. If we do this, without doubt God will

quickly respond."
A. W. Tozer

"It seems to me that doubt is worse than trial. I had sooner suffer any affliction than be left to question the gospel or my own interest in it."
C.H. Spurgeon

"You must cast yourself on God's gospel with all your weight, without any hanging back, without any doubt, without even the shadow of a suspicion that it will give."
Alexander MacLaren

"Doubt discovers difficulties which it never solves; it creates hesitancy, despondency, despair. Its progress is the decay of comfort, the death of peace. "Believe!" is the word which speaks life into a man, but doubt nails down his coffin."
C.H. Spurgeon

Without doubt the mightiest thought the mind can entertain is the thought of God.
A. W. Tozer

"I believe that the happiest of all Christians and the truest of Christians are those who never dare to doubt God, but take His Word simply as it stands, and believe it, and ask no questions, just feeling assured that if God has said it, it will be so."
C.H. Spurgeon

"For some reason, we think of doubt and worry as "small" sins. But when a Christian displays unbelief...or an inability to cope with life, he is saying to the world, "My God cannot be trusted," and that kind of disrespect makes one guilty of a fundamental error, the heinous sin of dishonoring God. That is no small sin."
John MacArthur
The Ultimate Priority, Moody Press 1983, p. 140.

Encouragement

Encouragement - Bible Verses

Deuteronomy 31:6 ESV
Be strong and courageous. Do not fear or be in dread of them, for it is the LORD your God who goes with you. He will not leave you or forsake you."

Isaiah 41:10 ESV
fear not, for I am with you; be not dismayed, for I am your God; I will strengthen you, I will help you, I will uphold you with my righteous right hand.

1 Corinthians 10:13 NIV
No temptation has overtaken you except what is common to mankind. And God is faithful; he will not let you be tempted beyond what you can bear. But when you are tempted, he will also provide a way out so that you can endure it.

2 Corinthians 4:16-18 NIV
Therefore we do not lose heart. Though outwardly we are wasting away, yet inwardly we are being renewed day by day. For our light and momentary troubles are achieving for us an eternal glory that far outweighs them all. So we fix our eyes not on what is seen, but on what is unseen, since what is seen is temporary, but what is unseen is eternal.

Deuteronomy 31:8 ESV
It is the LORD who goes before you. He will be with you; he will not leave you or forsake you. Do not fear or be dismayed."

Zephaniah 3:17 ESV
The LORD your God is in your midst, a mighty one who will save; he will rejoice over you with gladness; he will quiet you by his love; he will exult over you with loud singing.

Psalm 9:9 ESV
The LORD is a stronghold for the oppressed, a stronghold in times of trouble.

Psalm 55:22 ESV
Cast your burden on the LORD, and he will sustain you; he will never permit the righteous to be moved.

Matthew 11:28-29 NIV
"Come to me, all you who are weary and burdened, and I will give you rest. Take my yoke upon you and learn from me, for I am gentle and humble in heart, and you will find rest for your souls.

John 14:27 ESV
Peace I leave with you; my peace I give to you. Not as the world gives do I give to you. Let not your hearts be troubled, neither let them be afraid.

Psalm 23:4 ESV
Even though I walk through the valley of the shadow of death, I will fear no evil, for you are with me; your rod and your staff, they comfort me.

Romans 8:6 ESV
For to set the mind on the flesh is death, but to set the mind on the Spirit is life and peace.

Philippians 4:6-7 NASB
Be anxious for nothing, but in everything by prayer and supplication with thanksgiving let your requests be made known to God. And the peace of God, which surpasses all comprehension, will guard your hearts and your minds in Christ Jesus.

Colossians 3:15 NASB
Let the peace of Christ rule in your hearts, to which indeed you were called in one body; and be thankful.

John 6:47 ESV
Truly, truly, I say to you, he who believes has eternal life.

Deuteronomy 7:9 ESV
Know therefore that the LORD your God is God, the faithful God who keeps covenant and steadfast love with those who love him and keep his commandments, to a thousand generations

1 John 5:14 NASB
This is the confidence which we have before Him, that, if we ask anything according to His will, He hears us.

Excellent site for additional Bible translations:
http://www.biblegateway.com/resources/commentaries/
Excellent resource for additional Bible study:
(Be sure to read the instructions on their page)
http://www.blueletterbible.org/commentaries/

Encouragement- Christian Quotes

God will not be absent when His people are on trial; he will stand in court as their advocate, to plead on their behalf.
Charles Spurgeon

"Let us but feel that He has His heart set upon us, that He is watching us from those heavens with tender interest, that He is following us day by day as a mother follows her babe in his first attempt to walk alone, that He has set His love upon us, and in spite of ourselves is working out for us His higher will and blessing, as far as we will let Him – and then nothing can discourage us."
A.B. Simpson

You are valuable because you exist. Not because of what you do or what you have done, but simply because you are.
Max Lucado

Be assured, if you walk with Him and look to Him, and expect help from Him, He will never fail you.
George Mueller

The stars may fall, but God's promises will stand and be fulfilled.
J. I. Packer

Enemies

Enemies - Bible Verses

Exodus 23:5 ESV
If you see the donkey of one who hates you lying down under its burden, you shall refrain from leaving him with it; you shall rescue it with him.

Acts 7:60 NASB
Then falling on his knees, he cried out with a loud voice, "Lord, do not hold this sin against them!" Having said this, he fell asleep.

Romans 12:20 ESV
To the contrary, "if your enemy is hungry, feed him; if he is thirsty, give him something to drink; for by so doing you will heap burning coals on his head."

1 Samuel 26:21 ESV
Then Saul said, "I have sinned. Return, my son David, for I will no more do you harm, because my life was precious in your eyes this day. Behold, I have acted foolishly, and have made a great mistake."

Job 31:29 ESV
"If I have rejoiced at the ruin of him who hated me, or exulted when evil overtook him

Proverbs 24:17 ESV
Do not rejoice when your enemy falls, and let not your heart be glad when he stumbles,

Job 31:30 NASB
"No, I have not allowed my mouth to sin
By asking for his life in a curse.

Proverbs 26:26 ESV
though his hatred be covered with deception, his wickedness will be exposed in the assembly.

Psalm 59:9 ESV
O my Strength, I will watch for you, for you, O God, are my fortress.

Luke 6:27 NLT
 "But to you who are willing to listen, I say, love your enemies! Do good to those who hate you.

Exodus 23:4 ESV
"If you meet your enemy's ox or his donkey going astray, you shall bring it back to him.

Psalm 18:48 NLT
and rescues me from my enemies.
You hold me safe beyond the reach of my enemies;
    you save me from violent opponents.

Psalm 60:12 NLT
With God's help we will do mighty things,
    for he will trample down our foes.

Ephesians 4:32 NASB
Be kind to one another, tender-hearted, forgiving each other, just as God in Christ also has forgiven you.

Matthew 5:44 NASB
But I say to you, love your enemies and pray for those who persecute you,

Mark 11:25 NLT
But when you are praying, first forgive anyone you are holding a grudge against, so that your Father in heaven will forgive your sins, too."

Colossians 3:13 ESV

bearing with one another and, if one has a complaint against another, forgiving each other; as the Lord has forgiven you, so you also must forgive.

Psalm 136:24 ESV
and rescued us from our foes, for his steadfast love endures forever;

Luke 23:34 NIV
Jesus said, "Father, forgive them, for they don't know what they are doing." And the soldiers gambled for his clothes by throwing dice.

Romans 12:19 ESV
Beloved, never avenge yourselves, but leave it to the wrath of God, for it is written, "Vengeance is mine, I will repay, says the Lord."

Luke 17:4 NLT
Even if that person wrongs you seven times a day and each time turns again and asks forgiveness, you must forgive."

Excellent site for additional Bible translations:
http://www.biblegateway.com/resources/commentaries/
Excellent resource for additional Bible study:
(Be sure to read the instructions on their page)
http://www.blueletterbible.org/commentaries/

Enemies - Christian Quotes

"When principles that run against your deepest convictions begin to win the day, then battle is your calling, and peace has become sin; you must, at the price of dearest peace, lay your convictions bare before friend and enemy, with all the fire of your faith."
Abraham Kuyper

"The saints fare the better for the insolence and outrages of their enemies, whose ruin is thereby accelerated; and somewhat God will do the sooner for his people, lest the enemy exalt himself."
Abraham Wright

"Obey God in all things today ! Drive out the enemy ! Lay the ax to the root of the tree, and the capacity for Jesus Christ will be increased tomorrow."
Alan Redpath

"The enemy uses all his power to lead the Christian, and above all the minister, to neglect prayer. He knows that however admirable the sermon may be, however attractive the service, however faithful the pastoral visitation, none of these things can damage him or his kingdom if prayer is neglected."
Andrew Murray

"Forgiving and being forgiven are two names for the same thing. The important thing is that a discord has been resolved."
C. S. Lewis

"You are nothing better than deceitful hypocrites if you harbor in your minds a single unforgiving thought. There are some sins which may be in the heart, and yet you may be saved. But you cannot be saved unless you are forgiving. If we do not choose to forgive, we choose to be damned."
Charles Spurgeon

"Okay, here's how to do relationships - be kind to one another, tenderhearted, forgiving one another, just as God, in Christ, also has forgiven you."
Chip Ingram

"No prayers can be heard which do not come from a forgiving heart."
J. C. Ryle

"Who are you helping most when you forgive the person who hurt you? Actually, you're helping yourself more than the other person. I always looked at forgiving people who hurt me as being really hard. I thought it seemed so unfair for them to receive forgiveness when I had gotten hurt. I got pain, and they got freedom without having to pay for the pain they caused. Now I realize that I'm helping myself when I choose to forgive."
Joyce Meyers

Faith

Faith - Bible Verses

Ephesians 2:8-9 KJV
For by grace are ye saved through faith; and that not of yourselves: it is the gift of God:
Not of works, lest any man should boast.

Acts 6:5 ESV
And what they said pleased the whole gathering, and they chose Stephen, a man full of faith and of the Holy Spirit, and Philip, and Prochorus, and Nicanor, and Timon, and Parmenas, and Nicolaus, a proselyte of Antioch.

Acts 11:22-24 NIV
News of this reached the church in Jerusalem, and they sent Barnabas to Antioch. When he arrived and saw what the grace of God had done, he was glad and encouraged them all to remain true to the Lord with all their hearts. He was a good man, full of the Holy Spirit and faith, and a great number of people were brought to the Lord.

1 Corinthians 13:2 NIV
If I have the gift of prophecy and can fathom all mysteries and all knowledge, and if I have a faith that can move mountains, but do not have love, I am nothing.

1 Corinthians 16:13 ESV
Be watchful, stand firm in the faith, act like men, be strong.

2 Corinthians 5:6-7 NIV
Therefore we are always confident and know that as long as we are at home in the body we are away from the Lord. For we live by faith, not by sight.

Ephesians 6:16 KJV
Above all, taking the shield of faith, wherewith ye shall be able to quench all the fiery darts of the wicked.

Matthew 8:26 ESV
And he said to them, "Why are you afraid, O you of little faith?" Then he rose and rebuked the winds and the sea, and there was a great calm.

Matthew 14:29-31 NASB
And He said, "Come!" And Peter got out of the boat, and walked on the water and came toward Jesus. But seeing the wind, he became frightened, and beginning to sink, he cried out, "Lord, save me!" Immediately Jesus stretched out His hand and took hold of him, and *said to him, "You of little faith, why did you doubt?"

Matthew 17:20 ESV
He said to them, "Because of your little faith. For truly, I say to you, if you have faith like a grain of mustard seed, you will say to this mountain, 'Move from here to there,' and it will move, and nothing will be impossible for you."

Luke 12:27-28 NASB
Consider the lilies, how they grow: they neither toil nor spin; but I tell you, not even Solomon in all his glory clothed himself like one of these. But if God so clothes the grass in the field, which is alive today and tomorrow is thrown into the furnace, how much more will He clothe you? You men of little faith!

Matthew 9:22 ESV
Jesus turned, and seeing her he said, "Take heart, daughter; your faith has made you well." And instantly the woman was made well.

Matthew 15:28 ESV
Then Jesus answered her, "O woman, great is your faith! Be it done for you as you desire." And her daughter was healed instantly.

Matthew 21:21-22 NASB
And Jesus answered and said to them, "Truly I say to you, if you have faith and do not doubt, you will not only do what was done to the fig tree, but even if you say to this mountain, 'Be taken up and cast into the sea,' it will happen. And all things you ask in prayer, believing, you will receive."

Mark 10:52 ESV
And Jesus said to him, "Go your way; your faith has made you well." And immediately he recovered his sight and followed him on the way.

Acts 14:9-10 NASB
This man was listening to Paul as he spoke, who, when he had fixed his gaze on him and had seen that he had faith to be made well, said with a loud voice, "Stand upright on your feet." And he leaped up and began to walk.

Acts 15:8-9 NLT
God knows people's hearts, and he confirmed that he accepts Gentiles by giving them the Holy Spirit, just as he did to us. 9 He made no distinction between us and them, for he cleansed their hearts through faith.

Acts 20:18-21 NLT
When they arrived he declared, "You know that from the day I set foot in the province of Asia until now 19 I have done the Lord's work humbly and with many tears. I have endured the trials that came to me from the plots of the Jews. 20 I never shrank back from telling you what you needed to hear, either publicly or in your homes. 21 I have had one message for Jews and Greeks alike—the necessity of repenting from sin and turning to God, and of having faith in our Lord Jesus.

Romans 1:16-17 NLT
For I am not ashamed of this Good News about Christ. It is the power of God at work, saving everyone who believes—the Jew first and also the Gentile. This Good News tells us how God makes us right in his sight. This is accomplished from start to finish by faith. As the Scriptures say, "It is through faith that a righteous person has life."

2 Corinthians 4:13-14 NLT

But we continue to preach because we have the same kind of faith the psalmist had when he said, "I believed in God, so I spoke." We know that God, who raised the Lord Jesus, will also raise us with Jesus and present us to himself together with you.

Excellent site for additional Bible translations:
http://www.biblegateway.com/resources/commentaries/
Excellent resource for additional Bible study:
(Be sure to read the instructions on their page)
http://www.blueletterbible.org/commentaries/

Faith- Christian Quotes

"Let God be true but every man a liar" is the language of true faith."
A. W. Tozer

"Faith expects from God what is beyond all expectation."
Andrew Murray

"You must have faith in God."
A. B. Simpson

"Faith makes all things possible... love makes all things easy."
D.L. Moody

"We took our sins and drove them like nails through his hands and feet. We lifted him high up on the cross of our transgressions, and then we pierced his heart through with the spear of our unbelief."
C.H. Spurgeon

"Faith, mighty faith, the promise sees, And looks to God alone; Laughs at impossibilities, And cries it shall be done."
Charles Wesley

"Who can tell the misery that unbelief has brought on the world? Unbelief made Eve eat the forbidden fruit – she doubted the truth of God's word: "You will surely die." Unbelief made the old world reject Noah's warning, and so perish in their sin. Unbelief kept Israel in the wilderness – it was the barricade that kept them from entering the Promised Land. Unbelief made the Jews crucify the Lord of glory – they did not believe the voice of Moses and the prophets, even though they were read to them every day. And unbelief is the reigning sin of man's heart down to this very hour – unbelief in God's promises – unbelief in God's wrath and discipline – unbelief in our own sinfulness – unbelief in our own danger – unbelief in everything that runs counter to the pride and worldliness of our evil hearts."
J.C. Ryle

"To learn strong faith is to endure great trials. I have learned my faith by standing firm amid severe testings."
George Mueller

"Christ never failed to distinguish between doubt and unbelief. Doubt is can't believe. Unbelief is won't believe. Doubt is honesty. Unbelief is obstinacy. Doubt is looking for light. Unbelief is content with darkness."
Henry Drummond

Fathers

Fathers- Bible Verses

Deuteronomy 1:29-31 NIV
Then I said to you, "Do not be terrified; do not be afraid of them. The Lord your God, who is going before you, will fight for you, as he did for you in Egypt, before your very eyes, and in the wilderness. There you saw how the Lord your God carried you, as a father carries his son, all the way you went until you reached this place."

Psalm 127:3-5 ESV
Behold, children are a heritage from the LORD, the fruit of the womb a reward. Like arrows in the hand of a warrior are the children of one's youth. Blessed is the man who fills his quiver with them! He shall not be put to shame when he speaks with his enemies in the gate.

Proverbs 23:24 ESV
The father of the righteous will greatly rejoice; he who fathers a wise son will be glad in him.

Proverbs 20:7 ESV
The righteous who walks in his integrity—blessed are his children after him!

1 Thessalonians 2:11-12 ESV
For you know that we dealt with each of you as a father deals with his own children, encouraging, comforting and urging you to live lives worthy of God, who calls you into his kingdom and glory.

Proverbs 10:1 ESV
The proverbs of Solomon. A wise son makes a glad father, but a foolish son is a sorrow to his mother.

Luke 15:20 -23 NASB
So he got up and came to his father. But while he was still a long way off, his father saw him and felt compassion for him, and ran and embraced him and kissed him. And the son said to him, 'Father, I have sinned against heaven and in your sight; I am no longer worthy to be called your son.' But the father said to his slaves, 'Quickly bring out the best robe and put it on him, and put a ring on his hand and sandals on his feet; and bring the fattened calf, kill it, and let us eat and celebrate;

Exodus 20:12 ESV
"Honor your father and your mother, that your days may be long in the land that the LORD your God is giving you.

Proverbs 3:11-12 ESV
My son, do not despise the LORD's discipline or be weary of his reproof, 12 for the LORD reproves him whom he loves, as a father the son in whom he delights.

Proverbs 23:22 ESV
Listen to your father who gave you life, and do not despise your mother when she is old.

Proverbs 4:1-4 ESV
Hear, O sons, a father's instruction, and be attentive, that you may gain insight, for I give you good precepts; do not forsake my teaching. When I was a son with my father, tender, the only one in the sight of my mother, he taught me and said to me,"Let your heart hold fast my words; keep my commandments, and live.

Proverbs 19:18 ESV
Discipline your son, for there is hope; do not set your heart on putting him to death.

Ephesians 6:2-4 NASB
Honor your father and mother (which is the first commandment with a promise), so that it may be well with you, and that you may live long on the

earth. Fathers, do not provoke your children to anger, but bring them up in the discipline and instruction of the Lord.

Colossians 3:21 KJV
Fathers, provoke not your children to anger, lest they be discouraged.

Hebrews 12:7 NLT
As you endure this divine discipline, remember that God is treating you as his own children. Who ever heard of a child who is never disciplined by its father?

Malachi 4:6 NLT
His preaching will turn the hearts of fathers to their children, and the hearts of children to their fathers. Otherwise I will come and strike the land with a curse."

Matthew 7:9-11 NLT
"You parents—if your children ask for a loaf of bread, do you give them a stone instead? Or if they ask for a fish, do you give them a snake? Of course not! So if you sinful people know how to give good gifts to your children, how much more will your heavenly Father give good gifts to those who ask him.

Galatians 4:6 NASB
And because ye are sons, God hath sent forth the Spirit of his Son into your hearts, crying, Abba, Father.

Ephesians 4:4 KJV
There is one body, and one Spirit, even as ye are called in one hope of your calling;

Excellent site for additional Bible translations:
http://www.biblegateway.com/resources/commentaries/
Excellent resource for additional Bible study:
(Be sure to read the instructions on their page)

http://www.blueletterbible.org/commentaries/

Fathers - Christian Quotes

"A famous cigarette billboard pictures a curly-headed, bronze-faced, muscular macho with a cigarette hanging out the side of his mouth. The sign says, "Where a man belongs." That is a lie. Where a man belongs is at the bedside of his children, leading in devotion and prayer. Where a man belongs is leading his family to the house of God. Where a man belongs is up early and alone with God seeking vision and direction for the family."
John Piper

"Men are never manlier than when they are tender with their children – whether holding a baby in their arms, loving their grade-schooler, or hugging their teenager or adult children."
Kent Hughes
Disciplines of a Godly Man, Crossway Books, 1991, p. 51.

"The happiest and holiest children in the world are the children whose fathers succeed in winning both their tender affection and their reverential and loving fear. And they are the children who will come to understand most easily the mystery of the fatherhood of God."
John Piper

Fear

Fear - Bible Verses

Psalm 111:10 ESV
The fear of the LORD is the beginning of wisdom; all those who practice it have a good understanding. His praise endures forever!

2 Timothy 1:7 KJV
For God hath not given us the spirit of fear; but of power, and of love, and of a sound mind.

Genesis 3:8-10 NLT
When the cool evening breezes were blowing, the man and his wife heard the Lord God walking about in the garden. So they hid from the Lord God among the trees. Then the Lord God called to the man, "Where are you?"
He replied, "I heard you walking in the garden, so I hid. I was afraid because I was naked."

Proverbs 12:25 ESV
Anxiety in a man's heart weighs him down, but a good word makes him glad.

Matthew 28:4 NIV
The guards were so afraid of him that they shook and became like dead men.

Luke 2:8-9 NIV
And there were shepherds living out in the fields nearby, keeping watch over their flocks at night. An angel of the Lord appeared to them, and the glory of the Lord shone around them, and they were terrified.

Romans 8:15 NIV
The Spirit you received does not make you slaves, so that you live in fear again; rather, the Spirit you received brought about your adoption to sonship. And by him we cry, "Abba, Father."

2 Timothy 1:7 KJV
For God hath not given us the spirit of fear; but of power, and of love, and of a sound mind.

1 John 4:18 ESV
There is no fear in love, but perfect love casts out fear. For fear has to do with punishment, and whoever fears has not been perfected in love.

Revelation 11:11 NASB
But after the three and a half days, the breath of life from God came into them, and they stood on their feet; and great fear fell upon those who were watching them.

Genesis 22:11-13 NASB
But the angel of the Lord called to him from heaven and said, "Abraham, Abraham!" And he said, "Here I am." He said, "Do not stretch out your hand against the lad, and do nothing to him; for now I know that you fear God, since you have not withheld your son, your only son, from Me." Then Abraham raised his eyes and looked, and behold, behind him a ram caught in the thicket by his horns; and Abraham went and took the ram and offered him up for a burnt offering in the place of his son.

Exodus 1:16-18 NASB
and he said, "When you are helping the Hebrew women to give birth and see them upon the birthstool, if it is a son, then you shall put him to death; but if it is a daughter, then she shall live." But the midwives feared God, and did not do as the king of Egypt had commanded them, but let the boys live. So the king of Egypt called for the midwives and said to them, "Why have you done this thing, and let the boys live?"

Proverbs 2:1-6 ESV
My son, if you receive my words and treasure up my commandments with you, making your ear attentive to wisdom and inclining your heart to understanding; yes, if you call out for insight and raise your voice for understanding, if you seek it like silver and search for it as for hidden

treasures, then you will understand the fear of the LORD and find the knowledge of God. For the LORD gives wisdom; from his mouth come knowledge and understanding;

Ephesians 5:18-21 KJV
And be not drunk with wine, wherein is excess; but be filled with the Spirit; Speaking to yourselves in psalms and hymns and spiritual songs, singing and making melody in your heart to the Lord; Giving thanks always for all things unto God and the Father in the name of our Lord Jesus Christ; Submitting yourselves one to another in the fear of God.

1 Peter 2:17 NASB
Honor all people, love the brotherhood, fear God, honor the king.

Deuteronomy 31:6 ESV
Be strong and courageous. Do not fear or be in dread of them, for it is the LORD your God who goes with you. He will not leave you or forsake you."

1 Samuel 12:14 NASB
If you will fear the Lord and serve Him, and listen to His voice and not rebel against the command of the Lord, then both you and also the king who reigns over you will follow the Lord your God.

2 Kings 17:37-39 NLT
Be careful at all times to obey the decrees, regulations, instructions, and commands that he wrote for you. You must not worship other gods. Do not forget the covenant I made with you, and do not worship other gods. You must worship only the Lord your God. He is the one who will rescue you from all your enemies."

Psalm 27:1 ESV
The LORD is my light and my salvation; whom shall I fear? The LORD is the stronghold of my life; of whom shall I be afraid?

Psalm 40:3 ESV

He put a new song in my mouth, a song of praise to our God. Many will see and fear, and put their trust in the LORD.

Psalm 56:3-4 ESV

When I am afraid, I put my trust in you. In God, whose word I praise, in God I trust; I shall not be afraid. What can flesh do to me?

Psalm 61:5 ESV

For you, O God, have heard my vows; you have given me the heritage of those who fear your name.

Acts 10:1-2 NLT

In Caesarea there lived a Roman army officer named Cornelius, who was a captain of the Italian Regiment. He was a devout, God-fearing man, as was everyone in his household. He gave generously to the poor and prayed regularly to God.

Excellent site for additional Bible translations:
http://www.biblegateway.com/resources/commentaries/
Excellent resource for additional Bible study:
(Be sure to read the instructions on their page)
http://www.blueletterbible.org/commentaries/

Fear- Christian Quotes

"Faith, which is trust, and fear are opposite poles. If a man has the one, he can scarcely have the other in vigorous operation. He that has his trust set upon God does not need to dread anything except the weakening or the paralyzing of that trust."
Alexander MacLaren

"God incarnate is the end of fear; and the heart that realizes that He is in the midst... will be quiet in the middle of alarm."
F.B. Meyer

" If my attitude be one of fear, not faith, about one who has disappointed me; if I say, 'Just what I expected,' if a fall occurs, then I know nothing of Calvary love."
Amy Carmichael

"Fear is the response of the human heart when its one thing is threatened."
Augustine

"Fear is born of Satan, and if we would only take time to think a moment we would see that everything Satan says is founded upon a falsehood."
A. B. Simpson

"Worry is a cycle of inefficient thoughts whirling around a center of fear."
Corrie Ten Boom

"How strange this fear of death is! We are never frightened at a sunset."
George Macdonald

"Fear of something is at the root of hate for others, and hate within will eventually destroy the hater."
George Washington Carver

"No one ever told me that grief felt so like fear."
C.S. Lewis

Forgiveness

Forgiveness - Bible Verses

Mark 11:25 ESV
And whenever you stand praying, forgive, if you have anything against anyone, so that your Father also who is in heaven may forgive you your trespasses."

Ephesians 4:32 ESV
Be kind to one another, tenderhearted, forgiving one another, as God in Christ forgave you.

1 John 1:9 ESV
If we confess our sins, he is faithful and just to forgive us our sins and to cleanse us from all unrighteousness.

Matthew 18:21-22 NIV
Then Peter came to Jesus and asked, "Lord, how many times shall I forgive my brother or sister who sins against me? Up to seven times?"
22 Jesus answered, "I tell you, not seven times, but seventy-seven times.

Matthew 6:15 ESV
But if you do not forgive others their trespasses, neither will your Father forgive your trespasses.

James 5:16 ESV
Therefore, confess your sins to one another and pray for one another, that you may be healed. The prayer of a righteous person has great power as it is working.

1 Corinthians 10:13 ESV
No temptation has overtaken you that is not common to man. God is faithful, and he will not let you be tempted beyond your ability, but with the

temptation he will also provide the way of escape, that you may be able to endure it.

Matthew 6:14-15 NASB
For if you forgive others for their transgressions, your heavenly Father will also forgive you. But if you do not forgive others, then your Father will not forgive your transgressions.

Colossians 3:13 ESV
Bearing with one another and, if one has a complaint against another, forgiving each other; as the Lord has forgiven you, so you also must forgive.

Acts 2:38 KJV
Then Peter said unto them, Repent, and be baptized every one of you in the name of Jesus Christ for the remission of sins, and ye shall receive the gift of the Holy Ghost.

Luke 6:27 ESV
"But I say to you who hear, Love your enemies, do good to those who hate you,

Excellent site for additional Bible translations:
http://www.biblegateway.com/resources/commentaries/
Excellent resource for additional Bible study:
(Be sure to read the instructions on their page)
http://www.blueletterbible.org/commentaries/

Forgiveness - Christian Quotes

You are nothing better than deceitful hypocrites if you harbor in your minds a single unforgiving thought. There are some sins which may be in the heart, and yet you may be saved. But you cannot be saved unless you are forgiving. If we do not choose to forgive, we choose to be damned.
C.H. Spurgeon

Our forgiving others is not a cause of God's forgiving us, but it is a condition without which He will not forgive us (Mt. 6:12).
Thomas Watson

Forgiveness is not that stripe which says, "I will forgive, but not forget." It is not to bury the hatchet with the handle sticking out of the ground, so you can grasp it the minute you want it.
D.L. Moody

When I become bitter or unforgiving toward others, I'm assuming that the sins of others are more serious than my sins against God. The cross transforms my perspective. Through the cross I realize that no sin committed against me will ever be as serious as the innumerable sins I've committed against God. When we understand how much God has forgiven us, it's not difficult to forgive others.
C.J. Mahaney
The Cross Centered Life, 2002, Sovereign Grace Ministries, p. 81.

Forgiveness of others in the believer is so standard, so much a part of what it means to be a Christian, that no true believer is without it. If you are not a forgiver, you are not forgiven. To not be forgiven is to be damned to spend eternity in hell.
Jim Elliff

A stiff apology is a second insult.
G.K. Chesterton

It is the experience of having been forgiven (by Christ) which releases the generous impulses to forgive others (Matt. 18:23-35), just as it is the refusal to forgive which betrays the reality that forgiveness has not been received, that the individual has not even recognized the need for forgiveness (Matt. 6:14-15). A community has hope of holding together and growing together only when the need for forgiveness is recognized on each side where fault has been committed and only when forgiveness is both offered and received.
James Dunn

We need not climb up into heaven to see whether our sins are forgiven: let us look into our hearts, and see if we can forgive others. If we can, we need not doubt but God as forgiven us.
Thomas Watson

Mercy, like the regions of space, has no limit, and as these stretch away before the traveler who looks out from the farthest star, so the loftiest intellect and the largest heart can discover no bounds to mercy. Like our Father in heaven, we are to forgive without stint, forgiving as we expect to be forgiven.
Donald Guthrie

God's forgiveness is an outpouring of abundant grace and mercy that provides pardon to the guilty. Although God's forgiveness does not necessarily release the offender from the physical or material consequences of his sin, it provides full release from the guilt of the wrongdoing. For you to practice biblical forgiveness, you must understand and accept God's gracious forgiveness of you and must follow His example in providing forgiveness to others.
Biblical Counseling Foundation
Self-Confrontation Manuel, Lesson 12, Page 3,

The practice of comprehensive forgiveness overcomes our love of being right, our actual enjoyment and treasuring of our sense of being wronged... The constant practice of forgiveness leaves no room for self-righteousness. Frustrated condemnation of others and treasuring of old wrongs are not

part of the artillery of God, but the slithering, slimy, deadly creatures of the Prince of Darkness.
C. John Miller and Barbara Miller Juliani
Come Back, Barbara, P&R, 1997, p. 79-80.

[True forgiveness means] laying down our right to remain angry and giving up our claim to future repayment of the debt we have suffered.
Brian J. Dodd
Taken from Praying Jesus' Way: A Guide for Beginners and Veterans, © 1997,

Whenever I see myself before God and realize something of what my blessed Lord has done for me at Calvary, I am ready to forgive anybody anything. I cannot withhold it. I do not even want to withhold it.
Martin Lloyd-Jones

Forgiveness may be described as a decision to make four promises:
"I will not dwell on this incident."
"I will not bring up this incident again and use it against you."
"I will not talk to others about this incident."
"I will not let this incident stand between us or hinder our personal relationship."
Ken Sande
The Peacemaker: A Biblical Guide to Resolving Personal Conflict, 2004, p. 209.

Forgive, forget. Bear with the faults of others as you would have them bear with yours. Be patient and understanding. Life is too short to be vengeful or malicious.
Phillips Brooks

Forgiving costs us our sense of justice. We all have this innate sense deep within our souls, but it has been perverted by our selfish sinful natures. We want to see "justice" done, but the justice we envision satisfies our own interests. We must realize that justice has been done. God is the only rightful administrator of justice in all of creation, and His justice has been satisfied. In order to forgive our brother, we must be satisfied with God's justice and forego the satisfaction of our own.
Jerry Bridges

The Practice of Godliness, p. 207-208

Friendship

Friendship - Bible Verses

John 15:12-15 NASB
"This is My commandment, that you love one another, just as I have loved you. Greater love has no one than this, that one lay down his life for his friends. You are My friends if you do what I command you. No longer do I call you slaves, for the slave does not know what his master is doing; but I have called you friends, for all things that I have heard from My Father I have made known to you.."

James 4:8 NASB
Draw near to God and He will draw near to you. Cleanse your hands, you sinners; and purify your hearts, you double-minded.

Proverbs 12:26 ESV
One who is righteous is a guide to his neighbor, but the way of the wicked leads them astray.

Proverbs 13:20 ESV
Whoever walks with the wise becomes wise, but the companion of fools will suffer harm.

Proverbs 14:6-7 ESV
A scoffer seeks wisdom in vain, but knowledge is easy for a man of understanding. Leave the presence of a fool, for there you do not meet words of knowledge.

Proverbs 22:24-25 ESV
Make no friendship with a man given to anger, nor go with a wrathful man, lest you learn his ways and entangle yourself in a snare.

1 Corinthians 15:33 NASB
Do not be deceived: "Bad company ruins good morals."

Luke 6:31 NASB
Treat others the same way you want them to treat you.

Romans 12:10 ESV
Love one another with brotherly affection. Outdo one another in showing honor.

Ephesians 4:29-32 NLT
Don't use foul or abusive language. Let everything you say be good and helpful, so that your words will be an encouragement to those who hear them.
And do not bring sorrow to God's Holy Spirit by the way you live. Remember, he has identified you as his own, guaranteeing that you will be saved on the day of redemption.
Get rid of all bitterness, rage, anger, harsh words, and slander, as well as all types of evil behavior. Instead, be kind to each other, tenderhearted, forgiving one another, just as God through Christ has forgiven you.

Colossians 3:12-14 NLT
Since God chose you to be the holy people he loves, you must clothe yourselves with tenderhearted mercy, kindness, humility, gentleness, and patience. Make allowance for each other's faults, and forgive anyone who offends you. Remember, the Lord forgave you, so you must forgive others. Above all, clothe yourselves with love, which binds us all together in perfect harmony.

Proverbs 11:14 ESV
Where there is no guidance, a people falls, but in an abundance of counselors there is safety.

Proverbs 17:17 NASB
A friend loves at all times, And a brother is born for adversity.

Proverbs 24:5 ESV
A wise man is full of strength, and a man of knowledge enhances his might,

Proverbs 27:17 NASB
Iron sharpens iron, So one man sharpens another.

Ruth 1:16-17 ESV
But Ruth said, "Do not urge me to leave you or to return from following you. For where you go I will go, and where you lodge I will lodge. Your people shall be my people, and your God my God. Where you die I will die, and there will I be buried. May the LORD do so to me and more also if anything but death parts me from you."

1 Samuel 18:1-3 ESV
As soon as he had finished speaking to Saul, the soul of Jonathan was knit to the soul of David, and Jonathan loved him as his own soul. And Saul took him that day and would not let him return to his father's house. Then Jonathan made a covenant with David, because he loved him as his own soul.

Job 2:11 ESV
Now when Job's three friends heard of all this evil that had come upon him, they came each from his own place, Eliphaz the Temanite, Bildad the Shuhite, and Zophar the Naamathite. They made an appointment together to come to show him sympathy and comfort him.

2 Kings 2:2 NLT
And Elijah said to Elisha, "Stay here, for the Lord has told me to go to Bethel."
But Elisha replied, "As surely as the Lord lives and you yourself live, I will never leave you!" So they went down together to Bethel.

Excellent site for additional Bible translations:
http://www.biblegateway.com/resources/commentaries/
Excellent resource for additional Bible study:
(Be sure to read the instructions on their page)
http://www.blueletterbible.org/commentaries/

Friendship - Christian Quotes

"Friendship is unnecessary, like philosophy, like art... It has no survival value; rather it is one of those things that give value to survival."
C.S. Lewis

"A judicious friend, into whose heart we may pour out our souls, and tell our corruptions as well as our comforts, is a very great privilege."
George Whitefield

"Is any pleasure on earth as great as a circle of Christian friends by a good fire?"
C.S. Lewis

"A blessed thing it is for any man or woman to have a friend; one human soul whom we can trust utterly; who knows the best and the worst of us, and who loves us in spite of all our faults; who will speak the honest truth to us, while the world flatters us to our face, and laughs at us behind our back."
Charles Kingsley

"The next best thing to being wise oneself is to live in a circle of those who are."
C.S. Lewis

"The loss of a friend is like that of a limb; time may heal the anguish of the wound, but the loss cannot be repaired."
Robert Southey

"Next to hypocrisy in religion, there is nothing worse than hypocrisy in friendship."
Joseph Hall

"By friendship you mean the greatest love, the greatest usefulness, the most open communication, the noblest sufferings, the severest truth, the heartiest counsel, and the greatest union of minds of which brave men and women

are capable."
Jeremy Taylor

"Satan can use your nonChristian friends in [many] ways to get to you. God wants you to rub off on them, but the Enemy wants them to rub off on you. So remember: You can have friends outside the faith, but for your deepest comrades you should look to your brothers and sisters in Christ. Hang out with the holy. Get in with the godly. Spend time with the saved. Know who your real family is – the one where the Father is God."
J. Budziszewski
How to Stay Christian in College by J. Budziszewski p.75.

"What is a friend? A single soul dwelling in two bodies."
Augustine

Funerals

Funerals - Bible Verses

Job 19:25 NLT
"But as for me, I know that my Redeemer lives,
  and he will stand upon the earth at last.

Ecclesiastes 7:1 NLT
A good reputation is more valuable than costly perfume.
  And the day you die is better than the day you are born.

Matthew 5:4 NASB
"Blessed are those who mourn, for they shall be comforted

John 14:1-4 NIV
"Do not let your hearts be troubled. You believe in God; believe also in me. My Father's house has many rooms; if that were not so, would I have told you that I am going there to prepare a place for you? And if I go and prepare a place for you, I will come back and take you to be with me that you also may be where I am. You know the way to the place where I am going."

1 Corinthians 15:56-57 NIV
The sting of death is sin, and the power of sin is the law. But thanks be to God! He gives us the victory through our Lord Jesus Christ.

1 Thessalonians 4:14-17 NIV
For we believe that Jesus died and rose again, and so we believe that God will bring with Jesus those who have fallen asleep in him. According to the Lord's word, we tell you that we who are still alive, who are left until the coming of the Lord, will certainly not precede those who have fallen asleep. For the Lord himself will come down from heaven, with a loud command, with the voice of the archangel and with the trumpet call of God, and the dead in Christ will rise first. After that, we who are still alive and are left will

be caught up together with them in the clouds to meet the Lord in the air. And so we will be with the Lord forever.

Psalm 61:1-2 ESV
Hear my cry, O God, listen to my prayer; from the end of the earth I call to you when my heart is faint. Lead me to the rock that is higher than I

Psalm 94:19 ESV
When the cares of my heart are many, your consolations cheer my soul.

Isaiah 41:10 ESV
fear not, for I am with you; be not dismayed, for I am your God; I will strengthen you, I will help you, I will uphold you with my righteous right hand ...

Isaiah 41:13 ESV
For I, the LORD your God, hold your right hand; it is I who say to you, "Fear not, I am the one who helps you."

Romans 8:31 ESV
What then shall we say to these things? If God is for us, who can be against us?

2 Corinthians 1:3-4 NASB
Blessed be the God and Father of our Lord Jesus Christ, the Father of mercies and God of all comfort, who comforts us in all our affliction so that we will be able to comfort those who are in any affliction with the comfort with which we ourselves are comforted by God.

Psalm 119:50 KJV
This is my comfort in my affliction: for thy word hath quickened me.

Ecclesiastes 3:1-2 ESV
For everything there is a season, and a time for every matter under heaven: a time to be born, and a time to die; a time to plant, and a time to pluck up what is planted;

Romans 14:7-9 NLT

For we don't live for ourselves or die for ourselves. If we live, it's to honor the Lord. And if we die, it's to honor the Lord. So whether we live or die, we belong to the Lord. Christ died and rose again for this very purpose—to be Lord both of the living and of the dead.

Philippians 1:21-23 ESV

For to me to live is Christ, and to die is gain. If I am to live in the flesh, that means fruitful labor for me. Yet which I shall choose I cannot tell. I am hard pressed between the two. My desire is to depart and be with Christ, for that is far better.

Excellent site for additional Bible translations:
http://www.biblegateway.com/resources/commentaries/
Excellent resource for additional Bible study:
(Be sure to read the instructions on their page)
http://www.blueletterbible.org/commentaries/

Funerals - Christian Quotes

"They that love beyond the world cannot be separated by it. Death cannot kill what never dies."
Williams Penn

"When the time comes for you to die, you need not be afraid, because death cannot separate you from God's love."
Charles H. Spurgeon

"Many Christians dread the thought of leaving this world. Why? Because so many have stored up their treasures on earth, not in heaven. Each day brings us closer to death. If your treasures are on earth, that means each day brings you closer to losing your treasures."
Randy Alcorn
Excerpted from The Treasure Principle by Randy Alcorn © 2002 by Eternal Perspective Ministries, p. 40.

Let us consider this settled, that no one has made progress in the school of Christ who does not joyfully await the day of death and final resurrection.
John Calvin

"It is better for me to die in behalf of Jesus Christ, than to reign over all the ends of the earth."
Ignatius of Antioch

"He whose head is in heaven need not fear to put his feet into the grave."
Matthew Henry

"Has this world been so kind to you that you should leave with regret? There are better things ahead than any we leave behind."
C.S. Lewis

"The very happiest persons I have ever met with have been departing believers. The only people for whom I have felt any envy have been dying members of this very church, whose hands I have grasped in their passing

away. Almost without exception I have seen in them holy delight and triumph. And in the exceptions to this exceeding joy I have seen deep peace, exhibited in a calm and deliberate readiness to enter into the presence of their God."
C.H. Spurgeon

"The best moment of a Christian's life is his last one, because it is the one that is nearest heaven. And then it is that he begins to strike the keynote of the song which he shall sing to all eternity. "
C.H. Spurgeon

"Death in its substance has been removed, and only the shadow of it remains… Nobody is afraid of a shadow, for a shadow cannot block a man's pathway for even a moment. The shadow of a dog can't bite; the shadow of a sword can't kill."
C.H. Spurgeon

"We see his smile of love even when others see nothing but the black hand of Death smiting our best beloved."
C.H. Spurgeon

"Depend upon it, your dying hour will be the best hour you have ever known! Your last moment will be your richest moment, better than the day of your birth will be the day of your death. It shall be the beginning of heaven, the rising of a sun that shall go no more down forever!"
C.H. Spurgeon

"This is our comfort. We are "immortal until our work is done;" mortal still, but immortal also. Let us never fear death, then, but rather rejoice at the approach of it, since it comes at our dear Bridegroom's bidding!"
C.H. Spurgeon

"Death is never sudden to a saint; no guest comes unawares to him who keeps a constant table."
George Swinnock

"Let thy hope of heaven master they fear of death. Why shouldst thou be afraid to die, who hopest to live by dying!"
William Gurnall

Generosity

Generosity - Bible Verses

Acts 20:35 NIV
In everything I did, I showed you that by this kind of hard work we must help the weak, remembering the words the Lord Jesus himself said: 'It is more blessed to give than to receive.' "

Matthew 10:42 ESV
And whoever gives one of these little ones even a cup of cold water because he is a disciple, truly, I say to you, he will by no means lose his reward."

2 Corinthians 9:13 NIV
Because of the service by which you have proved yourselves, others will praise God for the obedience that accompanies your confession of the gospel of Christ, and for your generosity in sharing with them and with everyone else.

Proverbs 11:24 ESV
One gives freely, yet grows all the richer;
another withholds what he should give, and only suffers want.

2 Corinthians 9:7 ESV
Each one must give as he has decided in his heart, not reluctantly or under compulsion, for God loves a cheerful giver.

Luke 6:37-38 NASB
"Do not judge, and you will not be judged; and do not condemn, and you will not be condemned; pardon, and you will be pardoned. Give, and it will be given to you. They will pour into your lap a good measure—pressed down, shaken together, and running over. For by your standard of measure it will be measured to you in return."

Luke 19:8 NASB
Zaccheus stopped and said to the Lord, "Behold, Lord, half of my possessions I will give to the poor, and if I have defrauded anyone of anything, I will give back four times as much."

Deuteronomy 8:18 ESV
You shall remember the LORD your God, for it is he who gives you power to get wealth, that he may confirm his covenant that he swore to your fathers, as it is this day.

Proverbs 19:17 ESV
Whoever is generous to the poor lends to the LORD,
and he will repay him for his deed.

1 Timothy 6:17-19 NASB
Instruct those who are rich in this present world not to be conceited or to fix their hope on the uncertainty of riches, but on God, who richly supplies us with all things to enjoy. Instruct them to do good, to be rich in good works, to be generous and ready to share, storing up for themselves the treasure of a good foundation for the future, so that they may take hold of that which is life indeed.

Excellent site for additional Bible translations
http://www.biblegateway.com/resources/commentaries/
Excellent resource for additional Bible study:
(Be sure to read the instructions on their page)
http://www.blueletterbible.org/commentaries/

Generosity - Christian Quotes

"Never be afraid of giving up your best, and God will give you His better. "
James Hinton

"The greatest pleasure I have known is to do a good action by stealth, and to have it found out by accident."
Charles Lamb

"Charity is, indeed, a great thing, and a gift of God, and when it is rightly ordered likens us to God Himself, as far as that is possible; for it is charity which makes the man."
John Chrysostom

"Generosity always wins favor, particularly when accompanied by modesty."
John Goethe

"Giving is true having."
C.H. Spurgeon

"He is no fool who gives what he cannot keep to gain what he cannot lose."
Jim Elliot

"When we come to the end of life, the question will be, "How much have you given?" not "How much have you gotten?"
George Sweeting
Men of Integrity

"Christian giving is to be marked by self-sacrifice and self-forgetfulness, not by self-congratulation."
John Stott

"Nothing that you have not given away will ever be really yours."
C.S. Lewis

"You can always give without loving, but you can never love without giving."
Amy Carmichael

Gentleness

Gentleness - Bible Verses

Proverbs 15:1 ESV
A soft answer turns away wrath, but a harsh word stirs up anger.

Matthew 11:29-30 NASB
Take My yoke upon you and learn from Me, for I am gentle and humble in heart, and you will find rest for your souls. For My yoke is easy and My burden is light."

Philippians 4:5 NIV
Let your gentleness be evident to all. The Lord is near.

1 Peter 3:15 NASB
but sanctify Christ as Lord in your hearts, always being ready to make a defense to everyone who asks you to give an account for the hope that is in you, yet with gentleness and reverence;

Titus 3:2 ESV
to speak evil of no one, to avoid quarreling, to be gentle, and to show perfect courtesy toward all people.

James 3:17 ESV
But the wisdom from above is first pure, then peaceable, gentle, open to reason, full of mercy and good fruits, impartial and sincere.

Galatians 6:1 NIV
Brothers and sisters, if someone is caught in a sin, you who live by the Spirit should restore that person gently. But watch yourselves, or you also may be tempted.

1 Corinthians 13:4-5 NLT

Love is patient and kind. Love is not jealous or boastful or proud or rude. It does not demand its own way. It is not irritable, and it keeps no record of being wronged.

John 16:33 ESV

I have said these things to you, that in me you may have peace. In the world you will have tribulation. But take heart; I have overcome the world."

John 14:27 NLT

"I am leaving you with a gift—peace of mind and heart. And the peace I give is a gift the world cannot give. So don't be troubled or afraid.

Excellent site for additional Bible translations:
http://www.biblegateway.com/resources/commentaries/
Excellent resource for additional Bible study:
(Be sure to read the instructions on their page)
http://www.blueletterbible.org/commentaries/

Gentleness - Christian Quotes

"Meekness is not to be confused with weakness: the meek are not simply submissive because they lack the resources to be anything else. Meekness is quite compatible with great strength and ability as humans measure strength, but whatever strength or weakness the meek person has is accompanied by humility and a genuine dependence on God. True meekness may be a quality of the strong, those who could assert themselves but choose not to do so."
Leon Morris

"The meek man is not a human mouse afflicted with a sense of his own inferiority. Rather he may be in his moral life as bold as a lion and as strong as Samson; but he has stopped being fooled about himself. He has accepted God's estimate of his own life. He knows he is as weak and helpless as God declared him to be, but paradoxically, he knows at the same time that he is in the sight of God of more importance than angels. In himself, nothing; in God, everything. That is his motto."
A.W. Tozer

"The higher people are in the favor of God, the more tender they are."
Martin Luther

"Only the truly strong and great can be truly tender. Tenderness is a mark of nobility, not of weakness."
James Phillip

"Rudeness, yelling, anger, and swearing are a weak man's imitation of strength."
Unknown

"The meek are those who quietly submit themselves to God, to His Word and to His rod, who follow His directions, and comply with His designs, and are gentle toward all men."
Matthew Henry

"Gentleness is an active trait, describing the manner in which we should treat others. Meekness is a passive trait, describing the proper Christian response when others mistreat us."
Jerry Bridges
The Practice of Godliness p. 181

Gossip

Gossip- Bible Verses

Proverbs 16:28 ESV
A dishonest man spreads strife, and a whisperer separates close friends.

Leviticus 19:16 ESV
You shall not go around as a slanderer among your people, and you shall not stand up against the life of your neighbor: I am the LORD.

Proverbs 11:13 ESV
Whoever goes about slandering reveals secrets, but he who is trustworthy in spirit keeps a thing covered.

Proverbs 20:19 ESV
Whoever goes about slandering reveals secrets; therefore do not associate with a simple babbler.

Proverbs 26:20-22 ESV
For lack of wood the fire goes out, and where there is no whisperer, quarreling ceases. As charcoal to hot embers and wood to fire, so is a quarrelsome man for kindling strife. The words of a whisperer are like delicious morsels; they go down into the inner parts of the body.

Jeremiah 6:28 NLT
They are the worst kind of rebel,
　full of slander.
They are as hard as bronze and iron,
　and they lead others into corruption.

Jeremiah 9:4 NLT
"Beware of your neighbor!
　Don't even trust your brother!

For brother takes advantage of brother,
   and friend slanders friend.

Psalm 41:7 ESV
All who hate me whisper together about me; they imagine the worst for me.

Proverbs 25:23 ESV
The north wind brings forth rain, and a backbiting tongue, angry looks.

Romans 1:28-32 NIV
Furthermore, just as they did not think it worthwhile to retain the knowledge of God, so God gave them over to a depraved mind, so that they do what ought not to be done. They have become filled with every kind of wickedness, evil, greed and depravity. They are full of envy, murder, strife, deceit and malice. They are gossips, slanderers, God-haters, insolent, arrogant and boastful; they invent ways of doing evil; they disobey their parents; they have no understanding, no fidelity, no love, no mercy. Although they know God's righteous decree that those who do such things deserve death, they not only continue to do these very things but also approve of those who practice them.

2 Corinthians 12:20 ESV
For I fear that perhaps when I come I may find you not as I wish, and that you may find me not as you wish—that perhaps there may be quarreling, jealousy, anger, hostility, slander, gossip, conceit, and disorder.

1 Timothy 5:13-14 NIV
Besides, they get into the habit of being idle and going about from house to house. And not only do they become idlers, but also busybodies who talk nonsense, saying things they ought not to. So I counsel younger widows to marry, to have children, to manage their homes and to give the enemy no opportunity for slander.

2 Timothy 3:1-5 NIV
But mark this: There will be terrible times in the last days. People will be lovers of themselves, lovers of money, boastful, proud, abusive, disobedient

to their parents, ungrateful, unholy, without love, unforgiving, slanderous, without self-control, brutal, not lovers of the good, treacherous, rash, conceited, lovers of pleasure rather than lovers of God— having a form of godliness but denying its power. Have nothing to do with such people.

Titus 2:2-3 ESV
Older men are to be sober-minded, dignified, self-controlled, sound in faith, in love, and in steadfastness. Older women likewise are to be reverent in behavior, not slanderers or slaves to much wine. They are to teach what is good,

Excellent site for additional Bible translations:
http://www.biblegateway.com/resources/commentaries/
Excellent resource for additional Bible study:
(Be sure to read the instructions on their page)
http://www.blueletterbible.org/commentaries/

Gossip - Christian Quotes

"If there were no gratified hearers of ill reports, there would be an end of the trade of spreading them."
C.H. Spurgeon

"We will not listen or willingly inquire after ill concerning one another; that, if we do hear any ill of each other, we will not be forward to believe it; that as soon as possible we will communicate what we hear by speaking or writing to the person concerned; that until we have done this, we will not write or speak a syllable of it to any other person; that neither will we mention it, after we have done this, to any other person; that we will not make any exception to any of these rules unless we think ourselves absolutely obligated in conference."
John Wesley

"If there were no gratified hearers of ill reports, there would be an end of the trade of spreading them."
C.H. Spurgeon

"Three essential rules when speaking of others are: Is it true? Is it kind? Is it necessary?"
Unknown

"The best way to deal with slander is to pray about it: God will either remove it, or remove the sting from it. Our own attempts at clearing ourselves are usually failures; we are like the boy who wished to remove the blot from his copy, and by his bungling made it ten times worse."
C.H. Spurgeon

"Notice, we never pray for folks we gossip about, and we never gossip about the folk for whom we pray! For prayer is a great deterrent."
Leonard Ravenhill

"It is required of us that we be tender of the good name of our brethren; where we cannot speak well, we had better say nothing than speak evil; we must not take pleasure in making known the faults of others, divulging

things that are secret, merely to expose them, nor in making more of their known faults than really they deserve, and, least of all, in making false stories, and spreading things concerning them of which they are altogether innocent. What is this but to raise the hatred and encourage the persecutions of the world, against those who are engaged in the same interests with ourselves, and therefore with whom we ourselves must stand or fall?"
Matthew Henry

"It is a sign of a perverse and treacherous disposition to wound the good name of another, when he has no opportunity of defending himself."
John Calvin

"Despite our seemingly casual attitude toward it, slander is a particularly destructive sin. Writing in the 1828 edition of his dictionary, Noah Webster defined slander as "a false tale or report maliciously uttered, and tending to injure the reputation of another by lessening him in the esteem of his fellow citizens, by exposing him to impeachment and punishment, or by impairing his means of living." Slander strikes at people's dignity, defames their character, and destroys their reputation – their most priceless worldly asset (Proverbs 22:1; Ecclesiastes 7:1)."
John MacArthur

"A real Christian is a person who can give his pet parrot to the town gossip."
Billy Graham

"What good does it do to speak in tongues on Sunday if you have been using your tongue during the week to curse and gossip?"
Leonard Ravenhill

Grief

Grief - Bible Verses

Isaiah 53:4-6 ESV
Surely he has borne our griefs and carried our sorrows; yet we esteemed him stricken, smitten by God, and afflicted. But he was pierced for our transgressions; he was crushed for our iniquities; upon him was the chastisement that brought us peace, and with his wounds we are healed. All we like sheep have gone astray; we have turned—every one—to his own way; and the Lord has laid on him the iniquity of us all.

Genesis 37:34-35 NIV
Then Jacob tore his clothes, put on sackcloth and mourned for his son many days. All his sons and daughters came to comfort him, but he refused to be comforted. "No," he said, "I will continue to mourn until I join my son in the grave." So his father wept for him.

Deuteronomy 34:8 KJV
And the children of Israel wept for Moses in the plains of Moab thirty days: so the days of weeping and mourning for Moses were ended.

2 Samuel 12:16-17 ESV
David therefore sought God on behalf of the child. And David fasted and went in and lay all night on the ground. 17 And the elders of his house stood beside him, to raise him from the ground, but he would not, nor did he eat food with them.

Ecclesiastes 3:1-4 KJV
To every thing there is a season, and a time to every purpose under the heaven:
A time to be born, and a time to die; a time to plant, and a time to pluck up that which is planted;
A time to kill, and a time to heal; a time to break down, and a time to build up;

A time to weep, and a time to laugh; a time to mourn, and a time to dance;

Ecclesiastes 7:4 ESV
The heart of the wise is in the house of mourning, but the heart of fools is in the house of mirth.

Psalm 77:2 ESV
In the day of my trouble I seek the Lord; in the night my hand is stretched out without wearying; my soul refuses to be comforted.

Psalm 119:92 NASB
If your law had not been my delight, Then I would have perished in my affliction.

Proverbs 15:13-14 ESV
A glad heart makes a cheerful face, but by sorrow of heart the spirit is crushed. The heart of him who has understanding seeks knowledge, but the mouths of fools feed on folly.

Isaiah 41:10 ESV
Don't be afraid, for I am with you.
   Don't be discouraged, for I am your God.
I will strengthen you and help you.
   I will hold you up with my victorious right hand.

Philippians 3:13-14 NLT
No, dear brothers and sisters, I have not achieved it, but I focus on this one thing: Forgetting the past and looking forward to what lies ahead, I press on to reach the end of the race and receive the heavenly prize for which God, through Christ Jesus, is calling us.

James 4:7 ESV
Submit yourselves therefore to God. Resist the devil, and he will flee from you.

Psalm 116:15 ESV
Precious in the sight of the Lord is the death of his saints.

Psalm 119:50 ESV
This is my comfort in my affliction, that your promise gives me life.

Isaiah 51:11 ESV
And the ransomed of the Lord shall return and come to Zion with singing; everlasting joy shall be upon their heads; they shall obtain gladness and joy, and sorrow and sighing shall flee away.

Romans 8:18 NLT
Yet what we suffer now is nothing compared to the glory he will reveal to us later.

1 Corinthians 15:54-55 NASB
But when this perishable will have put on the imperishable, and this mortal will have put on immortality, then will come about the saying that is written, "Death is swallowed up in victory. O death, where is your victory? O death, where is your sting?"

1 Thessalonians 4:13 ESV
But we do not want you to be uninformed, brothers, about those who are asleep, that you may not grieve as others do who have no hope.

Revelation 14:13 NASB
And I heard a voice from heaven, saying, "Write, 'Blessed are the dead who die in the Lord from now on!'" "Yes," says the Spirit, "so that they may rest from their labors, for their deeds follow with them."

Revelation 21:4 NASB
and He will wipe away every tear from their eyes; and there will no longer be any death; there will no longer be any mourning, or crying, or pain; the first things have passed away."

Excellent site for additional Bible translations:
http://www.biblegateway.com/resources/commentaries/
Excellent resource for additional Bible study:
(Be sure to read the instructions on their page)
http://www.blueletterbible.org/commentaries/

Grief - Christian Quotes

"Too many Christians feel that grief is wrong, that we're supposed to rejoice when a loved one goes to be with the Lord. While we can rejoice in their homegoing, we can also grieve our loss."
Bruce Barton

"We are told that it is perfectly legitimate for believers to suffer grief. Our Lord Himself was a man of sorrows and acquainted with grief. Though grief may reach to the roots of our souls, it must not result in bitterness. Grief is a legitimate emotion, at times even a virtue, but there must be no place in the soul for bitterness."
R.C. Sproul

"Oh, when we are journeying through the murky night and the dark woods of affliction and sorrow, it is something to find here and there a spray broken, or a leafy stem bent down with the tread of His foot and the brush of His hand as He passed; and to remember that the path He trod He has hallowed, and thus to find lingering fragrance and hidden strength in the remembrance of Him as "in all points tempted like as we are," bearing grief for us, bearing grief with us, bearing grief like us."
Alexander Maclaren

"No one ever told me that grief felt so like fear."
C. S. Lewis

"Part of every misery is, so to speak, the misery's shadow or reflection: the fact that you don't merely suffer but have to keep on thinking about the fact that you suffer. I not only live each endless day in grief, but live each day thinking about living each day in grief."
C. S. Lewis

Guidance

Guidance - Bible Verses

Genesis 18:14 NASB
Is anything too difficult for the Lord? At the appointed time I will return to you, at this time next year, and Sarah will have a son."

Psalm 25:5 ESV
Lead me in your truth and teach me, for you are the God of my salvation; for you I wait all the day long.

Psalm 32:8 NASB
I will instruct you and teach you in the way which you should go; I will counsel you with my eye upon you.

Psalm 37:23-24 ESV
The steps of a man are established by the Lord, when he delights in his way; 24 though he fall, he shall not be cast headlong, for the Lord upholds his hand.

Proverbs 3:5-6 ESV
Trust in the Lord with all your heart, and do not lean on your own understanding. In all your ways acknowledge him, and he will make straight your paths.

Jeremiah 1:7-8 NIV
But the Lord said to me, "Do not say, 'I am too young.' You must go to everyone I send you to and say whatever I command you. 8 Do not be afraid of them, for I am with you and will rescue you," declares the Lord.

James 1:5-8 NIV
But if any of you lacks wisdom, let him ask of God, who gives to all generously and without reproach, and it will be given to him. But he must ask in faith without any doubting, for the one who doubts is like the surf of

the sea, driven and tossed by the wind. For that man ought not to expect that he will receive anything from the Lord, being a double-minded man, unstable in all his ways.

Leviticus 19:31 ESV
"Do not turn to mediums or necromancers; do not seek them out, and so make yourselves unclean by them: I am the Lord your God.

1 Samuel 7:3 NASB
Then Samuel spoke to all the house of Israel, saying, "If you return to the Lord with all your heart, remove the foreign gods and the Ashtaroth from among you and direct your hearts to the Lord and serve Him alone; and He will deliver you from the hand of the Philistines."

1 Chronicles 10:13-14 NIV
Saul died because he was unfaithful to the Lord; he did not keep the word of the Lord and even consulted a medium for guidance, and did not inquire of the Lord. So the Lord put him to death and turned the kingdom over to David son of Jesse.

Proverbs 11:14 ESV
Where there is no guidance, a people falls, but in an abundance of counselors there is safety.

Proverbs 14:12 ESV
There is a way that seems right to a man, but its end is the way to death.

Isaiah 30:19-22 NIV
People of Zion, who live in Jerusalem, you will weep no more. How gracious he will be when you cry for help! As soon as he hears, he will answer you. Although the Lord gives you the bread of adversity and the water of affliction, your teachers will be hidden no more; with your own eyes you will see them. Whether you turn to the right or to the left, your ears will hear a voice behind you, saying, "This is the way; walk in it." Then you will desecrate your idols overlaid with silver and your images covered with gold;

you will throw them away like a menstrual cloth and say to them, "Away with you!"

1 John 4:1 ESV
Beloved, do not believe every spirit, but test the spirits to see whether they are from God, for many false prophets have gone out into the world.

1 Corinthians 1:25 NIV
For the foolishness of God is wiser than human wisdom, and the weakness of God is stronger than human strength.

Isaiah 11:2 NLT
And the Spirit of the Lord shall rest upon him, the Spirit of wisdom and understanding, the Spirit of counsel and might, the Spirit of knowledge and the fear of the Lord.

John 14:26 ESV
But the Helper, the Holy Spirit, whom the Father will send in my name, he will teach you all things and bring to your remembrance all that I have said to you.

Romans 8:26 NIV
In the same way, the Spirit helps us in our weakness. We do not know what we ought to pray for, but the Spirit himself intercedes for us through wordless groans.

Excellent site for additional Bible translations:
http://www.biblegateway.com/resources/commentaries/
Excellent resource for additional Bible study:
(Be sure to read the instructions on their page)
http://www.blueletterbible.org/commentaries/

Guidance - Christian Quotes

"Superficial Christians are apt to be eccentric. Mature Christians are so near the Lord that they are not afraid of missing His guidance. They are not always trying to promote their loyalty to God by their independence from others."
A. B. Simpson

"For not only does sound reason direct us to refuse the guidance of those who do or teach anything wrong, but it is by all means vital for the lover of truth, regardless of the threat of death, to choose to do and say what is right even before saving his own life."
A. W. Tozer

"We have all been encouraged to feel in the guardianship and guidance of that Almighty Being whose power regulates the destiny of nations, whose blessings have been so conspicuously dispensed to this rising Republic."
James Madison

"All should work and ask God's guidance."
D. L. Moody

"The Word of God is creative. It is a hammer that crushes the hardness of our insubordination. It is medicine that heals the broken-hearted. And it is light that gives us guidance and hope on our way."
John Piper

"The fundamental mode whereby our rational Creator guides his rational creatures is by rational understanding and application of his written Word."
J. I. Packer

"Being a godly father requires much perseverance and prayer as we seek God's guidance in being the types of fathers He wants us to be."
Jonathan Falwell

Hard Times

Hard Times - Bible Verses

Psalm 119:67-68 ESV
Before I was afflicted I went astray, but now I keep your word. You are good and do good; teach me your statutes

Psalm 3:4 ESV
I cried aloud to the LORD, and he answered me from his holy hill. Selah

Psalm 34:17 ESV
When the righteous cry for help, the LORD hears and delivers them out of all their troubles.

Psalm 50:15 ESV
call upon me in the day of trouble; I will deliver you, and you shall glorify me.

Proverbs 3:5-6 ESV
Trust in the LORD with all your heart, and do not lean on your own understanding. In all your ways acknowledge him, and he will make straight your paths.

Isaiah 55:6 NASB
Seek the Lord while he may be found;
    call on him while he is near.

Psalm 42:5 ESV
Why are you cast down, O my soul, and why are you in turmoil within me? Hope in God; for I shall again praise him, my salvation

Psalm 66:17-20 ESV
I cried to him with my mouth, and high praise was on my tongue. If I had cherished iniquity in my heart, the Lord would not have listened. But truly

God has listened; he has attended to the voice of my prayer. Blessed be God, because he has not rejected my prayer or removed his steadfast love from me!

Psalm 146:5-6 ESV
Blessed is he whose help is the God of Jacob, whose hope is in the LORD his God, who made heaven and earth, the sea, and all that is in them, who keeps faith forever

Acts 16:25 ESV
About midnight Paul and Silas were praying and singing hymns to God, and the other prisoners were listening to them.

Ephesians 3:20-21 NIV
Now to him who is able to do immeasurably more than all we ask or imagine, according to his power that is at work within us, to him be glory in the church and in Christ Jesus throughout all generations, for ever and ever! Amen.

2 Corinthians 9:8 NIV
And God is able to bless you abundantly, so that in all things at all times, having all that you need, you will abound in every good work.

2 Corinthians 1:10 NIV
He has delivered us from such a deadly peril, and he will deliver us again. On him we have set our hope that he will continue to deliver us,

Colossians 1:13 ESV
He has delivered us from the domain of darkness and transferred us to the kingdom of his beloved Son

Hebrews 6:19-20 NASB
This hope we have as an anchor of the soul, a hope both sure and steadfast and one which enters within the veil, where Jesus has entered as a forerunner for us, having become a high priest forever according to the order of Melchizedek.

James 1:12 NASB
Blessed is a man who perseveres under trial; for once he has been approved, he will receive the crown of life which the Lord has promised to those who love Him.

James 1:2-4 NLT
Dear brothers and sisters, when troubles come your way, consider it an opportunity for great joy. For you know that when your faith is tested, your endurance has a chance to grow. So let it grow, for when your endurance is fully developed, you will be perfect and complete, needing nothing.

Psalm 119:71-72 ESV
It is good for me that I was afflicted, that I might learn your statutes. The law of your mouth is better to me than thousands of gold and silver pieces.

Psalm 119:75-76 ESV
I know, O LORD, that your rules are righteous, and that in faithfulness you have afflicted me. Let your steadfast love comfort me according to your promise to your servant.

Romans 5:2-5 NLT
Because of our faith, Christ has brought us into this place of undeserved privilege where we now stand, and we confidently and joyfully look forward to sharing God's glory.
We can rejoice, too, when we run into problems and trials, for we know that they help us develop endurance. And endurance develops strength of character, and character strengthens our confident hope of salvation. And this hope will not lead to disappointment. For we know how dearly God loves us, because he has given us the Holy Spirit to fill our hearts with his love.

Romans 8:28 ESV
And we know that for those who love God all things work together for good, for those who are called according to his purpose.

Excellent site for additional Bible translations:
http://www.biblegateway.com/resources/commentaries/
Excellent resource for additional Bible study:
(Be sure to read the instructions on their page)
http://www.blueletterbible.org/commentaries/

Hard Times - Christian Quotes

"A century or so since, they spoke of sharing our Lord with the heathen, and the world rocked with laughter at so crazy a scheme, with the Church joining loudly in the merriment. Yet today, who laughs now? We ought to be the gladdest and the most exultant people in the world; for we have found the key to our difficulties, and it turns; have come on a solution of life's problems, and it works."
A. J. Gossip

"What then are we to do about our problems? We must learn to live with them until such time as God delivers us from them. We must pray for grace to endure them without murmuring. Problems patiently endured will work for our spiritual perfecting. They harm us only when we resist them or endure them unwillingly."
A. W. Tozer

"I can only hope that every minister could come to know friends as true, as faithful, and as genuine as I have come to know in C. J., Mark, and Lig. We are exhilarated in being together, and we take tremendous delight in each other. One of the problems we face in today's church is that men are not often sustained by authentic friendships. This is especially deadly for pastors."
Albert Mohler

"Heaven will solve our problems, but not, I think, by showing us subtle reconciliations between all our apparently contradictory notions."
C. S. Lewis

"If we rationalize our problems when He points them out, we will spend less and less time meditating because we won't want to face God in that area of our lives."
Charles Stanley

"Difficulties and obstacles are God's challenges to faith. When hindrances confront us in the path of duty, we are to recognize them as vessels for faith to fill with the fullness and all-sufficiency of Jesus."
A. B. Simpson

"Let us not be surprised when we have to face difficulties. When the wind blows hard on a tree, the roots stretch and grow the stronger, Let it be so with us. Let us not be weaklings, yielding to every wind that blows, but strong in spirit to resist."
Amy Carmichael

"God knows our situation; He will not judge us as if we had no difficulties to overcome. What matters is the sincerity and perseverance of our will to overcome them."
C. S. Lewis

"Many men owe the grandeur of their lives to their tremendous difficulties."
Charles Spurgeon

"Doubt discovers difficulties which it never solves; it creates hesitancy, despondency, despair. Its progress is the decay of comfort, the death of peace. "Believe!" is the word which speaks life into a man, but doubt nails down his coffin."
Charles Spurgeon

Healing

Healing - Bible Verses

Matthew 7:7-11 ESV
"Ask, and it will be given to you; seek, and you will find; knock, and it will be opened to you. For everyone who asks receives, and the one who seeks finds, and to the one who knocks it will be opened. Or which one of you, if his son asks him for bread, will give him a stone? Or if he asks for a fish, will give him a serpent? If you then, who are evil, know how to give good gifts to your children, how much more will your Father who is in heaven give good things to those who ask him!"

Mark 11:23-26 NIV
"Truly I tell you, if anyone says to this mountain, 'Go, throw yourself into the sea,' and does not doubt in their heart but believes that what they say will happen, it will be done for them. Therefore I tell you, whatever you ask for in prayer, believe that you have received it, and it will be yours. And when you stand praying, if you hold anything against anyone, forgive them, so that your Father in heaven may forgive you your sins."

John 15:7 NIV
If you remain in me and my words remain in you, ask whatever you wish, and it will be done for you.

Matthew 6:5-8 NIV
"And when you pray, do not be like the hypocrites, for they love to pray standing in the synagogues and on the street corners to be seen by others. Truly I tell you, they have received their reward in full. But when you pray, go into your room, close the door and pray to your Father, who is unseen. Then your Father, who sees what is done in secret, will reward you. And when you pray, do not keep on babbling like pagans, for they think they will be heard because of their many words. Do not be like them, for your Father knows what you need before you ask him.

James 5:14-15 NASB
Is anyone among you sick? Then he must call for the elders of the church and they are to pray over him, anointing him with oil in the name of the Lord; and the prayer offered in faith will restore the one who is sick, and the Lord will raise him up, and if he has committed sins, they will be forgiven him.

Matthew 9:20-22 ESV
And behold, a woman who had suffered from a discharge of blood for twelve years came up behind him and touched the fringe of his garment, for she said to herself, "If I only touch his garment, I will be made well." Jesus turned, and seeing her he said, "Take heart, daughter; your faith has made you well." And instantly the woman was made well.

Mark 2:8-12 NLT
Jesus knew immediately what they were thinking, so he asked them, "Why do you question this in your hearts? 9 Is it easier to say to the paralyzed man 'Your sins are forgiven,' or 'Stand up, pick up your mat, and walk'? 10 So I will prove to you that the Son of Man has the authority on earth to forgive sins." Then Jesus turned to the paralyzed man and said, 11 "Stand up, pick up your mat, and go home!"
12 And the man jumped up, grabbed his mat, and walked out through the stunned onlookers. They were all amazed and praised God, exclaiming, "We've never seen anything like this before!"

Luke 17:11-19 ESV
On the way to Jerusalem he was passing along between Samaria and Galilee. And as he entered a village, he was met by ten lepers, who stood at a distance and lifted up their voices, saying, "Jesus, Master, have mercy on us." When he saw them he said to them, "Go and show yourselves to the priests." And as they went they were cleansed. Then one of them, when he saw that he was healed, turned back, praising God with a loud voice; and he fell on his face at Jesus' feet, giving him thanks. Now he was a Samaritan. Then Jesus answered, "Were not ten cleansed? Where are the nine? Was no one found to return and give praise to God except this foreigner?" And he said to him, "Rise and go your way; your faith has made you well."

John 9:1-7 NASB
As He passed by, He saw a man blind from birth. And His disciples asked Him, "Rabbi, who sinned, this man or his parents, that he would be born blind?" Jesus answered, "It was neither that this man sinned, nor his parents; but it was so that the works of God might be displayed in him. We must work the works of Him who sent Me as long as it is day; night is coming when no one can work. While I am in the world, I am the Light of the world." When He had said this, He spat on the ground, and made clay of the spittle, and applied the clay to his eyes, and said to him, "Go, wash in the pool of Siloam" (which is translated, Sent). So he went away and washed, and came back seeing.

Acts 9:40-42 ESV
But Peter put them all outside, and knelt down and prayed; and turning to the body he said, "Tabitha, arise." And she opened her eyes, and when she saw Peter she sat up. And he gave her his hand and raised her up. Then calling the saints and widows, he presented her alive. And it became known throughout all Joppa, and many believed in the Lord.

Acts 14:8-10 NLT
While they were at Lystra, Paul and Barnabas came upon a man with crippled feet. He had been that way from birth, so he had never walked. He was sitting and listening as Paul preached. Looking straight at him, Paul realized he had faith to be healed. So Paul called to him in a loud voice, "Stand up!" And the man jumped to his feet and started walking.

Excellent site for additional Bible translations:
http://www.biblegateway.com/resources/commentaries/
Excellent resource for additional Bible study:
(Be sure to read the instructions on their page)
http://www.blueletterbible.org/commentaries/

Healing - Christian Quotes

"We must leave room for mystery in God's ways. Some things will always remain unexplained. Why God does or does not choose to heal is ultimately subject to his wisdom and sovereign purposes. Why God chooses to heal in part or in whole, now or later, this person but not that one, is often beyond our capacity to understand. Resist the tendency to replace divine mystery with human formulas."
Sam Storms

"Health is a good thing; but sickness is far better, if it leads us to God."
J.C. Ryle

"Begin to rejoice in the Lord, and your bones will flourish like an herb, and your cheeks will glow with the bloom of health and freshness. Worry, fear, distrust, care-all are poisonous! Joy is balm and healing, and if you will but rejoice, God will give power."
A. B. Simpson

"I venture to say that the greatest earthly blessing that God can give to any of us is health, with the exception of sickness. Sickness has frequently been of more use to the saints of God than health has."
C.H. Spurgeon

"The storms of winter often bring out the defects in a man's dwelling, and sickness often exposes the gracelessness of a man's soul. Surely anything that makes us find out the real character of our faith is a good."
 J.C. Ryle

"Healing was a miraculous sign gift to be used for special purposes. It was not intended as a permanent way to keep the Christian community in perfect health. Yet today most charismatics teach that God wants every Christian well. If that is true, why does God allow Christians to get sick in the first place?"
John MacArthur

Hope

Hope - Bible Verses

Proverbs 24:20 ESV
for the evil man has no future; the lamp of the wicked will be put out.

Proverbs 24:14 ESV
Know that wisdom is such to your soul; if you find it, there will be a future, and your hope will not be cut off.

Jeremiah 29:11-12 ESV
For I know the plans I have for you, declares the Lord, plans for welfare and not for evil, to give you a future and a hope. Then you will call upon me and come and pray to me, and I will hear you.

Titus 1:1-2 ESV
Paul, a servant of God and an apostle of Jesus Christ, for the sake of the faith of God's elect and their knowledge of the truth, which accords with godliness, in hope of eternal life, which God, who never lies,promised before the ages began

Titus 3:7 ESV
so that being justified by his grace we might become heirs according to the hope of eternal life.

1 Corinthians 15:19 NASB
If we have hoped in Christ in this life only, we are of all men most to be pitied.

2 Corinthians 4:16-18 NIV
Therefore we do not lose heart. Though outwardly we are wasting away, yet inwardly we are being renewed day by day. For our light and momentary troubles are achieving for us an eternal glory that far outweighs them all. So

we fix our eyes not on what is seen, but on what is unseen, since what is seen is temporary, but what is unseen is eternal.

1 Peter 1:3 NIV
Praise be to the God and Father of our Lord Jesus Christ! In his great mercy he has given us new birth into a living hope through the resurrection of Jesus Christ from the dead,

Romans 5:2-5 NASB
through whom also we have obtained our introduction by faith into this grace in which we stand; and we exult in hope of the glory of God. And not only this, but we also exult in our tribulations, knowing that tribulation brings about perseverance; and perseverance, proven character; and proven character, hope; and hope does not disappoint, because the love of God has been poured out within our hearts through the Holy Spirit who was given to us.

Romans 8:24-25 NLT
We were given this hope when we were saved. (If we already have something, we don't need to hope for it. But if we look forward to something we don't yet have, we must wait patiently and confidently.)

Romans 12:12 ESV
Rejoice in hope, be patient in tribulation, be constant in prayer.

Romans 15:4 ESV
For whatever was written in former days was written for our instruction, that through endurance and through the encouragement of the Scriptures we might have hope.

Romans 15:13 ESV
May the God of hope fill you with all joy and peace in believing, so that by the power of the Holy Spirit you may abound in hope.

Psalm 27:4-5 ESV
One thing have I asked of the LORD, that will I seek after: that I may dwell in the house of the LORD all the days of my life, to gaze upon the beauty of the LORD and to inquire in his temple. For he will hide me in his shelter in the day of trouble; he will conceal me under the cover of his tent; he will lift me high upon a rock.

Mark 5:35-36 NLT
While he was still speaking to her, messengers arrived from the home of Jairus, the leader of the synagogue. They told him, "Your daughter is dead. There's no use troubling the Teacher now."
But Jesus overheard them and said to Jairus, "Don't be afraid. Just have faith."

Numbers 23:19 ESV
God is not man, that he should lie, or a son of man, that he should change his mind. Has he said, and will he not do it? Or has he spoken, and will he not fulfill it?

Zephaniah 3:17 ESV
The LORD your God is in your midst, a mighty one who will save; he will rejoice over you with gladness; he will quiet you by his love; he will exult over you with loud singing.

John 4:13-14 NASB
Jesus answered, "Everyone who drinks this water will be thirsty again, but whoever drinks the water I give them will never thirst. Indeed, the water I give them will become in them a spring of water welling up to eternal life."

Job 13:15 ESV
Though he slay me, I will hope in him; yet I will argue my ways to his face.

Hebrews 11:1 ESV
Now faith is the assurance of things hoped for, the conviction of things not seen.

Excellent site for additional Bible translations:
http://www.biblegateway.com/resources/commentaries/
Excellent resource for additional Bible study:
(Be sure to read the instructions on their page)
http://www.blueletterbible.org/commentaries/

Hope - Christian Quotes

"Most people, if they had really learned to look into their own hearts, would know that they do want, and want acutely, something that cannot be had in this world. There are all sorts of things in this world that offer to give it to you, but they never quite keep their promise.
C.S. Lewis

"Do not look to your hope, but to Christ, the source of your hope."
C.H. Spurgeon

"At present we are on the outside... the wrong side of the door. We discern the freshness and purity of morning, but they do not make us fresh and pure. We cannot mingle with the pleasures we see. But all the pages of the New Testament are rustling with the rumor that it will not always be so. Someday, God willing, we shall get "in"... We will put on glory... that greater glory of which Nature is only the first sketch.
C.S. Lewis

We do not want to merely "see" beauty—though, God knows, even that is bounty enough. We want something else which can hardly be put into words—to be united with the beauty we see, to pass into it, to receive it into ourselves, to bathe in it, to become part of it.
C.S. Lewis

"Hope: A trusting expectation that God is going to keep His word."
Unknown

"The Christmas message is that there is hope for a ruined humanity - hope of pardon, hope of peace with God, hope of glory - because at the Father's will Jesus Christ became poor, and was born in a stable so that thirty years later He might hang on a cross."
J. I. Packer

"Just as the sinner's despair of any hope from himself is the first prerequisite of a sound conversion, so the loss of all confidence in himself is the first essential in the believer's growth in grace."
A. W. Pink

"Let this one great, gracious, glorious fact lie in your spirit until it permeates all your thoughts and makes you rejoice even though you are without strength. Rejoice that the Lord Jesus has become your strength and your song - He has become your salvation."
Charles Spurgeon

"Hope is like the sun, which, as we journey toward it, casts the shadow of our burden behind us."
Samuel Smiles

"Without Christ there is no hope."
Charles Spurgeon

Humility

Humility - Bible Verses

Deuteronomy 8:2-3 ESV
And you shall remember the whole way that the LORD your God has led you these forty years in the wilderness, that he might humble you, testing you to know what was in your heart, whether you would keep his commandments or not. And he humbled you and let you hunger and fed you with manna, which you did not know, nor did your fathers know, that he might make you know that man does not live by bread alone, but man lives by every word that comes from the mouth of the LORD.

2 Chronicles 7:14 ESV
if my people who are called by my name humble themselves, and pray and seek my face and turn from their wicked ways, then I will hear from heaven and will forgive their sin and heal their land.

Psalm 25:9 ESV
He leads the humble in what is right, and teaches the humble his way.

Psalm 55:19 ESV
God will give ear and humble them, he who is enthroned from of old, Selah because they do not change and do not fear God.

1 Peter 5:5 NIV
In the same way, you who are younger, submit yourselves to your elders. All of you, clothe yourselves with humility toward one another, because,
"God opposes the proud but shows favor to the humble."

Zechariah 9:9 ESV
Rejoice greatly, O daughter of Zion! Shout aloud, O daughter of Jerusalem! Behold, your king is coming to you; righteous and having salvation is he, humble and mounted on a donkey, on a colt, the foal of a donkey.

Mark 10:45 NASB
For even the Son of Man did not come to be served, but to serve, and to give his life as a ransom for many."

Philippians 2:5-8 NIV
Have this mind among yourselves, which is yours in Christ Jesus, who, though he was in the form of God, did not count equality with God a thing to be grasped, but emptied himself, by taking the form of a servant, being born in the likeness of men. And being found in human form, he humbled himself by becoming obedient to the point of death, even death on a cross.

Genesis 18:27 NIV
Then Abraham spoke up again: "Now that I have been so bold as to speak to the Lord, though I am nothing but dust and ashes,

Genesis 41:16 KJV
And Joseph answered Pharaoh, saying, It is not in me: God shall give Pharaoh an answer of peace.

Exodus 3:11 KJV
And Moses said unto God, Who am I, that I should go unto Pharaoh, and that I should bring forth the children of Israel out of Egypt?

1 Kings 21:29 ESV
"Have you seen how Ahab has humbled himself before me? Because he has humbled himself before me, I will not bring the disaster in his days; but in his son's days I will bring the disaster upon his house."

Luke 1:43 KJV
And whence is this to me, that the mother of my Lord should come to me?

Mark 1:7 NASB
And he was preaching, and saying, "After me One is coming who is mightier than I, and I am not fit to stoop down and untie the thong of His sandals.

2 Corinthians 10:1 NASB

Now I, Paul, myself urge you by the meekness and gentleness of Christ—I who am meek when face to face with you, but bold toward you when absent!

2 Chronicles 12:12 ESV
And when he humbled himself the wrath of the LORD turned from him, so as not to make a complete destruction. Moreover, conditions were good in Judah.

Job 22:29 NASB
"When you are cast down, you will speak with confidence, And the humble person He will save.

Psalm 18:27 ESV
For you save a humble people, but the haughty eyes you bring down.

Proverbs 11:2 ESV
When pride comes, then comes disgrace, but with the humble is wisdom.

Excellent site for additional Bible translations:
http://www.biblegateway.com/resources/commentaries/
Excellent resource for additional Bible study:
(Be sure to read the instructions on their page)
http://www.blueletterbible.org/commentaries/

Humility - Christian Quotes

"The greatest test of whether the holiness we profess to seek or to attain is truth and life will be whether it produces an increasing humility in us. In man, humility is the one thing needed to allow God's holiness to dwell in him and shine through him. The chief mark of counterfeit holiness is lack of humility. The holiest will be the humblest."
Andrew Murray

"The very design of the gospel is to abase us; and the work of grace is begun and carried on in humiliation. Humility is not a mere ornament of a Christian, but an essential part of the new creature. It is a contradiction in terms, to be a Christian, and not humble."
Richard Baxter

"Christian humility does not consist in denying what there is of good in us; but in an abiding sense of ill-desert, and the consciousness that what we have of good is due to the grace of God."
Charles Hodge

"Humility is a strange thing. As a rule, once you discover you have it you lose it. Humility is like a rare flower -- put it on display and it instantly wilts and loses its fragrance! Humility is one character trait that can never come out of the closest; it is not something to announce from the rooftop...No, humility is not something to be announced. For then, if you can imagine the irony of this, you have become proud of your humility."
Unknown

"Without Christ there is no hope."
Charles Spurgeon

"Humility is a paradox. The moment you think you've finally found it, you've lost it. There has yet to be written a book entitled, 'Humility and How I Achieved It.' And yet, God expects (and rewards) an attitude of servant-like humility in His followers."
Unknown

"In our sad condition our only consolation is the expectancy of another life."
Martin Luther

"Humility: The beginning of perfection is to be little in self. The increase in perfection is to be less. The end of perfection is to be nothing at all."
Unknown

"I am persuaded that love and humility are the highest attainments in the school of Christ and the brightest evidences that He is indeed our Master."
John Newton

"There was no part of creature holiness that I had so great a sense of loveliness as humility, as brokenness of heart and poverty in spirit. There is nothing that I longed for more earnestly. My heart panted after this, to lie low before God as in the dust that I might be nothing and that God might be all."
Jonathan Edwards

"Nothing sets a Christian so much out of the devil's reach than humility."
Jonathan Edwards

"Humility may be defined to be a habit of mind and heart corresponding to our comparative unworthiness and vileness before God, or a sense of our own comparative meanness in His sight, with the disposition to a behavior answerable thereto."
Jonathan Edwards

"Humility is the repentance of pride."
Nehemiah Rogers

Inspirational

Inspirational - Bible Verses

Psalm 136:26 NASB
Give thanks to the God of heaven,
For His lovingkindness is everlasting.

Jeremiah 29:11 NASB
For I know the plans that I have for you,' declares the Lord, 'plans for welfare and not for calamity to give you a future and a hope.

Zephaniah 3:17 ESV
The LORD your God is in your midst, a mighty one who will save; he will rejoice over you with gladness; he will quiet you by his love; he will exult over you with loud singing.

Romans 15:13 NASB
Now may the God of hope fill you with all joy and peace in believing, so that you will abound in hope by the power of the Holy Spirit.

Isaiah 41:10 ESV
fear not, for I am with you; be not dismayed, for I am your God; I will strengthen you, I will help you, I will uphold you with my righteous right hand.

Psalm 18:32-34 ESV
the God who equipped me with strength and made my way blameless. He made my feet like the feet of a deer and set me secure on the heights. He trains my hands for war, so that my arms can bend a bow of bronze.

1 Corinthians 10:13 NIV
No temptation has overtaken you except what is common to mankind. And God is faithful; he will not let you be tempted beyond what you can bear. But

when you are tempted, he will also provide a way out so that you can endure it.

Deuteronomy 7:9 ESV
Know therefore that the LORD your God is God, the faithful God who keeps covenant and steadfast love with those who love him and keep his commandments, to a thousand generations

Psalm 32:8 ESV
I will instruct you and teach you in the way you should go; I will counsel you with my eye upon you.

John 6:47 NIV
Very truly I tell you, the one who believes has eternal life.

1 John 5:14 NIV
This is the confidence we have in approaching God: that if we ask anything according to his will, he hears us.

1 Corinthians 2:7-9 ESV
But we impart a secret and hidden wisdom of God, which God decreed before the ages for our glory. None of the rulers of this age understood this, for if they had, they would not have crucified the Lord of glory. But, as it is written,"What no eye has seen, nor ear heard, nor the heart of man imagined, what God has prepared for those who love him"

Philippians 1:21-23 NASB
For to me, to live is Christ and to die is gain. But if I am to live on in the flesh, this will mean fruitful labor for me; and I do not know which to choose. But I am hard-pressed from both directions, having the desire to depart and be with Christ, for that is very much better;

Philippians 3:20-21 NASB
For our citizenship is in heaven, from which also we eagerly wait for a Savior, the Lord Jesus Christ; who will transform the body of our humble

state into conformity with the body of His glory, by the exertion of the power that He has even to subject all things to Himself.

Revelation 21:4 NLT
He will wipe every tear from their eyes, and there will be no more death or sorrow or crying or pain. All these things are gone forever."

Romans 8:37-39 NLT
No, despite all these things, overwhelming victory is ours through Christ, who loved us.
And I am convinced that nothing can ever separate us from God's love. Neither death nor life, neither angels nor demons, neither our fears for today nor our worries about tomorrow—not even the powers of hell can separate us from God's love. No power in the sky above or in the earth below—indeed, nothing in all creation will ever be able to separate us from the love of God that is revealed in Christ Jesus our Lord.

1 John 4:7-8 NIV
Dear friends, let us continue to love one another, for love comes from God. Anyone who loves is a child of God and knows God. But anyone who does not love does not know God, for God is love.

Psalm 136:26 ESV
Give thanks to the God of heaven, for his steadfast love endures forever.

Galatians 2:20 NLT
My old self has been crucified with Christ. It is no longer I who live, but Christ lives in me. So I live in this earthly body by trusting in the Son of God, who loved me and gave himself for me.

Deuteronomy 31:6 ESV
Be strong and courageous. Do not fear or be in dread of them, for it is the LORD your God who goes with you. He will not leave you or forsake you."

Joshua 1:7-9 ESV
Only be strong and very courageous, being careful to do according to all the law that Moses my servant commanded you. Do not turn from it to the right

hand or to the left, that you may have good success wherever you go. This Book of the Law shall not depart from your mouth, but you shall meditate on it day and night, so that you may be careful to do according to all that is written in it. For then you will make your way prosperous, and then you will have good success. Have I not commanded you? Be strong and courageous. Do not be frightened, and do not be dismayed, for the LORD your God is with you wherever you go."

Psalm 27:1 ESV
The LORD is my light and my salvation; whom shall I fear? The LORD is the stronghold of my life of whom shall I be afraid?

Excellent site for additional Bible translations:
http://www.biblegateway.com/resources/commentaries/
Excellent resource for additional Bible study:
(Be sure to read the instructions on their page)
http://www.blueletterbible.org/commentaries/

Inspirational- Christian Quotes

"Faith sees the invisible, believes the unbelievable, and receives the impossible."
Corrie Ten Boom

"The only way to learn strong faith is to endure great trials."
George Muller

"I believe in Christianity as I believe that the sun has risen: not only because I see it, but because by it I see everything else."
C. S. Lewis

"We may ignore, but we can nowhere evade, the presence of God."
C.S.Lewis

"Immanuel, God with us in our nature, in our sorrow, in our lifework, in our punishment, in our grave, and now with us, or rather we with Him, in resurrection, ascension, triumph, and Second Advent splendor."
Charles Spurgeon

"He shows much more of Himself to some people than to others-not because He has favourites, but because it is impossible for Him to show Himself to a man whose whole mind and character are in the wrong condition."
C. S. Lewis

The doctrine of the Kingdom of Heaven, which was the main teaching of Jesus, is certainly one of the most revolutionary doctrines that ever stirred and changed human thought.
H. G. Wells

"Within the covers of the Bible are the answers for all the problems men face."
Ronald Reagan

"Christ is not a reservoir but a spring. His life is continual, active and ever passing on with an outflow as necessary as its inflow. If we do not perpetually draw the fresh supply from the living Fountain, we shall either grow stagnant or empty, It is, therefore, not so much a perpetual fullness as a perpetual filling."
A. B. Simpson

Integrity

Integrity - Bible Verses

1 Kings 9:4-5 ESV
And as for you, if you will walk before me, as David your father walked, with integrity of heart and uprightness, doing according to all that I have commanded you, and keeping my statutes and my rules, then I will establish your royal throne over Israel forever, as I promised David your father, saying, 'You shall not lack a man on the throne of Israel.'

Psalm 41:11-13 ESV
By this I know that you delight in me: my enemy will not shout in triumph over me. But you have upheld me because of my integrity, and set me in your presence forever. Blessed be the LORD, the God of Israel, from everlasting to everlasting! Amen and Amen.

Proverbs 2:6-8 ESV
For the LORD gives wisdom; from his mouth come knowledge and understanding; he stores up sound wisdom for the upright; he is a shield to those who walk in integrity, guarding the paths of justice and watching over the way of his saints.

Proverbs 2:20-21 NLT
Follow the steps of good men instead,
   and stay on the paths of the righteous.
For only the godly will live in the land,
   and those with integrity will remain in it.

Genesis 20:5-6 ESV
Did he not himself say to me, 'She is my sister'? And she herself said, 'He is my brother.' In the integrity of my heart and the innocence of my hands I have done this." Then God said to him in the dream, "Yes, I know that you have done this in the integrity of your heart, and it was I who kept you from sinning against me. Therefore I did not let you touch her.

Job 2:3 ESV
And the LORD said to Satan, "Have you considered my servant Job, that there is none like him on the earth, a blameless and upright man, who fears God and turns away from evil? He still holds fast his integrity, although you incited me against him to destroy him without reason."

Psalm 25:19-21 ESV
Consider how many are my foes, and with what violent hatred they hate me. Oh, guard my soul, and deliver me! Let me not be put to shame, for I take refuge in you. May integrity and uprightness preserve me, for I wait for you.

Psalm 26:8-12 ESV
O LORD, I love the habitation of your house and the place where your glory dwells. Do not sweep my soul away with sinners, nor my life with bloodthirsty men, in whose hands are evil devices, and whose right hands are full of bribes. But as for me, I shall walk in my integrity; redeem me, and be gracious to me. My foot stands on level ground; in the great assembly I will bless the LORD.

Psalm 26:1-3 ESV
Vindicate me, O LORD, for I have walked in my integrity, and I have trusted in the LORD without wavering. Prove me, O LORD, and try me; test my heart and my mind. For your steadfast love is before my eyes, and I walk in your faithfulness.

Job 2:9 ESV
Then his wife said to him, "Do you still hold fast your integrity? Curse God and die."

Psalm 7:8 ESV
The LORD judges the peoples; judge me, O LORD, according to my righteousness and according to the integrity that is in me.

Proverbs 10:9 ESV
Whoever walks in integrity walks securely, but he who makes his ways crooked will be found out.

Proverbs 11:3 ESV
The integrity of the upright guides them, but the crookedness of the treacherous destroys them.

Job 27:1-5 ESV
And Job again took up his discourse, and said: "As God lives, who has taken away my right, and the Almighty, who has made my soul bitter, as long as my breath is in me, and the spirit of God is in my nostrils, my lips will not speak falsehood, and my tongue will not utter deceit. Far be it from me to say that you are right; till I die I will not put away my integrity from me.

Psalm 101:1-2 ESV
I will sing of steadfast love and justice; to you, O LORD, I will make music. I will ponder the way that is blameless. Oh when will you come to me? Will walk with integrity of heart within my house;

Proverbs 20:7 ESV
The righteous who walks in his integrity— blessed are his children after him!

Proverbs 28:18 ESV
Whoever walks in integrity will be delivered, but he who is crooked in his ways will suddenly fall.

1 Timothy 2:1-4 KJV
I exhort therefore, that, first of all, supplications, prayers, intercessions, and giving of thanks, be made for all men; For kings, and for all that are in authority; that we may lead a quiet and peaceable life in all godliness and honesty. For this is good and acceptable in the sight of God our Saviour; Who will have all men to be saved, and to come unto the knowledge of the truth.

Titus 2:7-8 ESV
Show yourself in all respects to be a model of good works, and in your teaching show integrity, dignity, and sound speech that cannot be

condemned, so that an opponent may be put to shame, having nothing evil to say about us.

Excellent site for additional Bible translations:
http://www.biblegateway.com/resources/commentaries/
Excellent resource for additional Bible study:
(Be sure to read the instructions on their page)
http://www.blueletterbible.org/commentaries/

Integrity - Christian Quotes

"We must be the same person in private and in public. Only the Christian worldview gives us the basis for this kind of integrity."
Chuck Colson

Few things are more infectious than a godly lifestyle. The people you rub shoulders with everyday need that kind of challenge. Not prudish. Not preachy. Just cracker jack clean living. Just honest to goodness, bone - deep, non-hypocritical integrity.
Chuck Swindoll

"Integrity is keeping a commitment even after circumstances have changed."
David Jeremiah

"According to Scripture, virtually everything that truly qualifies a person for leadership is directly related to character. It's not about style, status, personal charisma, clout, or worldly measurements of success. Integrity is the main issue that makes the difference between a good leader and a bad one."
John MacArthur

"Few things are more infectious than a godly lifestyle. The people you rub shoulders with everyday need that kind of challenge. Not prudish. Not preachy. Just cracker jack clean living. Just honest to goodness, bone – deep, non-hypocritical integrity."
Chuck Swindoll

"Integrity is built by defeating the temptation to be dishonest; humility grows when we refuse to be prideful; and endurance develops every time you reject the temptation to give up."
Rick Warren

Jealousy

Jealousy- Bible Verses

Song of Solomon 8:6 ESV
Set me as a seal upon your heart, as a seal upon your arm, for love is strong as death, jealousy is fierce as the grave. Its flashes are flashes of fire, the very flame of the LORD.

1 Corinthians 13:4 NIV
Love is patient, love is kind. It does not envy, it does not boast, it is not proud.

Philippians 2:3 NIV
Do nothing out of selfish ambition or vain conceit. Rather, in humility value others above yourselves,

James 3:14-15 NIV
But if you harbor bitter envy and selfish ambition in your hearts, do not boast about it or deny the truth. Such "wisdom" does not come down from heaven but is earthly, unspiritual, demonic.

James 3:16 NLT
For wherever there is jealousy and selfish ambition, there you will find disorder and evil of every kind.

Psalm 37:1-3 KJV
Fret not thyself because of evildoers, neither be thou envious against the workers of iniquity.
For they shall soon be cut down like the grass, and wither as the green herb.
Trust in the Lord, and do good; so shalt thou dwell in the land, and verily thou shalt be fed.

Proverbs 6:34 KJV
For jealousy is the rage of a man: therefore he will not spare in the day of vengeance.

James 4:1-2 NASB
What is the source of quarrels and conflicts among you? Is not the source your pleasures that wage war in your members? You lust and do not have; so you commit murder. You are envious and cannot obtain; so you fight and quarrel. You do not have because you do not ask.

Proverbs 14:30 ESV
A tranquil heart gives life to the flesh, but envy makes the bones rot.

Exodus 20:5 NASB
You shall not worship them or serve them; for I, the Lord your God, am a jealous God, visiting the iniquity of the fathers on the children, on the third and the fourth generations of those who hate Me,

Exodus 34:14 NASB
—for you shall not worship any other god, for the Lord, whose name is Jealous, is a jealous God—

Deuteronomy 4:24 KJV
For the Lord thy God is a consuming fire, even a jealous God.

Psalm 79:5 KJV
How long, Lord? wilt thou be angry for ever? shall thy jealousy burn like fire?

Exodus 20:17 ESV
"You shall not covet your neighbor's house; you shall not covet your neighbor's wife, or his male servant, or his female servant, or his ox, or his donkey, or anything that is your neighbor's."

Proverbs 27:4 KJV
Wrath is cruel, and anger is outrageous; but who is able to stand before envy?

Acts 7:9 KJV
And the patriarchs, moved with envy, sold Joseph into Egypt: but God was with him,

1 Corinthians 3:3-5 NLT
for you are still controlled by your sinful nature. You are jealous of one another and quarrel with each other. Doesn't that prove you are controlled by your sinful nature? Aren't you living like people of the world? When one of you says, "I am a follower of Paul," and another says, "I follow Apollos," aren't you acting just like people of the world?
After all, who is Apollos? Who is Paul? We are only God's servants through whom you believed the Good News. Each of us did the work the Lord gave us.

Ephesians 5:3-5 NLT
Let there be no sexual immorality, impurity, or greed among you. Such sins have no place among God's people. Obscene stories, foolish talk, and coarse jokes—these are not for you. Instead, let there be thankfulness to God. You can be sure that no immoral, impure, or greedy person will inherit the Kingdom of Christ and of God. For a greedy person is an idolater, worshiping the things of this world.

Galatians 5:19-21 NLT
When you follow the desires of your sinful nature, the results are very clear: sexual immorality, impurity, lustful pleasures, idolatry, sorcery, hostility, quarreling, jealousy, outbursts of anger, selfish ambition, dissension, division, envy, drunkenness, wild parties, and other sins like these. Let me tell you again, as I have before, that anyone living that sort of life will not inherit the Kingdom of God.

Romans 13:13 NASB

Let us behave properly as in the day, not in carousing and drunkenness, not in sexual promiscuity and sensuality, not in strife and jealousy.

Excellent site for additional Bible translations:
http://www.biblegateway.com/resources/commentaries/
Excellent resource for additional Bible study:
(Be sure to read the instructions on their page)
http://www.blueletterbible.org/commentaries/

Jealousy- Christian Quotes

"Self-love is, no doubt, the usual foundation of human jealousy...the fear lest another should by any means supplant us."
C.H. Spurgeon

"Envy is a spirit of dissatisfaction or opposition to the prosperity or happiness of other people."
Jonathan Edwards

"How much of hell is there in the temper of an envious man! The happiness of another is his misery; the good of another is his affliction. He looks upon the virtue of another with an evil eye, and is as sorry at the praise of another as if that praise were taken away from himself. Envy makes him a hater of his neighbor, and his own tormentor."
Nathaniel Vincent

"Can you serve your boss and others at work, helping them to succeed and be happy, even when they are promoted and you are overlooked? Can you work to make others look good without envy filling your heart? Can you minister to the needs of those whom God exalts and men honor when you yourself are neglected? Can you pray for the ministry of others to prosper when it would cast yours in the shadows?"
Donald Whitney

"Sins such as envy, jealousy, covetousness, and greed very markedly reveal a focus on self. Instead you are to please God and bless others by practicing biblical stewardship which is to care for and give of the physical and spiritual resources that God has provided for you."
John Broger

"If there is any sin more deadly than envy, it is being pleased at being envied."
Richard Armour

Joy

Joy - Bible Verses

Deuteronomy 16:15 NASB
Seven days you shall celebrate a feast to the Lord your God in the place which the Lord chooses, because the Lord your God will bless you in all your produce and in all the work of your hands, so that you will be altogether joyful.

Nehemiah 8:10 NASB
Then he said to them, "Go, eat of the fat, drink of the sweet, and send portions to him who has nothing prepared; for this day is holy to our Lord. Do not be grieved, for the joy of the Lord is your strength."

Esther 8:17 ESV
And in every province and in every city, wherever the king's command and his edict reached, there was gladness and joy among the Jews, a feast and a holiday. And many from the peoples of the country declared themselves Jews, for fear of the Jews had fallen on them.

Ecclesiastes 9:7 NIV
Go, eat your food with gladness, and drink your wine with a joyful heart, for God has already approved what you do.

Isaiah 9:3 ESV
You have multiplied the nation; you have increased its joy; they rejoice before you as with joy at the harvest, as they are glad when they divide the spoil.

Psalm 5:11-12 ESV
But let all who take refuge in you rejoice; let them ever sing for joy, and spread your protection over them, that those who love your name may exult in you. For you bless the righteous, O LORD; you cover him with favor as with a shield.

Psalm 47:1 ESV

Clap your hands, all peoples! Shout to God with loud songs of joy!

Psalm 63:5-7 ESV

My soul will be satisfied as with fat and rich food, and my mouth will praise you with joyful lips, when I remember you upon my bed, and meditate on you in the watches of the night; for you have been my help, and in the shadow of your wings I will sing for joy.

Psalm 96:11-13 NLT

Let the heavens be glad, and the earth rejoice!
    Let the sea and everything in it shout his praise!
Let the fields and their crops burst out with joy!
    Let the trees of the forest rustle with praise
before the Lord, for he is coming!
    He is coming to judge the earth.
He will judge the world with justice,
    and the nations with his truth.

Isaiah 12:6 NLT

Let all the people of Jerusalem shout his praise with joy!
    For great is the Holy One of Israel who lives among you."

1 Samuel 18:6 NIV

When the men were returning home after David had killed the Philistine, the women came out from all the towns of Israel to meet King Saul with singing and dancing, with joyful songs and with timbrels and lyres.

Luke 15:7 NIV

I tell you that in the same way there will be more rejoicing in heaven over one sinner who repents than over ninety-nine righteous persons who do not need to repent.

John 16:21 NLT
It will be like a woman suffering the pains of labor. When her child is born, her anguish gives way to joy because she has brought a new baby into the world.

Philippians 1:3-5 NLT
Every time I think of you, I give thanks to my God. Whenever I pray, I make my requests for all of you with joy, for you have been my partners in spreading the Good News about Christ from the time you first heard it until now.

Philemon 1:7 NLT
Your love has given me much joy and comfort, my brother, for your kindness has often refreshed the hearts of God's people.

Proverbs 10:28 KJV
The hope of the righteous shall be gladness: but the expectation of the wicked shall perish.

Romans 15:13 KJV
Now the God of hope fill you with all joy and peace in believing, that ye may abound in hope, through the power of the Holy Ghost.

1 Thessalonians 2:17-20 NIV
But, brothers and sisters, when we were orphaned by being separated from you for a short time (in person, not in thought), out of our intense longing we made every effort to see you. For we wanted to come to you—certainly I, Paul, did, again and again—but Satan blocked our way. For what is our hope, our joy, or the crown in which we will glory in the presence of our Lord Jesus when he comes? Is it not you? Indeed, you are our glory and joy.

1 Peter 1:8-9 NIV
Though you have not seen him, you love him; and even though you do not see him now, you believe in him and are filled with an inexpressible and glorious joy, for you are receiving the end result of your faith, the salvation of your souls.

2 John 1:12 ESV
Though I have much to write to you, I would rather not use paper and ink. Instead I hope to come to you and talk face to face, so that our joy may be complete.

Excellent site for additional Bible translations:
http://www.biblegateway.com/resources/commentaries/
Excellent resource for additional Bible study:
(Be sure to read the instructions on their page)
http://www.blueletterbible.org/commentaries/

Joy - Christian Quotes

"When the heart is full of joy, it always allows its joy to escape. It is like the fountain in the marketplace; whenever it is full it runs away in streams, and so soon as it ceases to overflow, you may be quite sure that it has ceased to be full. The only full heart is the overflowing heart."
C.H. Spurgeon

"The out-and-out Christian is a joyful Christian. The half-and-half Christian is the kind of Christian that a great many of you are~~~little acquainted with the Lord. Why should we live halfway up the hill and swathed in the mists, when we might have an unclouded sky and a radiant sun over our heads if we would climb higher and walk in the light of His face?"
Alexander Maclaren

"The men whom I have seen succeed best in life have always been cheerful and hopeful men, who went about their business with a smile on their faces, and took the changes and chances of this mortal life like men, facing rough and smooth alike as it came."
Charles Kingsley

"It is His joy that remains in us that makes our joy full."
A. B. Simpson

"What I am anxious to see in Christian believers is a beautiful paradox. I want to see in them the joy of finding God while at the same time they are blessedly pursuing Him. I want to see in them the great joy of having God yet always wanting Him."
A. W. Tozer

"Joy is the serious business of Heaven."
C. S. Lewis

"No man should desire to be happy who is not at the same time holy. He should spend his efforts in seeking to know and do the will of God, leaving

to Christ the matter of how happy he should be."
A.W. Tozer

"Holy joy will be oil to the wheels of our obedience."
Matthew Henry

"Joy is not necessarily the absence of suffering, it is the presence of God."
Sam Storms

"Happiness is like manna; it is to be gathered in grains, and enjoyed every day. It will not keep; it cannot be accumulated; nor have we got to go out of ourselves or into remote places to gather it, since it is rained down from Heaven, at our very doors."
Tyron Edwards

"There's nothing more contradictory than an unenthusiastic Christian. The Bible tells us that God loves us so much, in fact, that God gave his only son so that all who believe in him will have everlasting life. Nothing not even death can separate us from God's love! If we really believe that, we can't help but overflow with joy!"
Ronald Newhouse

"Begin to rejoice in the Lord, and your bones will flourish like an herb, and your cheeks will glow with the bloom of health and freshness. Worry, fear, distrust, care-all are poisonous! Joy is balm and healing, and if you will but rejoice, God will give power."
A. B. Simpson

"I have not suffered a lot for Christ, but I want to tell you that those times that I have suffered and I knew it was for Jesus, have been some of the happiest times of my entire life. I cannot tell you the indescribable joy that has come into my heart and my life."
Adrian Rogers

Judgment

Judgment - Bible Verses

Exodus 6:6 ESV
Say therefore to the people of Israel, 'I am the LORD, and I will bring you out from under the burdens of the Egyptians, and I will deliver you from slavery to them, and I will redeem you with an outstretched arm and with great acts of judgment.

Exodus 12:12 ESV
For I will pass through the land of Egypt that night, and I will strike all the firstborn in the land of Egypt, both man and beast; and on all the gods of Egypt I will execute judgments: I am the LORD.

Psalm 51:4 KJV
Against thee, thee only, have I sinned, and done this evil in thy sight: that thou mightest be justified when thou speakest, and be clear when thou judgest.

Psalm 97:8 KJV
Zion heard, and was glad; and the daughters of Judah rejoiced because of thy judgments, O Lord.

Ecclesiastes 12:14 KJV
For God shall bring every work into judgment, with every secret thing, whether it be good, or whether it be evil.

Revelation 19:1-3 KJV
And after these things I heard a great voice of much people in heaven, saying, Alleluia; Salvation, and glory, and honour, and power, unto the Lord our God:
For true and righteous are his judgments: for he hath judged the great whore, which did corrupt the earth with her fornication, and hath avenged the blood of his servants at her hand.

And again they said, Alleluia And her smoke rose up for ever and ever.

John 5:21-31 NIV
For just as the Father raises the dead and gives them life, even so the Son gives life to whom he is pleased to give it. Moreover, the Father judges no one, but has entrusted all judgment to the Son, that all may honor the Son just as they honor the Father. Whoever does not honor the Son does not honor the Father, who sent him.

"Very truly I tell you, whoever hears my word and believes him who sent me has eternal life and will not be judged but has crossed over from death to life. Very truly I tell you, a time is coming and has now come when the dead will hear the voice of the Son of God and those who hear will live. For as the Father has life in himself, so he has granted the Son also to have life in himself. And he has given him authority to judge because he is the Son of Man.

"Do not be amazed at this, for a time is coming when all who are in their graves will hear his voice and come out—those who have done what is good will rise to live, and those who have done what is evil will rise to be condemned. By myself I can do nothing; I judge only as I hear, and my judgment is just, for I seek not to please myself but him who sent me. "If I testify about myself, my testimony is not true.

John 9:38-39 NIV
Then the man said, "Lord, I believe," and he worshiped him.
Jesus said, "For judgment I have come into this world, so that the blind will see and those who see will become blind."

John 12:30-32 NASB
Jesus answered and said, "This voice has not come for My sake, but for your sakes. Now judgment is upon this world; now the ruler of this world will be cast out. And I, if I am lifted up from the earth, will draw all men to Myself."

John 16:7-9 NASB
But I tell you the truth, it is to your advantage that I go away; for if I do not go away, the Helper will not come to you; but if I go, I will send Him to you. And He, when He comes, will convict the world concerning sin and

righteousness and judgment; concerning sin, because they do not believe in Me;

Deuteronomy 1:13-18 ESV
Choose for your tribes wise, understanding, and experienced men, and I will appoint them as your heads.' And you answered me, 'The thing that you have spoken is good for us to do.' So I took the heads of your tribes, wise and experienced men, and set them as heads over you, commanders of thousands, commanders of hundreds, commanders of fifties, commanders of tens, and officers, throughout your tribes. And I charged your judges at that time, 'Hear the cases between your brothers, and judge righteously between a man and his brother or the alien who is with him. You shall not be partial in judgment. You shall hear the small and the great alike. You shall not be intimidated by anyone, for the judgment is God's. And the case that is too hard for you, you shall bring to me, and I will hear it.' And I commanded you at that time all the things that you should do.

2 Chronicles 19:8 NASB
In Jerusalem also Jehoshaphat appointed some of the Levites and priests, and some of the heads of the fathers' households of Israel, for the judgment of the Lord and to judge disputes among the inhabitants of Jerusalem.

Proverbs 20:7-9 ESV
The righteous who walks in his integrity— blessed are his children after him! A king who sits on the throne of judgment winnows all evil with his eyes. Who can say, "I have made my heart pure; I am clean from my sin"?

Romans 13:1-3 KJV
Let every soul be subject unto the higher powers. For there is no power but of God: the powers that be are ordained of God. Whosoever therefore resisteth the power, resisteth the ordinance of God: and they that resist shall receive to themselves damnation. For rulers are not a terror to good works, but to the evil. Wilt thou then not be afraid of the power? do that which is good, and thou shalt have praise of the same:

Matthew 7:2-4 NASB
For in the way you judge, you will be judged; and by your standard of measure, it will be measured to you. Why do you look at the speck that is in your brother's eye, but do not notice the log that is in your own eye? Or how can you say to your brother, 'Let me take the speck out of your eye,' and behold, the log is in your own eye?

Romans 14:1-4 NIV
Accept the one whose faith is weak, without quarreling over disputable matters. One person's faith allows them to eat anything, but another, whose faith is weak, eats only vegetables. The one who eats everything must not treat with contempt the one who does not, and the one who does not eat everything must not judge the one who does, for God has accepted them. Who are you to judge someone else's servant? To their own master, servants stand or fall. And they will stand, for the Lord is able to make them stand.

Romans 14:12-14 NIV
So then, each of us will give an account of ourselves to God.
Therefore let us stop passing judgment on one another. Instead, make up your mind not to put any stumbling block or obstacle in the way of a brother or sister. I am convinced, being fully persuaded in the Lord Jesus, that nothing is unclean in itself. But if anyone regards something as unclean, then for that person it is unclean.

1 Corinthians 4:5 NIV
Therefore judge nothing before the appointed time; wait until the Lord comes. He will bring to light what is hidden in darkness and will expose the motives of the heart. At that time each will receive their praise from God.

1 Peter 4:17 ESV
For it is time for judgment to begin at the household of God; and if it begins with us, what will be the outcome for those who do not obey the gospel of God?

Excellent site for additional Bible translations:
http://www.biblegateway.com/resources/commentaries/
Excellent resource for additional Bible study:
(Be sure to read the instructions on their page)
http://www.blueletterbible.org/commentaries/

Judgment - Christian Quotes

"The most tremendous judgment of God in this world is the hardening of the hearts of men."
John Owen

"An individual Christian may see fit to give up all sorts of things for special reasons – marriage, or meat, or beer, or cinema; but the moment he stars saying the things are bad in themselves, or looking down his nose at other people who do use them, he has taken the wrong turning."
C.S. Lewis

"The day of judgment will be a day when the skeletons come out of the closets! And each of us will be standing there to face the record."
Adrian Rogers

"Take your stand on the Rock of Ages. Let death, let the judgment come: the victory is Christ's and yours through Him."
D. L. Moody

"A Pharisee is hard on others and easy on himself, but a spiritual man is easy on others and hard on himself."
A.W. Tozer

"Thus was the King and the Lord of glory judged by man's judgment, when manifest in flesh: far be it from any of his ministers to expect better treatment."
George Whitfield

"[Christians are] not to be hasty in making negative judgments on their fellows. It is a dangerous procedure because it invites a similar judgment in return. And it is a difficult procedure because our own faults make it hard for us to see precisely what is amiss in our fellows. Jesus is not, of course, forbidding all judgments; He is warning against the hasty condemnations that are so easy to make, and so characteristic of the human race."
Leon Morris

"When the author walks on the stage the play is over. God is going to invade, all right...something so beautiful to some of us and so terrible to others that none of us will have any choice left? For this time it will be God without disguise...it will be too late then to choose your side. There is no use saying you choose to lie down when it has become impossible to stand up."
C. S. Lewis

"[The one] who judges according to the word and law of the Lord, and forms his judgments by the rule of charity, always begins with subjecting himself to examination, and preserves a proper medium and order in his judgments."
John Calvin

"Mere are so many stony ground hearers, who receive the Word with joy that I have determined to suspend my judgment till I know the tree by its fruits. I cannot believe they are converts till I see fruit brought back; it will never do a sincere soul any harm."
George Whitfield

"What Jesus prohibits...is sinful, improper judging. It is the hypocrisy of condemning others but failing to see one's own glaring sins. Jesus forbids self-righteous criticism, a hypercritical spirit, and a harsh, fault-finding mindset."
Alexander Strauch

"Holiness is the habit of being of one mind with God, according as we find His mind described in Scripture. It is the habit of agreeing in God's judgment, hating what He hates, loving what He loves, and measuring everything in this world by the standard of His Word."
J. C. Ryle

Knowledge

Knowledge - Bible Verses

Proverbs 2:10-11 ESV
for wisdom will come into your heart, and knowledge will be pleasant to your soul; discretion will watch over you, understanding will guard you,

Proverbs 1:7 ESV
The fear of the LORD is the beginning of knowledge; fools despise wisdom and instruction.

Job 28:28 NASB
"And to man He said, 'Behold, the fear of the Lord, that is wisdom;
And to depart from evil is understanding.'"

James 1:5 NASB
But if any of you lacks wisdom, let him ask of God, who gives to all generously and without reproach, and it will be given to him.

1 Kings 3:5-12 ESV
At Gibeon the LORD appeared to Solomon in a dream by night, and God said, "Ask what I shall give you." And Solomon said, "You have shown great and steadfast love to your servant David my father, because he walked before you in faithfulness, in righteousness, and in uprightness of heart toward you. And you have kept for him this great and steadfast love and have given him a son to sit on his throne this day. And now, O LORD my God, you have made your servant king in place of David my father, although I am but a little child. I do not know how to go out or come in. And your servant is in the midst of your people whom you have chosen, a great people, too many to be numbered or counted for multitude. Give your servant therefore an understanding mind to govern your people, that I may discern between good and evil, for who is able to govern this your great people?" It pleased the Lord that Solomon had asked this. And God said to him, "Because you have asked this, and have not asked for yourself long life

or riches or the life of your enemies, but have asked for yourself understanding to discern what is right, behold, I now do according to your word. Behold, I give you a wise and discerning mind, so that none like you has been before you and none like you shall arise after you.

Daniel 2:21 NASB
"It is He who changes the times and the epochs;
He removes kings and establishes kings;
He gives wisdom to wise men
And knowledge to men of understanding.

Psalm 119:66 NASB
Teach me good discernment and knowledge,
For I believe in Your commandments.

Proverbs 16:22 NASB
Understanding is a fountain of life to one who has it,
But the discipline of fools is folly.

Proverbs 1:5 NASB
A wise man will hear and increase in learning,
And a man of understanding will acquire wise counsel,

Ecclesiastes 7:12 ESV
For the protection of wisdom is like the protection of money, and the advantage of knowledge is that wisdom preserves the life of him who has it.

Excellent site for additional Bible translations:
http://www.biblegateway.com/resources/commentaries/
Excellent resource for additional Bible study:
(Be sure to read the instructions on their page)
http://www.blueletterbible.org/commentaries/

Knowledge - Christian Quotes

"The ultimate ground of faith and knowledge is confidence in God. ~ Charles Hodge

Wisdom is the right use of knowledge. To know is not to be wise. Many men know a great deal, and are all the greater fools for it. There is no fool so great a fool as a knowing fool. But to know how to use knowledge is to have wisdom."
Charles Spurgeon

"Knowledge is indispensable to Christian life and service. If we do not use the mind that God has given us, we condemn ourselves to spiritual superficiality and cut ourselves off from many of the riches of God's grace."
John Stott

"Knowledge, not improved and well employed, will only increase our condemnation at the last day."
J.C. Ryle

"Prayer and praise are the oars by which a man may row his boat into the deep waters of the knowledge of Christ."
C.H. Spurgeon

"Seek not to grow in knowledge chiefly for the sake of applause, and to enable you to dispute with others; but seek it for the benefit of your souls."
Jonathan Edwards

"The Bible was not given to increase our knowledge but to change our lives."
D.L. Moody

"Knowledge is power."
Francis Bacon

"Knowledge is but folly unless it is guided by grace."
George Herbert

"Wisdom is the right of knowledge. To know is not to be wise. Many men know a great deal, and are all the greater fools for it. There is no fool so great a fool as a knowing fool. But to know how to use knowledge is to have wisdom."
C.H. Spurgeon

"Modern mankind can go anywhere, do everything and be completely curious about the universe. But only a rare person now and then is curious enough to want to know God."
A. W. Tozer

"The knowledge of God is the great hope of sinners. Oh, if you knew Him better, you would fly to Him! If you understood how gracious He is, you would seek Him. If you could have any idea of His holiness, you would loathe your self-righteousness. If you knew anything of His power, you would not venture to contend with Him. If you knew anything of His grace, you would not hesitate to yield yourself to Him."
C.H. Spurgeon

Life

Life - Bible Verses

Genesis 1:20 KJV
And God said, Let the waters bring forth abundantly the moving creature that hath life, and fowl that may fly above the earth in the open firmament of heaven.

Genesis 2:9 NIV
The Lord God made all kinds of trees grow out of the ground—trees that were pleasing to the eye and good for food. In the middle of the garden were the tree of life and the tree of the knowledge of good and evil.

Genesis 3:14 ESV
The LORD God said to the serpent, "Because you have done this, cursed are you above all livestock and above all beasts of the field; on your belly you shall go, and dust you shall eat all the days of your life.

Genesis 3:17-18 NIV
To Adam he said, "Because you listened to your wife and ate fruit from the tree about which I commanded you, 'You must not eat from it,'
"Cursed is the ground because of you;
   through painful toil you will eat food from it
   all the days of your life.
It will produce thorns and thistles for you,
   and you will eat the plants of the field.

Genesis 3:22-23 ESV
Then the LORD God said, "Behold, the man has become like one of us in knowing good and evil. Now, lest he reach out his hand and take also of the tree of life and eat, and live forever — " therefore the LORD God sent him out from the garden of Eden to work the ground from which he was taken.

Leviticus 24:17-18 ESV
"Whoever takes a human life shall surely be put to death. Whoever takes an animal's life shall make it good, life for life."

Deuteronomy 30:19-20 NASB
I call heaven and earth to witness against you today, that I have set before you life and death, the blessing and the curse. So choose life in order that you may live, you and your descendants, by loving the Lord your God, by obeying His voice, and by holding fast to Him; for this is your life and the length of your days, that you may live in the land which the Lord swore to your fathers, to Abraham, Isaac, and Jacob, to give them."

Proverbs 14:27 NASB
The fear of the Lord is a fountain of life,
That one may avoid the snares of death.

Proverbs 18:21 ESV
Death and life are in the power of the tongue,
And those who love it will eat its fruit.

Romans 5:10 NASB
For if while we were enemies we were reconciled to God through the death of His Son, much more, having been reconciled, we shall be saved by His life.

John 3:16 KJV
For God so loved the world, that he gave his only begotten Son, that whosoever believeth in him should not perish, but have everlasting life.

John 3:36 KJV
He that believeth on the Son hath everlasting life: and he that believeth not the Son shall not see life; but the wrath of God abideth on him.

Romans 6:23 KJV
For the wages of sin is death; but the gift of God is eternal life through Jesus Christ our Lord.

1 Timothy 6:12 NIV
Fight the good fight of the faith. Take hold of the eternal life to which you were called when you made your good confession in the presence of many witnesses.

1 John 5:13 NIV
I write these things to you who believe in the name of the Son of God so that you may know that you have eternal life.

John 6:35 NLT
Jesus replied, "I am the bread of life. Whoever comes to me will never be hungry again. Whoever believes in me will never be thirsty.

John 8:12 NLT
Jesus spoke to the people once more and said, "I am the light of the world. If you follow me, you won't have to walk in darkness, because you will have the light that leads to life."

John 11:25-26 ESV
Jesus said to her, "I am the resurrection and the life. Whoever believes in me, though he die, yet shall he live, and everyone who lives and believes in me shall never die. Do you believe this?"

John 14:6 ESV
Jesus said to him, "I am the way, and the truth, and the life. No one comes to the Father except through me."

1 John 5:20 NLT
And we know that the Son of God has come, and he has given us understanding so that we can know the true God. And now we live in fellowship with the true God because we live in fellowship with his Son, Jesus Christ. He is the only true God, and he is eternal life.

Excellent site for additional Bible translations:
http://www.biblegateway.com/resources/commentaries/
Excellent resource for additional Bible study:

(Be sure to read the instructions on their page)
http://www.blueletterbible.org/commentaries/

Life - Christian Quotes

"There is no blessed way of living, than the life of faith upon a covenant-keeping God - to know that we have no care, for he cares for us; that we need have no fear, except to fear him; that we need have no troubles, because we have cast our burdens upon the Lord, and are conscious that he will sustain us."
C. H. Spurgeon

"How far you go in life depends on your being tender with the young, compassionate with the aged, sympathetic with the striving, and tolerant of the weak and the strong. Because someday in life you will have been all of these."
George Washington

"We begin life with the natural, next we come into the spiritual; but then, when we have truly received the kingdom of God and His righteousness, the natural is added to the spiritual, and we are able to receive the gifts of His providence and the blessings of life without becoming centered in them or allowing them to separate us from Him."
A. B. Simpson

"Go forth today, by the help of God's Spirit, vowing and declaring that in life —-come poverty, come wealth, in death—come pain or come what may, you are and ever must be the Lord's. For this is written on your heart, 'We love Him because He first loved us.'"
Charles H. Spurgeon

"In almost everything that touches our everyday life on earth, God is pleased when we're pleased. He wills that we be as free as birds to soar and sing our maker's praise without anxiety."
A.W. Tozer

"Where I was born and where and how I have lived is unimportant. It is what I have done with where I have been that should be of interest."
D.L. Moody

"Perils as well as privileges attend the higher Christian life. The nearer we come to God, the thicker the hosts of darkness in heavenly places."
A. B. Simpson

Love

Love- Bible Verses

John 3:16 ESV
"For God so loved the world, that he gave his only Son, that whoever believes in him should not perish but have eternal life.

Romans 5:8 NASB
But God demonstrates His own love toward us, in that while we were yet sinners, Christ died for us.

Romans 8:37-39 NASB
But in all these things we overwhelmingly conquer through Him who loved us. For I am convinced that neither death, nor life, nor angels, nor principalities, nor things present, nor things to come, nor powers, nor height, nor depth, nor any other created thing, will be able to separate us from the love of God, which is in Christ Jesus our Lord.

Galatians 2:20 ESV
I have been crucified with Christ. It is no longer I who live, but Christ who lives in me. And the life I now live in the flesh I live by faith in the Son of God, who loved me and gave himself for me.

1 John 3:1 ESV
See what kind of love the Father has given to us, that we should be called children of God; and so we are. The reason why the world does not know us is that it did not know him.

Romans 13:8 NIV
Let no debt remain outstanding, except the continuing debt to love one another, for whoever loves others has fulfilled the law.

Galatians 5:13 NIV
You, my brothers and sisters, were called to be free. But do not use your freedom to indulge the flesh; rather, serve one another humbly in love.

Ephesians 4:2 NIV
Be completely humble and gentle; be patient, bearing with one another in love.

1 Peter 1:22 NASB
Since you have in obedience to the truth purified your souls for a sincere love of the brethren, fervently love one another from the heart,

1 John 4:7 NASB
Beloved, let us love one another, for love is from God; and everyone who loves is born of God and knows God.

Matthew 5:43-48 ESV
"You have heard that it was said, 'You shall love your neighbor and hate your enemy.' But I say to you, love your enemies and pray for those who persecute you, so that you may be sons of your Father who is in heaven; for He causes His sun to rise on the evil and the good, and sends rain on the righteous and the unrighteous. For if you love those who love you, what reward do you have? Do not even the tax collectors do the same? If you greet only your brothers, what more are you doing than others? Do not even the Gentiles do the same? Therefore you are to be perfect, as your heavenly Father is perfect.

Matthew 6:24-25 NLT
"No one can serve two masters. For you will hate one and love the other; you will be devoted to one and despise the other. You cannot serve both God and money.
"That is why I tell you not to worry about everyday life—whether you have enough food and drink, or enough clothes to wear. Isn't life more than food, and your body more than clothing?

Mark 12:28-30 ESV
And one of the scribes came up and heard them disputing with one another, and seeing that he answered them well, asked him, "Which commandment is the most important of all?" Jesus answered, "The most important is, 'Hear, O Israel: The Lord our God, the Lord is one. And you shall love the Lord your God with all your heart and with all your soul and with all your mind and with all your strength.'

John 14:21-24 NIV
Whoever has my commands and keeps them is the one who loves me. The one who loves me will be loved by my Father, and I too will love them and show myself to them."
Then Judas (not Judas Iscariot) said, "But, Lord, why do you intend to show yourself to us and not to the world?"
Jesus replied, "Anyone who loves me will obey my teaching. My Father will love them, and we will come to them and make our home with them. Anyone who does not love me will not obey my teaching. These words you hear are not my own; they belong to the Father who sent me.

John 15:9-17 NIV
"As the Father has loved me, so have I loved you. Now remain in my love. If you keep my commands, you will remain in my love, just as I have kept my Father's commands and remain in his love. I have told you this so that my joy may be in you and that your joy may be complete. My command is this: Love each other as I have loved you. Greater love has no one than this: to lay down one's life for one's friends. You are my friends if you do what I command. I no longer call you servants, because a servant does not know his master's business. Instead, I have called you friends, for everything that I learned from my Father I have made known to you. You did not choose me, but I chose you and appointed you so that you might go and bear fruit—fruit that will last—and so that whatever you ask in my name the Father will give you. This is my command: Love each other.

Song of Solomon 8:6-7 ESV
Set me as a seal upon your heart, as a seal upon your arm, for love is strong as death, jealousy is fierce as the grave. Its flashes are flashes of fire, the very

flame of the LORD. Many waters cannot quench love, neither can floods drown it. If a man offered for love all the wealth of his house, he would be utterly despised.

Ephesians 4:2-3 ESV
with all humility and gentleness, with patience, bearing with one another in love, eager to maintain the unity of the Spirit in the bond of peace.

Philippians 2:2 ESV
complete my joy by being of the same mind, having the same love, being in full accord and of one mind.

1 John 3:18 ESV
Little children, let us not love in word or talk but in deed and in truth.

Psalm 23:5-6 ESV
You prepare a table before me in the presence of my enemies; you anoint my head with oil; my cup overflows. Surely goodness and mercy shall follow me all the days of my life, and I shall dwell in the house of the LORD forever.

Psalm 63:3 KJV
Because thy lovingkindness is better than life, my lips shall praise thee.

Proverbs 10:12 ESV
Hatred stirs up strife, but love covers all offenses.

Proverbs 17:17 KJV
A friend loveth at all times, and a brother is born for adversity.

Excellent site for additional Bible translations:
http://www.biblegateway.com/resources/commentaries/
Excellent resource for additional Bible study:
(Be sure to read the instructions on their page)
http://www.blueletterbible.org/commentaries/

Love - Christian Quotes

"The hunger for love is much more difficult to remove than the hunger for bread."
Mother Teresa

"The way to love anything is to realize that it may be lost."
G.K. Chesterton

"What is the surest character of true, divine, supernatural love that distinguishes it from counterfeits that arise from a natural self-love? It is the Christian virtue of humility that shines in it. Divine love above all others renounces and abases what we term "self." Christian love or true love is a humble love... In that person we see a sense of his own smallness, vileness, weakness, and utter insufficiency. We see a lack of self-confidence. We see self-emptiness, self-denial, and poverty of spirit. These are the manifest tokens of the Spirit of God."
Jonathan Edwards

"For where love is wanting, the beauty of all virtue is mere tinsel, is empty sound, is not worth a straw, nay more, is offensive and disgusting."
John Calvin

"Since we were forged by the Lover, we should delight in loving and in being loved. It would be inhuman not to delight in love. It would also be inhuman if we didn't hurt deeply when rejected or sinned against by others. The problem is not that we desire love, the problem is how much we desire it or for what purpose we desire it. Do we desire it so much that it overshadows our desire to be imitators of God? Do we desire it for our own pleasure or for God's glory?"
Edward T. Welch

"Resolved, to examine carefully, and constantly, what that one thing in me is, which causes me in the least to doubt of the love of God; and to direct all my forces against it."
Jonathan Edwards

"Love is an act of endless forgiveness."
Jean Vanier

Lying

Lying - Bible Verses

Proverbs 6:16-19 NASB
There are six things which the Lord hates,
Yes, seven which are an abomination to Him:
Haughty eyes, a lying tongue,
And hands that shed innocent blood,
A heart that devises wicked plans,
Feet that run rapidly to evil,
A false witness who utters lies,
And one who spreads strife among brothers.

Proverbs 19:9 ESV
A false witness will not go unpunished, and he who breathes out lies will perish.

Proverbs 12:22 ESV
Lying lips are an abomination to the Lord, but those who act faithfully are his delight.

Colossians 3:9-10 NIV
Do not lie to each other, since you have taken off your old self with its practices 10 and have put on the new self, which is being renewed in knowledge in the image of its Creator.

Psalm 101:7 ESV
No one who practices deceit shall dwell in my house; no one who utters lies shall continue before my eyes.

1 John 2:4 KJV
He that saith, I know him, and keepeth not his commandments, is a liar, and the truth is not in him.

Ephesians 4:25 ESV
Therefore, having put away falsehood, let each one of you speak the truth with his neighbor, for we are members one of another.

Proverbs 24:28 ESV
Be not a witness against your neighbor without cause, and do not deceive with your lips.

Luke 8:17 ESV
For nothing is hidden that will not be made manifest, nor is anything secret that will not be known and come to light.

John 8:44 ESV
You are of your father the devil, and your will is to do your father's desires. He was a murderer from the beginning, and has nothing to do with the truth, because there is no truth in him. When he lies, he speaks out of his own character, for he is a liar and the father of lies.

Matthew 15:18-20 NLT
But the words you speak come from the heart—that's what defiles you. For from the heart come evil thoughts, murder, adultery, all sexual immorality, theft, lying, and slander. These are what defile you. Eating with unwashed hands will never defile you."

Revelation 21:8 ESV
But as for the cowardly, the faithless, the detestable, as for murderers, the sexually immoral, sorcerers, idolaters, and all liars, their portion will be in the lake that burns with fire and sulfur, which is the second death."

Exodus 20:16 ESV
"You shall not bear false witness against your neighbor.

James 3:14 ESV
But if you have bitter jealousy and selfish ambition in your hearts, do not boast and be false to the truth.

Psalm 109:2 ESV
For wicked and deceitful mouths are opened against me, speaking against me with lying tongues.

Proverbs 12:19 ESV
Truthful lips endure forever, but a lying tongue is but for a moment.

Romans 12:17-21 NASB
Never pay back evil for evil to anyone. Respect what is right in the sight of all men. If possible, so far as it depends on you, be at peace with all men. Never take your own revenge, beloved, but leave room for the wrath of God, for it is written, "Vengeance is Mine, I will repay," says the Lord. "But if your enemy is hungry, feed him, and if he is thirsty, give him a drink; for in so doing you will heap burning coals on his head." Do not be overcome by evil, but overcome evil with good.

Excellent site for additional Bible translations:
http://www.biblegateway.com/resources/commentaries/
Excellent resource for additional Bible study:
(Be sure to read the instructions on their page)
http://www.blueletterbible.org/commentaries/

Lying - Christian Quotes

A lie consists in speaking a falsehood with the intention of deceiving.
Augustine

I would not tell one lie to save the souls of all the world.
John Wesley

Think about how much falsehood and deceit there is in the world! How much exaggeration! How many untruths are added to a simple story! How many things are left out, if it does not serve the speaker's interest to tell them! How few there are around us of whom we can say, that we trust their word without question!
J.C. Ryle

Saints not only desire to love and speak truth with their lips, but they seek to be true within; they will not lie even in the closet of their hearts, for God is there to listen; they scorn double meanings, evasions, equivocations, white lies, flatteries, and deceptions.
C.H. Spurgeon

Christians don't tell lies they just go to church and sing them.
A.W. Tozer

It is more from carelessness about truth than from intentional lying that there is so much falsehood in the world.
Samuel Johnson

A lie is a snowball; the further you roll it, the bigger it becomes.
Martin Luther

Truth has no degrees or shades. A half truth is a whole lie, and a white lie is really black.
John MacArthur
Matthew 1-7, Moody, 1985, p. 326.

They hurt us in that lies deceive us, not just other people. They persuade us that we are on top of our problem. We think we can fool others, but we can't be fooled. With other people, the power of lies is obvious. Anyone who has been lied to knows that lies divide people; lies are the language of war. With God, lies provide evidence that our allegiances are not with Him. Instead, they show that our allegiance is to Satan – the Father of Lies – and to ourselves.
Edward T. Welch
Blame in on the Brain? P&R Publishing, 1998, p. 200.

If you are of the truth, if you have learned the truth, if you see the sanctity of the truth, then speak truth. We are not called to be deceivers or liars. God is a God of truth, and His people are called to have an enormously high standard of truth.
R.C. Sproul
The Purpose of God, An Exposition of Ephesians, Christian Focus Publications, 1994, p. 114.

Satan is the prince of this world, and since he not only is a liar himself but also "the father of lies" (John 8:44), it should not be surprising that the system he heads is characterized by lying... Our whole society is largely built on a network of fabrication, of manufactured "truth." We shade truth, we cheat, we exaggerate, we misrepresent income tax deductions, we make promises we have no intention of keeping, we make up excuses, and betray confidences – all as a matter of normal, everyday living.
John MacArthur
Matthew 1-7, Moody, 1985, p. 319-320.

Marriage

Marriage- Bible Verses

Hosea 2:19 NASB
"I will betroth you to Me forever;
Yes, I will betroth you to Me in righteousness and in justice,
In lovingkindness and in compassion,

Genesis 1:27-28 NASB
God created man in His own image, in the image of God He created him; male and female He created them. God blessed them; and God said to them, "Be fruitful and multiply, and fill the earth, and subdue it; and rule over the fish of the sea and over the birds of the sky and over every living thing that moves on the earth."

Genesis 2:21-25 NASB
So the Lord God caused a deep sleep to fall upon the man, and he slept; then He took one of his ribs and closed up the flesh at that place. The Lord God fashioned into a woman the rib which He had taken from the man, and brought her to the man. The man said,
"This is now bone of my bones,
And flesh of my flesh;
She shall be called Woman,
Because she was taken out of Man."
For this reason a man shall leave his father and his mother, and be joined to his wife; and they shall become one flesh. And the man and his wife were both naked and were not ashamed.

Malachi 2:14-15 NIV
You ask, "Why?" It is because the Lord is the witness between you and the wife of your youth. You have been unfaithful to her, though she is your partner, the wife of your marriage covenant.

Has not the one God made you? You belong to him in body and spirit. And what does the one God seek? Godly offspring. So be on your guard, and do not be unfaithful to the wife of your youth.

1 Corinthians 7:2 ESV
But because of the temptation to sexual immorality, each man should have his own wife and each woman her own husband.

Hebrews 13:4 ESV
Let marriage be held in honor among all, and let the marriage bed be undefiled, for God will judge the sexually immoral and adulterous.

Genesis 29:22-23 NIV
So Laban brought together all the people of the place and gave a feast. But when evening came, he took his daughter Leah and brought her to Jacob, and Jacob made love to her.

Judges 1:12 ESV
And Caleb said, "He who attacks Kiriath-sepher and captures it, I will give him Achsah my daughter for a wife." And Othniel the son of Kenaz, Caleb's younger brother, captured it. And he gave him Achsah his daughter for a wife.

1 Samuel 17:25 ESV
And the men of Israel said, "Have you seen this man who has come up? Surely he has come up to defy Israel. And the king will enrich the man who kills him with great riches and will give him his daughter and make his father's house free in Israel."

1 Samuel 18:20-21 NIV
Now Saul's daughter Michal was in love with David, and when they told Saul about it, he was pleased. "I will give her to him," he thought, "so that she may be a snare to him and so that the hand of the Philistines may be against him." So Saul said to David, "Now you have a second opportunity to become my son-in-law."

Genesis 24:67 ESV
Then Isaac brought her into the tent of Sarah his mother and took Rebekah, and she became his wife, and he loved her. So Isaac was comforted after his mother's death.

1 Samuel 25:40-42 ESV
When the servants of David came to Abigail at Carmel, they said to her, "David has sent us to you to take you to him as his wife." And she rose and bowed with her face to the ground and said, "Behold, your handmaid is a servant to wash the feet of the servants of my lord." And Abigail hurried and rose and mounted a donkey, and her five young women attended her. She followed the messengers of David and became his wife.

Ruth 4:13 SEV
So Boaz took Ruth, and she became his wife. And he went in to her, and the LORD gave her conception, and she bore a son.

Esther 2:16-18 ESV
And when Esther was taken to King Ahasuerus, into his royal palace, in the tenth month, which is the month of Tebeth, in the seventh year of his reign, the king loved Esther more than all the women, and she won grace and favor in his sight more than all the virgins, so that he set the royal crown on her head and made her queen instead of Vashti. Then the king gave a great feast for all his officials and servants; it was Esther's feast. He also granted a remission of taxes to the provinces and gave gifts with royal generosity.

Luke 2:4-5 KJV
And Joseph also went up from Galilee, out of the city of Nazareth, into Judaea, unto the city of David, which is called Bethlehem; (because he was of the house and lineage of David:) To be taxed with Mary his espoused wife, being great with child.

John 2:1-2 KJV
And the third day there was a marriage in Cana of Galilee; and the mother of Jesus was there:
And both Jesus was called, and his disciples, to the marriage.

Isaiah 54:5 KJV
For thy Maker is thine husband; the Lord of hosts is his name; and thy Redeemer the Holy One of Israel; The God of the whole earth shall he be called.

Ephesians 5:23-24 NLT
For a husband is the head of his wife as Christ is the head of the church. He is the Savior of his body, the church. As the church submits to Christ, so you wives should submit to your husbands in everything.

Revelation 19:7-9 NLT
Let us be glad and rejoice, and give honour to him: for the marriage of the Lamb is come, and his wife hath made herself ready.
And to her was granted that she should be arrayed in fine linen, clean and white: for the fine linen is the righteousness of saints.
And he saith unto me, Write, Blessed are they which are called unto the marriage supper of the Lamb. And he saith unto me, These are the true sayings of God.

Revelation 21:9-14 KJV
And there came unto me one of the seven angels which had the seven vials full of the seven last plagues, and talked with me, saying, Come hither, I will shew thee the bride, the Lamb's wife.
And he carried me away in the spirit to a great and high mountain, and shewed me that great city, the holy Jerusalem, descending out of heaven from God,
Having the glory of God: and her light was like unto a stone most precious, even like a jasper stone, clear as crystal;
And had a wall great and high, and had twelve gates, and at the gates twelve angels, and names written thereon, which are the names of the twelve tribes of the children of Israel:
On the east three gates; on the north three gates; on the south three gates; and on the west three gates.
And the wall of the city had twelve foundations, and in them the names of the twelve apostles of the Lamb.

Excellent site for additional Bible translations:
http://www.biblegateway.com/resources/commentaries/
Excellent resource for additional Bible study:
(Be sure to read the instructions on their page)
http://www.blueletterbible.org/commentaries/

Marriage - Christian Quotes

"Marriage is an exclusive union between one man and one woman, publicly acknowledged, permanently sealed, and physically consummated."
Selwyn Hughes

"Marriage is a picture of Christ and the church. It is a sacred mystery. In fact, the sacredness of Christ's church is linked to the sacredness of marriage. Christ is the heavenly Bridegroom and the church is His bride (Revelation 21:9). Marriage illustrates this union. The husband is called to be Christlike in his love for his wife because this protects the sacredness of the divine object lesson. The Christian husband therefore displays what he thinks of Christ by the way he treats his wife. And marriage itself is a sacred institution because of what it illustrates."
John MacArthur

"Marriage is not a human invention, it is the creation of God; it did not originate in the mind of man, but in the mind of God. This being the case, man cannot change the definition or purpose of marriage to suit himself. The redefinition of marriage is the negation of marriage."
William Einwechter

"The monstrosity of sexual intercourse outside marriage is that those who indulge in it are trying to isolate one kind of union (the sexual) from all the other kinds of union which were intended to go along with it and make up the total union."
C.S. Lewis

"Marriage is not a mere civil thing, but is partly spiritual and Divine, and therefore God alone has the power to appoint the beginning, the continuance, and the end thereof."
A.W. Pink

"A man doesn't own his marriage; he is only the steward of his wife's love."
Edwin Louis Cole

There is no more lovely, friendly or charming relationship, communion or company, than a good marriage.
Martin Luther

"Fifty-fifty marriages are an impossibility. They do not work. They cannot work. In marriage someone has to be the final decision maker. Someone has to delegate responsibility, and God has ordained that this should be the husband."
Wayne Mack

The Puritan ethic of marriage was first to look not for a partner whom you do love passionately at this moment but rather for one whom you can love steadily as your best friend for life, then to proceed with God's help to do just that.
J. I. Packer

God intends and expects marriage to be a lifetime commitment between a man and a woman, based on the principles of biblical love. The relationship between Jesus Christ and His church is the supreme example of the committed love that a husband and wife are to follow in their relationship with each other.
John Broger

Obedience

Obedience - Bible Verses

Deuteronomy 6:4-9 NIV
Hear, O Israel: The Lord our God, the Lord is one. Love the Lord your God with all your heart and with all your soul and with all your strength. These commandments that I give you today are to be on your hearts. Impress them on your children. Talk about them when you sit at home and when you walk along the road, when you lie down and when you get up. Tie them as symbols on your hands and bind them on your foreheads. Write them on the doorframes of your houses and on your gates.

Ephesians 6:1-3 NIV
Children, obey your parents in the Lord, for this is right. "Honor your father and mother"—which is the first commandment with a promise— "so that it may go well with you and that you may enjoy long life on the earth."

Colossians 3:22 NASB
Slaves, in all things obey those who are your masters on earth, not with external service, as those who merely please men, but with sincerity of heart, fearing the Lord.

Hebrews 13:17 KJV
Obey them that have the rule over you, and submit yourselves: for they watch for your souls, as they that must give account, that they may do it with joy, and not with grief: for that is unprofitable for you.

1 Peter 4:16-17 KJV
Yet if any man suffer as a Christian, let him not be ashamed; but let him glorify God on this behalf.
For the time is come that judgment must begin at the house of God: and if it first begin at us, what shall the end be of them that obey not the gospel of God?

Deuteronomy 4:1 ESV

"And now, O Israel, listen to the statutes and the rules that I am teaching you, and do them, that you may live, and go in and take possession of the land that the LORD, the God of your fathers, is giving you.

1 Samuel 15:22 ESV

And Samuel said, "Has the LORD as great delight in burnt offerings and sacrifices, as in obeying the voice of the LORD? Behold, to obey is better than sacrifice, and to listen than the fat of rams.

Galatians 5:13-14 NASB

For you were called to freedom, brethren; only do not turn your freedom into an opportunity for the flesh, but through love serve one another. For the whole Law is fulfilled in one word, in the statement, "You shall love your neighbor as yourself."

2 John 1:6 NASB

And this is love, that we walk according to His commandments. This is the commandment, just as you have heard from the beginning, that you should walk in it.

Numbers 20:7-12 NIV

The Lord said to Moses, "Take the staff, and you and your brother Aaron gather the assembly together. Speak to that rock before their eyes and it will pour out its water. You will bring water out of the rock for the community so they and their livestock can drink."

So Moses took the staff from the Lord's presence, just as he commanded him. He and Aaron gathered the assembly together in front of the rock and Moses said to them, "Listen, you rebels, must we bring you water out of this rock?" Then Moses raised his arm and struck the rock twice with his staff. Water gushed out, and the community and their livestock drank.

But the Lord said to Moses and Aaron, "Because you did not trust in me enough to honor me as holy in the sight of the Israelites, you will not bring this community into the land I give them."

Judges 2:1-3 NLT
The angel of the Lord went up from Gilgal to Bokim and said to the Israelites, "I brought you out of Egypt into this land that I swore to give your ancestors, and I said I would never break my covenant with you. For your part, you were not to make any covenants with the people living in this land; instead, you were to destroy their altars. But you disobeyed my command. Why did you do this? So now I declare that I will no longer drive out the people living in your land. They will be thorns in your sides, and their gods will be a constant temptation to you."

Joshua 5:6 ESV
For the people of Israel walked forty years in the wilderness, until all the nation, the men of war who came out of Egypt, perished, because they did not obey the voice of the LORD; the LORD swore to them that he would not let them see the land that the LORD had sworn to their fathers to give to us, a land flowing with milk and honey.

Romans 2:6-8 NLT
He will judge everyone according to what they have done. He will give eternal life to those who keep on doing good, seeking after the glory and honor and immortality that God offers. But he will pour out his anger and wrath on those who live for themselves, who refuse to obey the truth and instead live lives of wickedness.

Genesis 22:17-18 ESV
I will surely bless you, and I will surely multiply your offspring as the stars of heaven and as the sand that is on the seashore. And your offspring shall possess the gate of his enemies, and in your offspring shall all the nations of the earth be blessed, because you have obeyed my voice."

Proverbs 13:13 ESV
Whoever despises the word brings destruction on himself, but he who reveres the commandment will be rewarded.

Psalm 1:1-2 ESV

Blessed is the man who walks not in the counsel of the wicked, nor stands in the way of sinners, nor sits in the seat of scoffers; but his delight is in the law of the LORD, and on his law he meditates day and night.

Luke 11:28 NLT

Jesus replied, "But even more blessed are all who hear the word of God and put it into practice."

Ephesians 5:6 NLT

Don't be fooled by those who try to excuse these sins, for the anger of God will fall on all who disobey him.

Excellent site for additional Bible translations:
http://www.biblegateway.com/resources/commentaries/
Excellent resource for additional Bible study:
(Be sure to read the instructions on their page)
http://www.blueletterbible.org/commentaries/

Obedience - Christian Quotes

"When did the servant have the right to give orders to his master? When did the bondslave have a right to question the commands of his Lord? By what right do you who know Jesus Christ as a personal Savior sit in judgment on the Word of God and the will of God when God demands absolute obedience to it?"
J. Dwight Pentecost

"The Bible recognizes no faith that does not lead to obedience, nor does it recognize any obedience that does not spring from faith. The two are at opposite sides of the same coin."
A.W. Tozer

"Salvation apart from obedience is unknown in the sacred Scriptures… Apart from obedience there can be no salvation, for salvation without obedience is a self-contradictory impossibility."
A.W. Tozer

"You cannot obey God without your obedience spilling out in a blessing to all those around you."
Adrian Rogers

"I find the doing of the will of God leaves me no time for disputing about His plans."
George MacDonald

"How many observe Christ's birthday! How few, His precepts!"
Benjamin Franklin

"Beware of reasoning about God's Word – obey It."
Oswald Chambers

"Why do you need a voice when you have a verse."
Jim Elliot

"Just as a servant knows that he must first obey his master in all things, so the surrender to an implicit and unquestionable obedience must become the essential characteristic of our lives."
Andrew Murray

"The safe place lies in obedience to God's Word, singleness of heart and holy vigilance."
A. B. Simpson

"Trust in God's promises comes to light in obedience to his commands... It is therefore a contradiction in terms to say that we acknowledge Christ's rule in our lives if we do not submit to his word... There is no distinction in the Bible between knowing God or Jesus as our "Savior" and knowing him as our "Lord." Saving faith always expresses itself in obedience (James 2:21-24)."
Scott Hafemann

Pain

Pain - Bible Verses

Psalm 18:2 ESV
The LORD is my rock and my fortress and my deliverer, my God, my rock, in whom I take refuge, my shield, and the horn of my salvation, my stronghold.

Psalm 34:18 ESV
The LORD is near to the brokenhearted and saves the crushed in spirit.

Hebrews 2:18 NLT
Since he himself has gone through suffering and testing, he is able to help us when we are being tested.

2 Corinthians 7:9-10 NIV
yet now I am happy, not because you were made sorry, but because your sorrow led you to repentance. For you became sorrowful as God intended and so were not harmed in any way by us. Godly sorrow brings repentance that leads to salvation and leaves no regret, but worldly sorrow brings death.

Revelation 22:4-5 NIV
They will see his face, and his name will be on their foreheads. There will be no more night. They will not need the light of a lamp or the light of the sun, for the Lord God will give them light. And they will reign for ever and ever.

Romans 8:18 KJV
For I reckon that the sufferings of this present time are not worthy to be compared with the glory which shall be revealed in us.

Job 1:21 ESV
And he said, "Naked I came from my mother's womb, and naked shall I return. The LORD gave, and the LORD has taken away; blessed be the name of the LORD."

Job 6:10 ESV

This would be my comfort; I would even exult in pain unsparing, for I have not denied the words of the Holy One.

1 Corinthians 10:13 NIV

No temptation has overtaken you except what is common to mankind. And God is faithful; he will not let you be tempted beyond what you can bear. But when you are tempted, he will also provide a way out so that you can endure it.

1 Peter 5:9-10 NIV

Resist him, standing firm in the faith, because you know that the family of believers throughout the world is undergoing the same kind of sufferings.
And the God of all grace, who called you to his eternal glory in Christ, after you have suffered a little while, will himself restore you and make you strong, firm and steadfast.

Excellent site for additional Bible translations:
http://www.biblegateway.com/resources/commentaries/
Excellent resource for additional Bible study:
(Be sure to read the instructions on their page)
http://www.blueletterbible.org/commentaries/

Pain - Christian Quotes

"Though poor in this world's goods, though grieving the loss of loved ones, though suffering pain of body, though harassed by sin and Satan, though hated and persecuted by worldlings, whatever be the case and lot of the Christian, it is both his privilege and duty to rejoice in the Lord."
A.W. Pink

"We are certainly in a common class with the beasts; every action of animal life is concerned with seeking bodily pleasure and avoiding pain."
Augustine

"Pain removes the veil; it plants the flag of truth within the fortress of a rebel soul."
C.S. Lewis

"Pain is no evil, unless it conquers us."
Charles Kingsley

"I am certain that I never did grow in grace one-half so much anywhere as I have upon the bed of pain."
Charles Spurgeon

"I am not a theologian or a scholar, but I am very aware of the fact that pain is necessary to all of us. In my own life, I think I can honestly say that out of the deepest pain has come the strongest conviction of the presence of God and the love of God."
Elizabeth Elliot

"Go forth today, by the help of God's Spirit, vowing and declaring that in life - come poverty, come wealth, in death - come pain or come what may, you are and ever must be the Lord's. For this is written on your heart, 'We love Him because He first loved us."
Charles Spurgeon

"Pain is a kindly, hopeful thing, a certain proof of life, a clear assurance that all is not yet over, that there is still a chance. But if your heart has no pain — well, that may betoken health, as you suppose: but are you certain that it does not mean that your soul is dead? "
A. J. Gossip

"As I look back over fifty years of ministry, I recall innumerable tests, trials and times of crushing pain. But through it all, the Lord has proven faithful, loving, and totally true to all his promises."
David Wilkerson

Parents

Parents -Bible Verses

Deuteronomy 7:14 NIV
You will be blessed more than any other people; none of your men or women will be childless, nor will any of your livestock be without young.

Psalm 127:3-5 ESV
Behold, children are a heritage from the LORD, the fruit of the womb a reward. Like arrows in the hand of a warrior are the children of one's youth. Blessed is the man who fills his quiver with them! He shall not be put to shame when he speaks with his enemies in the gate.

Psalm 139:13-16 ESV
For you formed my inward parts; you knitted me together in my mother's womb. I praise you, for I am fearfully and wonderfully made. Wonderful are your works; my soul knows it very well. My frame was not hidden from you, when I was being made in secret, intricately woven in the depths of the earth. Your eyes saw my unformed substance; in your book were written, every one of them, the days that were formed for me, when as yet there was none of them.

Matthew 18:12-14 NIV
"What do you think? If a man owns a hundred sheep, and one of them wanders away, will he not leave the ninety-nine on the hills and go to look for the one that wandered off? And if he finds it, truly I tell you, he is happier about that one sheep than about the ninety-nine that did not wander off. In the same way your Father in heaven is not willing that any of these little ones should perish.

Ephesians 2:10 ESV
For we are his workmanship, created in Christ Jesus for good works, which God prepared beforehand, that we should walk in them.

Ephesians 6:1-3 NIV
Children, obey your parents in the Lord, for this is right. "Honor your father and mother"—which is the first commandment with a promise— "so that it may go well with you and that you may enjoy long life on the earth."

Romans 6:23 NASB
For the wages of sin is death, but the free gift of God is eternal life in Christ Jesus our Lord.

John 3:16 ESV
For God so loved the world, that he gave his only Son, that whoever believes in him should not perish but have eternal life.

Ephesians 2:8-9 NASB
For by grace you have been saved through faith; and that not of yourselves, it is the gift of God; not as a result of works, so that no one may boast.

Deuteronomy 6:6-9 NASB
These words, which I am commanding you today, shall be on your heart. You shall teach them diligently to your sons and shall talk of them when you sit in your house and when you walk by the way and when you lie down and when you rise up. You shall bind them as a sign on your hand and they shall be as frontals on your forehead. You shall write them on the doorposts of your house and on your gates.

Proverbs 1:8-9 ESV
Hear, my son, your father's instruction, and forsake not your mother's teaching, for they are a graceful garland for your head and pendants for your neck.

Proverbs 22:6 ESV
Train up a child in the way he should go; even when he is old he will not depart from it.

Ephesians 6:4 ESV
Fathers, do not provoke your children to anger, but bring them up in the discipline and instruction of the Lord.

Colossians 3:21 ESV
Fathers, do not exasperate your children, so that they will not lose heart.

Proverbs 13:24 ESV
Whoever spares the rod hates his son, but he who loves him is diligent to discipline him.

Proverbs 19:18 ESV
Discipline your son, for there is hope; do not set your heart on putting him to death.

Proverbs 22:15 NLT
A youngster's heart is filled with foolishness, but physical discipline will drive it far away.

Proverbs 23:13-14 KJV
Withhold not correction from the child: for if thou beatest him with the rod, he shall not die. Thou shalt beat him with the rod, and shalt deliver his soul from hell.

Proverbs 29:15 ESV
The rod and reproof give wisdom, but a child left to himself brings shame to his mother.

Proverbs 29:17 ESV
Discipline your son, and he will give you rest; he will give delight to your heart.

Excellent site for additional Bible translations:
http://www.biblegateway.com/resources/commentaries/
Excellent resource for additional Bible study:
(Be sure to read the instructions on their page)

http://www.blueletterbible.org/commentaries/

Parents - Christian Quotes

"Teach them to obey while they are young, or else they will be protesting against God all their lives, and wear themselves out with the vain idea of being independent of His control... That child's character in the end will be self-will, pride, and conceit. Is it any wonder that men refuse to obey their Father who is in heaven, if you allow them, when children, to disobey their father who is on earth."
J.C. Ryle

"I was cradled in the home of piety, nurtured with the tenderest care, taught the gospel from my youth up, with the holiest example of my parents, the best possible checks all around to prevent me running into sin."
C.H. Spurgeon

"Train up a child in the way he should go – but be sure you go that way yourself."
C.H. Spurgeon

"A man ought to live so that everybody knows he is a Christian...and most of all, his family ought to know."
D.L. Moody

"[The] most important duty, respecting both the temporal and spiritual good of your children, is fervent supplication to God for them. Without this all the rest will be ineffectual. Means are unavailing unless the Lord blesses them. The Throne of Grace is to be earnestly implored that your efforts to bring up your children for God may be crowned with success."
A.W. Pink

"A child who is allowed to be disrespectful to his parents will not have true respect for anyone."
Billy Graham

"As parents, you may confidently rear your children according to God's Word. While bringing up your children, you are to remember that your

children are not your "possessions" but instead are the Lord's gift to you. You are to exercise faithful stewardship in their lives."
John Broger

"If we, as parents, are not painstakingly investing in the lives of our children, we are doing them a disservice and pain will be the likely result."
Jonathan Falwell

Patience

Patience - Bible Verses

Numbers 14:18 ESV
'The LORD is slow to anger and abounding in steadfast love, forgiving iniquity and transgression, but he will by no means clear the guilty, visiting the iniquity of the fathers on the children, to the third and the fourth generation.'

Psalm 86:15 KJV
But thou, O Lord, art a God full of compassion, and gracious, long suffering, and plenteous in mercy and truth.

Nahum 1:3 NIV
The Lord is slow to anger but great in power;
    the Lord will not leave the guilty unpunished.
His way is in the whirlwind and the storm,
    and clouds are the dust of his feet.

Romans 2:3-4 NIV
So when you, a mere human being, pass judgment on them and yet do the same things, do you think you will escape God's judgment? Or do you show contempt for the riches of his kindness, forbearance and patience, not realizing that God's kindness is intended to lead you to repentance?

2 Peter 3:9 NIV
The Lord is not slow in keeping his promise, as some understand slowness. Instead he is patient with you, not wanting anyone to perish, but everyone to come to repentance.

Genesis 6:3 ESV
Then the LORD said, "My Spirit shall not abide in man forever, for he is flesh: his days shall be 120 years."

Proverbs 29:1 ESV
He who is often reproved, yet stiffens his neck, will suddenly be broken beyond healing.

Ecclesiastes 8:11 NIV
When the sentence for a crime is not quickly carried out, people's hearts are filled with schemes to do wrong.

Jeremiah 44:22 ESV
The LORD could no longer bear your evil deeds and the abominations that you committed. Therefore your land has become a desolation and a waste and a curse, without inhabitant, as it is this day.

Matthew 25:41 ESV
"Then he will say to those on his left, 'Depart from me, you cursed, into the eternal fire prepared for the devil and his angels."

2 Corinthians 12:12 ESV
The signs of a true apostle were performed among you with utmost patience, with signs and wonders and mighty works.

Galatians 5:22-23 NASB
But the fruit of the Spirit is love, joy, peace, patience, kindness, goodness, faithfulness, gentleness, self-control; against such things there is no law.

Ephesians 4:1-3 NIV
As a prisoner for the Lord, then, I urge you to live a life worthy of the calling you have received. Be completely humble and gentle; be patient, bearing with one another in love. Make every effort to keep the unity of the Spirit through the bond of peace.

Colossians 1:11-12 NIV
being strengthened with all power according to his glorious might so that you may have great endurance and patience, and giving joyful thanks to the Father, who has qualified you to share in the inheritance of his holy people in the kingdom of light.

Colossians 3:12-13 NIV
Therefore, as God's chosen people, holy and dearly loved, clothe yourselves with compassion, kindness, humility, gentleness and patience. Bear with each other and forgive one another if any of you has a grievance against someone. Forgive as the Lord forgave you.

Luke 8:15 NASB
But the seed in the good soil, these are the ones who have heard the word in an honest and good heart, and hold it fast, and bear fruit with perseverance.

Romans 2:6-7 ESV
He will render to each one according to his works: to those who by patience in well-doing seek for glory and honor and immortality, he will give eternal life;

Romans 8:24-25 ESV
For in this hope we were saved. Now hope that is seen is not hope. For who hopes for what he sees? But if we hope for what we do not see, we wait for it with patience.

1 Timothy 1:16 ESV
But I received mercy for this reason, that in me, as the foremost, Jesus Christ might display his perfect patience as an example to those who were to believe in him for eternal life.

Hebrews 6:11-12 NLT
Our great desire is that you will keep on loving others as long as life lasts, in order to make certain that what you hope for will come true. 12 Then you will not become spiritually dull and indifferent. Instead, you will follow the example of those who are going to inherit God's promises because of their faith and endurance.

Excellent site for additional Bible translations:
http://www.biblegateway.com/resources/commentaries/
Excellent resource for additional Bible study:
(Be sure to read the instructions on their page)

http://www.blueletterbible.org/commentaries/

Patience - Christian Quotes

"There is nothing which shows our ignorance so much as our impatience under trouble. We forget that every cross is a message from God, and intended to do us good in the end. Trials are intended to make us think – to wean us from the world, to send us to the Bible, to drive us to our knees. Health is a good thing; but sickness is far better, if it leads us to God. Prosperity is a great mercy, but adversity is a greater one, if it brings us to Christ. Anything, anything is better than living in carelessness, and dying in sin."
J.C. Ryle

"There are no sins God's people are more subject to than unbelief and impatience. They are ready either to faint through unbelief, or to fret through impatience."
Thomas Watson

"The faith of Christ offers no buttons to push for quick service. The new order must wait the Lord's own time, and that is too much for the man in a hurry. He just gives up and becomes interested in something else."
A.W. Tozer

"If I have not the patience of my Saviour with the souls who grow slowly; if I know little of travail (a sharp and painful thing) till Christ be fully formed in them, then I know nothing of Calvary love."
Amy Carmichael

"Have patience with all things, but chiefly have patience with yourself. Do not lose courage in considering your own imperfections but instantly set about remedying them– every day begin the task anew."
Francis de Sales

"Cast not away your confidence because God defers his performances. That which does not come in your time, will be hastened in his time, which is always the more convenient season. God will work when he pleases, how he pleases, and by what means he pleases. He is not bound to keep our time,

but he will perform his word, honour our faith, and reward them that diligently seek him."
Matthew Henry

"Timing is so important! If you are going to be successful in dance, you must be able to respond to rhythm and timing. It's the same in the Spirit. People who don't understand God's timing can become spiritually spastic, trying to make the right things happen at the wrong time. They don't get His rhythm – and everyone can tell they are out of step. They birth things prematurely, threatening the very lives of their God-given dreams."
T. D. Jakes

"Nothing is ever wasted in the kingdom of God. Not one tear, not all our pain, not the unanswered question or the seemingly unanswered prayers. Nothing will be wasted if we give our lives to God. And if we are willing to be patient until the grace of God is made manifest, whether it takes nine years or ninety, it will be worth the wait."
Unknown

If the Lord Jehovah makes us wait, let us do so with our whole hearts; for blessed are all they that wait for Him. He is worth waiting for. The waiting itself is beneficial to us: it tries faith, exercises patience, trains submission, and endears the blessing when it comes. The Lord's people have always been a waiting people.
Charles Spurgeon

Peace

Peace - Bible Verses

Matthew 5:9 NASB
"Blessed are the peacemakers, for they shall be called sons of God.

Matthew 11:28-30 NASB
"Come to Me, all who are weary and heavy-laden, and I will give you rest. Take My yoke upon you and learn from Me, for I am gentle and humble in heart, and you will find rest for your souls. For My yoke is easy and My burden is light."

John 14:27 NASB
Peace I leave with you; My peace I give to you; not as the world gives do I give to you. Do not let your heart be troubled, nor let it be fearful.

John 16:33 NASB
These things I have spoken to you, so that in Me you may have peace. In the world you have tribulation, but take courage; I have overcome the world."

John 20:19 ESV
On the evening of that day, the first day of the week, the doors being locked where the disciples were for fear of the Jews, Jesus came and stood among them and said to them, "Peace be with you."

Philippians 4:6-7 ESV
do not be anxious about anything, but in everything by prayer and supplication with thanksgiving let your requests be made known to God. And the peace of God, which surpasses all understanding, will guard your hearts and your minds in Christ Jesus.

Romans 14:17-19 NLT
For the Kingdom of God is not a matter of what we eat or drink, but of living a life of goodness and peace and joy in the Holy Spirit. If you serve Christ

with this attitude, you will please God, and others will approve of you, too. So then, let us aim for harmony in the church and try to build each other up.

2 Corinthians 13:11 NLT
Dear brothers and sisters, I close my letter with these last words: Be joyful. Grow to maturity. Encourage each other. Live in harmony and peace. Then the God of love and peace will be with you.

1 Peter 1:2 ESV
according to the foreknowledge of God the Father, in the sanctification of the Spirit, for obedience to Jesus Christ and for sprinkling with his blood: May grace and peace be multiplied to you.

Isaiah 12:2 NLT
See, God has come to save me.
  I will trust in him and not be afraid.
The Lord God is my strength and my song;
  he has given me victory."

Romans 5:1 ESV
Therefore, since we have been justified by faith, we have peace with God through our Lord Jesus Christ

Mark 9:50 NLT
Salt is good for seasoning. But if it loses its flavor, how do you make it salty again? You must have the qualities of salt among yourselves and live in peace with each other."

Luke 6:27 ESV
"But I say to you who hear, Love your enemies, do good to those who hate you,

Romans 12:17
Do not repay anyone evil for evil. Be careful to do what is right in the eyes of everyone.

1 Corinthians 7:15 NIV
But if the unbeliever leaves, let it be so. The brother or the sister is not bound in such circumstances; God has called us to live in peace.

James 3:18 ESV
And a harvest of righteousness is sown in peace by those who make peace.

Numbers 6:25-26 NIV
the Lord make his face shine on you
   and be gracious to you;
the Lord turn his face toward you
   and give you peace.'"

Isaiah 9:6 ESV
For to us a child is born, to us a son is given; and the government shall be upon his shoulder, and his name shall be called Wonderful Counselor, Mighty God,

Romans 8:6 NIV
The mind governed by the flesh is death, but the mind governed by the Spirit is life and peace.

Colossians 3:15 ESV
And let the peace of Christ rule in your hearts, to which indeed you were called in one body. And be thankful.

Excellent site for additional Bible translations:
http://www.biblegateway.com/resources/commentaries/
Excellent resource for additional Bible study:
(Be sure to read the instructions on their page)
http://www.blueletterbible.org/commentaries/

Peace - Christian Quotes

"So long as we are occupied with any other object than God Himself, there will be neither rest for the heart nor peace for the mind. But when we receive all that enters our lives as from His hand, then, no matter what may be our circumstances or surroundings--whether in a hovel or prison-dungeon, or at a martyr's stake--we shall be enabled to say, 'The lines are fallen unto me in pleasant places' (Ps. 16:6). But that is the language of faith, not of sight nor of sense."
A. W. Pink

"The labor of self-love is a heavy one indeed. Think whether much of your sorrow has not arisen from someone speaking slightingly of you. As long as you set yourself up as a little god to which you must be loyal, how can you hope to find inward peace."
A. W. Tozer

"When principles that run against your deepest convictions begin to win the day, then battle is your calling, and peace has become sin; you must, at the price of dearest peace, lay your convictions bare before friend and enemy, with all the fire of your faith."
Abraham Kuyper

"You do not really care for God's mercy or His comfort either, so long as you live in any sin. And it is well that you do not; for you can have neither. Your peace will be like a river, when you put away your sin; but not one word of true peace, not one drop of true comfort, can you have till then."
Alexander Whyte

"Riches have never yet given anybody either peace or rest."
Billy Sunday

"God cannot give us a happiness and peace apart from Himself, because it is not there. There is no such thing."
C. S. Lewis

"Peace comes when there is no cloud between us and God. Peace is the consequence of forgiveness, God's removal of that which obscures His face and so breaks union with Him."
Charles H. Bent

"Doubt discovers difficulties which it never solves; it creates hesitancy, despondency, despair. Its progress is the decay of comfort, the death of peace. "Believe!" is the word which speaks life into a man, but doubt nails down his coffin."
Charles Spurgeon

"Great thoughts of your sin alone will drive you to despair; but great thoughts of Christ will pilot you into the haven of peace."
Charles Spurgeon

"Prayer girds human weakness with divine strength, turns human folly into heavenly wisdom, and gives to troubled mortals the peace of God. We know not what prayer can do."
Charles Spurgeon

"A great many people are trying to make peace, but that has already been done. God has not left it for us to do; all we have to do is to enter into it."
D L. Moody

There cannot be any peace where there is uncertainty."
D L. Moody

"When our lives are filled with peace, faith and joy, people will want to know what we have."
David Jeremiah

"As we pour out our bitterness, God pours in his peace."
F. B. Meyer

"Never be in a hurry; do everything quietly and in a calm spirit. Do not lose your inner peace for anything whatsoever, even if your whole world seems upset."
Francis de Sales

Perseverance

Perseverance - Bible Verses

Psalm 27:14 KJV
Wait on the Lord: be of good courage, and he shall strengthen thine heart: wait, I say, on the Lord.

Romans 8:37-39 NASB
But in all these things we overwhelmingly conquer through Him who loved us. For I am convinced that neither death, nor life, nor angels, nor principalities, nor things present, nor things to come, nor powers, nor height, nor depth, nor any other created thing, will be able to separate us from the love of God, which is in Christ Jesus our Lord.

Romans 12:12 ESV
Rejoice in hope, be patient in tribulation, be constant in prayer.

Colossians 1:11-12 NASB
strengthened with all power, according to His glorious might, for the attaining of all steadfastness and patience; joyously giving thanks to the Father, who has qualified us to share in the inheritance of the saints in Light.

1 Thessalonians 1:3 NLT
As we pray to our God and Father about you, we think of your faithful work, your loving deeds, and the enduring hope you have because of our Lord Jesus Christ.

Hebrews 6:11-15 NASB
And we desire that each one of you show the same diligence so as to realize the full assurance of hope until the end, so that you will not be sluggish, but imitators of those who through faith and patience inherit the promises.
For when God made the promise to Abraham, since He could swear by no one greater, He swore by Himself, saying, "I will surely bless you and I will

surely multiply you." And so, having patiently waited, he obtained the promise.

Matthew 10:16-22 NASB
"Behold, I send you out as sheep in the midst of wolves; so be shrewd as serpents and innocent as doves. But beware of men, for they will hand you over to the courts and scourge you in their synagogues; and you will even be brought before governors and kings for My sake, as a testimony to them and to the Gentiles. But when they hand you over, do not worry about how or what you are to say; for it will be given you in that hour what you are to say. For it is not you who speak, but it is the Spirit of your Father who speaks in you.
"Brother will betray brother to death, and a father his child; and children will rise up against parents and cause them to be put to death. You will be hated by all because of My name, but it is the one who has endured to the end who will be saved.

Galatians 6:9 ESV
And let us not grow weary of doing good, for in due season we will reap, if we do not give up.

Ephesians 6:16-19 ESV
In all circumstances take up the shield of faith, with which you can extinguish all the flaming darts of the evil one; and take the helmet of salvation, and the sword of the Spirit, which is the word of God, praying at all times in the Spirit, with all prayer and supplication. To that end keep alert with all perseverance, making supplication for all the saints, and also for me, that words may be given to me in opening my mouth boldly to proclaim the mystery of the gospel,

2 Timothy 4:1-5 NIV
In the presence of God and of Christ Jesus, who will judge the living and the dead, and in view of his appearing and his kingdom, I give you this charge: Preach the word; be prepared in season and out of season; correct, rebuke and encourage—with great patience and careful instruction. For the time will come when people will not put up with sound doctrine. Instead, to suit

their own desires, they will gather around them a great number of teachers to say what their itching ears want to hear. They will turn their ears away from the truth and turn aside to myths. But you, keep your head in all situations, endure hardship, do the work of an evangelist, discharge all the duties of your ministry.

Romans 5:2-5 ESV
Through him we have also obtained access by faith into this grace in which we stand, and we rejoice in hope of the glory of God. Not only that, but we rejoice in our sufferings, knowing that suffering produces endurance, and endurance produces character, and character produces hope, and hope does not put us to shame, because God's love has been poured into our hearts through the Holy Spirit who has been given to us.

2 Corinthians 6:3-10 NIV
We put no stumbling block in anyone's path, so that our ministry will not be discredited. Rather, as servants of God we commend ourselves in every way: in great endurance; in troubles, hardships and distresses; in beatings, imprisonments and riots; in hard work, sleepless nights and hunger; in purity, understanding, patience and kindness; in the Holy Spirit and in sincere love; in truthful speech and in the power of God; with weapons of righteousness in the right hand and in the left; through glory and dishonor, bad report and good report; genuine, yet regarded as impostors; known, yet regarded as unknown; dying, and yet we live on; beaten, and yet not killed; sorrowful, yet always rejoicing; poor, yet making many rich; having nothing, and yet possessing everything.

James 1:2-4 ESV
Count it all joy, my brothers, when you meet trials of various kinds, for you know that the testing of your faith produces steadfastness. And let steadfastness have its full effect, that you may be perfect and complete, lacking in nothing.

James 1:12 ESV
Blessed is the man who remains steadfast under trial, for when he has stood the test he will receive the crown of life, which God has promised to those who love him.

Revelation 2:10 NIV
Do not be afraid of what you are about to suffer. I tell you, the devil will put some of you in prison to test you, and you will suffer persecution for ten days. Be faithful, even to the point of death, and I will give you life as your victor's crown.

Revelation 3:10 ESV
Because you have kept my word about patient endurance, I will keep you from the hour of trial that is coming on the whole world, to try those who dwell on the earth.

1 Corinthians 9:24 ESV
Do you not know that in a race all the runners run, but only one receives the prize? So run that you may obtain it.

2 Thessalonians 3:5 ESV
May the Lord direct your hearts to the love of God and to the steadfastness of Christ.

1 Timothy 6:11-12 NLT
But you, Timothy, are a man of God; so run from all these evil things. Pursue righteousness and a godly life, along with faith, love, perseverance, and gentleness. Fight the good fight for the true faith. Hold tightly to the eternal life to which God has called you, which you have confessed so well before many witnesses.

Hebrews 12:1-2 NLT
Therefore, since we are surrounded by such a huge crowd of witnesses to the life of faith, let us strip off every weight that slows us down, especially the sin that so easily trips us up. And let us run with endurance the race God has set before us. We do this by keeping our eyes on Jesus, the champion who

initiates and perfects our faith. Because of the joy awaiting him, he endured the cross, disregarding its shame. Now he is seated in the place of honor beside God's throne.

Excellent site for additional Bible translations:
http://www.biblegateway.com/resources/commentaries/
Excellent resource for additional Bible study:
(Be sure to read the instructions on their page)
http://www.blueletterbible.org/commentaries/

Perseverance - Christian Quotes

"It is the Holy Spirit who is causing you to persevere. In those times when you are lazy and have no enthusiasm for any Spiritual Discipline, or when you haven't practiced a particular Discipline as you habitually do, it is the Holy Spirit who prompts you to pick it up in spite of your feelings. Left to yourself you would have forsaken these means of sustaining grace long ago, but the Holy Spirit preserves you by granting to you the grace to persevere in them."
Donald Whitney

"If I did not believe the doctrine of the final perseverance of the saints, I think I should be of all men the most miserable, because I should lack any ground for comfort."
C.H. Spurgeon

"We are able to persevere only because God works within us, within our free wills. And because God is at work in us, we are certain to persevere. The decrees of God concerning election are immutable. They do not change, because He does not change. All whom He justifies He glorifies. None of the elect has ever been lost."
R.C. Sproul

God knows our situation; He will not judge us as if we had no difficulties to overcome. What matters is the sincerity and perseverance of our will to overcome them.
C. S. Lewis

I wish that saints would cling to Christ half as earnestly as sinners cling to the devil. If we were as willing to suffer for God as some are willing to suffer for their lusts, what perseverance and zeal would be seen on all sides!
Charles Spurgeon

Power of Prayer

Power of Prayer - Bible Verses

Matthew 7:7 NASB
"Ask, and it will be given to you seek, and you will find; knock, and it will be opened to you.

Matthew 21:22 ESV
And whatever you ask in prayer, you will receive, if you have faith."

Mark 9:29 NLT
Jesus replied, "This kind can be cast out only by prayer."

Mark 11:24 ESV
Therefore I tell you, whatever you ask in prayer, believe that you have received it, and it will be yours.

John 14:13-14 NIV
And I will do whatever you ask in my name, so that the Father may be glorified in the Son. You may ask me for anything in my name, and I will do it.

Acts 9:40 ESV
But Peter put them all outside, and knelt down and prayed; and turning to the body he said, "Tabitha, arise." And she opened her eyes, and when she saw Peter she sat up.

Ephesians 6:18 ESV
praying at all times in the Spirit, with all prayer and supplication. To that end keep alert with all perseverance, making supplication for all the saints,

Philippians 4:6-7 NIV
Do not be anxious about anything, but in every situation, by prayer and petition, with thanksgiving, present your requests to God. And the peace of

God, which transcends all understanding, will guard your hearts and your minds in Christ Jesus.

James 5:14-16 NLT

Are any of you sick? You should call for the elders of the church to come and pray over you, anointing you with oil in the name of the Lord. Such a prayer offered in faith will heal the sick, and the Lord will make you well. And if you have committed any sins, you will be forgiven.

Confess your sins to each other and pray for each other so that you may be healed. The earnest prayer of a righteous person has great power and produces wonderful results.

Excellent site for additional Bible translations:
http://www.biblegateway.com/resources/commentaries/
Excellent resource for additional Bible study:
(Be sure to read the instructions on their page)
http://www.blueletterbible.org/commentaries/

Power of Prayer - Christian Quotes

"Earnest intercession will be sure to bring love with it. I do not believe you can hate a man for whom you habitually pray. If you dislike any brother Christian, pray for him doubly, not only for his sake, but for your own, that you may be cured of prejudice and saved from all unkind feeling."
C.H. Spurgeon

"Men may spurn our appeals, reject our message, oppose our arguments, despise our persons, but they are helpless against our prayers."
J. Sidlow Baxter

"If you want that splendid power in prayer, you must remain in loving, living, lasting, conscious, practical, abiding union with the Lord Jesus Christ."
C.H. Spurgeon

"It is easy to criticize and find fault with the conduct of kings, and write furious articles against them in newspapers, or make violent speeches about them on platforms. Any fool can rip and rend a costly garment, but not every man can cut out and make one. To expect perfection in kings, prime ministers, or rulers of any king, is senseless and unreasonable. We would exhibit more wisdom if we prayed for them more, and criticized less."
J.C. Ryle

"Our God has boundless resources. The only limit is in us. Our asking, our thinking, our praying are too small. Our expectations are too limited."
A.B. Simpson

"I could no more doubt the power of prayer than I could disbelieve the law of gravity."
C.H. Spurgeon

"Time spent in prayer will yield more than that given to work. Prayer alone gives work its worth and its success. Prayer opens the way for God Himself to do His work in us and through us. Let our chief work as God's messengers

be intercession; in it we secure the presence and power of God to go with us."
Andrew Murray

"There is no way that Christians in a private capacity can do so much to promote the work of God and advance the kingdom of Christ, as by prayer."
Jonathan Edwards

"Prayer as it comes from the saint is weak and languid; but when the arrow of a saint's prayer is put into the bow of Christ's intercession it pierces the throne of grace."
Thomas Watson

"I have joyfully dedicated my whole life to the object of exemplifying how much may be accomplished by prayer and faith."
George Mueller

"If you are strangers to prayer you are strangers to power."
Billy Sunday

"Unless we are willing to pay the price, and sacrifice time and attention and what appear legitimate or necessary duties, for the sake of the heavenly gifts we need not look for a large experience of the power of the heavenly world in our work."
Andrew Murray

Pride

Pride - Bible Verses

James 4:6 NLT
But he gives us even more grace to stand against such evil desires. As the Scriptures say,
"God opposes the proud
  but favors the humble."

Isaiah 2:11 NIV
The eyes of the arrogant will be humbled
  and human pride brought low;
the Lord alone will be exalted in that day.

2 Chronicles 26:16 NIV
But after Uzziah became powerful, his pride led to his downfall. He was unfaithful to the Lord his God, and entered the temple of the Lord to burn incense on the altar of incense.

Psalm 10:3-4 ESV
For the wicked boasts of the desires of his soul, and the one greedy for gain curses and renounces the Lord.4 In the pride of his face the wicked does not seek him; all his thoughts are, "There is no God."

Psalm 59:12 ESV
For the sin of their mouths, the words of their lips, let them be trapped in their pride. For the cursing and lies that they utter

Proverbs 6:16-19 ESV
There are six things that the Lord hates, seven that are an abomination to him: haughty eyes, a lying tongue, and hands that shed innocent blood, a heart that devises wicked plans, feet that make haste to run to evil, a false witness who breathes out lies, and one who sows discord among brothers.

Proverbs 8:13 NIV
To fear the Lord is to hate evil;
    I hate pride and arrogance,
    evil behavior and perverse speech.

Isaiah 14:12-14 ESV
"How you are fallen from heaven, O Day Star, son of Dawn! How you are cut down to the ground, you who laid the nations low! 13 You said in your heart, 'I will ascend to heaven; above the stars of God I will set my throne on high; I will sit on the mount of assembly in the far reaches of the north; 14 I will ascend above the heights of the clouds; I will make myself like the Most High.'

Matthew 4:8-9 NASB
Again, the devil took Him to a very high mountain and showed Him all the kingdoms of the world and their glory; and he said to Him, "All these things I will give You, if You fall down and worship me."

2 Chronicles 32:25-26 NASB
But Hezekiah gave no return for the benefit he received, because his heart was proud; therefore wrath came on him and on Judah and Jerusalem. However, Hezekiah humbled the pride of his heart, both he and the inhabitants of Jerusalem, so that the wrath of the Lord did not come on them in the days of Hezekiah.

Isaiah 10:12 ESV
When the Lord has finished all his work on Mount Zion and on Jerusalem, he will punish the speech of the arrogant heart of the king of Assyria and the boastful look in his eyes.

Luke 18:9-14 NASB
And He also told this parable to some people who trusted in themselves that they were righteous, and viewed others with contempt: "Two men went up into the temple to pray, one a Pharisee and the other a tax collector. The Pharisee stood and was praying this to himself: 'God, I thank You that I am not like other people: swindlers, unjust, adulterers, or even like this tax

collector. I fast twice a week; I pay tithes of all that I get.' But the tax collector, standing some distance away, was even unwilling to lift up his eyes to heaven, but was beating his breast, saying, 'God, be merciful to me, the sinner!' I tell you, this man went to his house justified rather than the other; for everyone who exalts himself will be humbled, but he who humbles himself will be exalted."

Acts 12:21-23 NLT

and an appointment with Herod was granted. When the day arrived, Herod put on his royal robes, sat on his throne, and made a speech to them. The people gave him a great ovation, shouting, "It's the voice of a god, not of a man!"

Instantly, an angel of the Lord struck Herod with a sickness, because he accepted the people's worship instead of giving the glory to God. So he was consumed with worms and died.

Leviticus 26:18-20 NLT

"And if, in spite of all this, you still disobey me, I will punish you seven times over for your sins. I will break your proud spirit by making the skies as unyielding as iron and the earth as hard as bronze. All your work will be for nothing, for your land will yield no crops, and your trees will bear no fruit.

Isaiah 3:16-17 NLT

The Lord says, "Beautiful Zion is haughty:
craning her elegant neck,
    flirting with her eyes,
walking with dainty steps,
    tinkling her ankle bracelets.
So the Lord will send scabs on her head;
    the Lord will make beautiful Zion bald."

Zephaniah 3:11 NLT

On that day you will no longer need to be ashamed,
    for you will no longer be rebels against me.
I will remove all proud and arrogant people from among you.
    There will be no more haughtiness on my holy mountain.

Isaiah 4:2 ESV
In that day the branch of the LORD shall be beautiful and glorious, and the fruit of the land shall be the pride and honor of the survivors of Israel.

2 Corinthians 5:12 ESV
We are not commending ourselves to you again but giving you cause to boast about us, so that you may be able to answer those who boast about outward appearance and not about what is in the heart.

2 Corinthians 7:2-4 NLT
Please open your hearts to us. We have not done wrong to anyone, nor led anyone astray, nor taken advantage of anyone. I'm not saying this to condemn you. I said before that you are in our hearts, and we live or die together with you. I have the highest confidence in you, and I take great pride in you. You have greatly encouraged me and made me happy despite all our troubles.

2 Corinthians 8:24 NLT
So show them your love, and prove to all the churches that our boasting about you is justified.

Galatians 6:4 NLT
Pay careful attention to your own work, for then you will get the satisfaction of a job well done, and you won't need to compare yourself to anyone else.

Excellent site for additional Bible translations:
http://www.biblegateway.com/resources/commentaries/
Excellent resource for additional Bible study:
(Be sure to read the instructions on their page)
http://www.blueletterbible.org/commentaries/

Pride - Christian Quotes

"[Pride] comes from not knowing yourself and the world. The older you grow, and the more you see, the less reason you will find for being proud. Ignorance and inexperience are the pedestal of pride; once the pedestal is removed – pride will soon come down."
J.C. Ryle

"Be not proud of race, face, place, or grace."
C.H. Spurgeon

"Those who think too much of themselves don't think enough."
Amy Carmichael

"When a man thinks he has got a good deal of strength, and is self-confidence, you may look for his downfall. It may be years before it comes to light, but it is already commenced."
D.L. Moody

"There is nothing in the world that works such satanic, profound, God-defiant pride as false assurance; nothing works such utter humility, or brings to such utter self-emptiness, as the child-like spirit of true assurance."
A. A. Hodge

"It was pride that changed angels into devils; it is humility that makes men as angels."
Augustine

"Pride gets no pleasure out of having something, only out of having more of it than the next man."
C. S. Lewis

"A man who is eating or lying with his wife or preparing to go to sleep in humility, thankfulness and temperance, is, by Christian standards, in an

infinitely higher state than one who is listening to Bach or reading Plato in a state of pride."
C. S. Lewis

"Pride may be set down as "the sin" of human nature."
C.H. Spurgeon

"No matter how dear you are to God, if pride is harbored in your spirit, He will whip it out of you. They that go up in their own estimation must come down again by His discipline."
C.H. Spurgeon

"There is nothing into which the heart of man so easily falls as pride, and yet there is no more vice which is more frequently, more emphatically, and more eloquently condemned in Scripture. Pride is a thing which should be unnatural to us, for we have nothing to be proud of. In almost every other sin, we gather us ashes when the fire is gone. But here, what is left? The covetous man has his shining gold, but what does the proud man have? He has less than he would have had without pride, and is no gainer whatever. Pride wins no crown."
C.H. Spurgeon

"I believe firmly that the moment our hearts are emptied of pride and selfishness and ambition and everything that is contrary to God's law, the Holy Spirit will fill every corner of our hearts. But if we are full of pride and conceit and ambition and the world, there is no room for the Spirit of God. We must be emptied before we can be filled."
D. L. Moody

"If we are full of pride and conceit and ambition and self-seeking and pleasure and the world, there is no room for the Spirit of God, and I believe many a man is praying to God to fill him when he is full already with something else."
D. L. Moody

Prayer

Prayer - Bible Verses

Ephesians 6:18 ESV
praying at all times in the Spirit, with all prayer and supplication. To that end keep alert with all perseverance, making supplication for all the saints,

Philippians 1:3-4 NLT
Every time I think of you, I give thanks to my God. Whenever I pray, I make my requests for all of you with joy,

Colossians 1:3 NLT
We give thanks to God and the Father of our Lord Jesus Christ, praying always for you,

1 Thessalonians 5:17 NASB
pray without ceasing;

Psalm 66:17 ESV
I cried to him with my mouth, and high praise was on my tongue.

Psalm 95:2 ESV
Let us come into his presence with thanksgiving; let us make a joyful noise to him with songs of praise!

Matthew 6:9-13 KJV
After this manner therefore pray ye: Our Father which art in heaven, Hallowed be thy name. Thy kingdom come, Thy will be done in earth, as it is in heaven. Give us this day our daily bread. And forgive us our debts, as we forgive our debtors. And lead us not into temptation, but deliver us from evil: For thine is the kingdom, and the power, and the glory, for ever. Amen.

1 Corinthians 14:15 NLT
Well then, what shall I do? I will pray in the spirit, and I will also pray in words I understand. I will sing in the spirit, and I will also sing in words I understand..

James 1:6 ESV
But let him ask in faith, with no doubting, for the one who doubts is like a wave of the sea that is driven and tossed by the wind.

Psalm 50:14-15 ESV
Offer to God a sacrifice of thanksgiving, and perform your vows to the Most High, and call upon me in the day of trouble; I will deliver you, and you shall glorify me."

Psalm 118:25 ESV
Save us, we pray, O LORD! O LORD, we pray, give us success!

Psalm 122:6 ESV
Pray for the peace of Jerusalem! May they be secure who love you!

Romans 10:1 NLT
Dear brothers and sisters, the longing of my heart and my prayer to God is for the people of Israel to be saved.

Romans 10:13 ESV
For "Everyone who calls on the name of the Lord will be saved."

Romans 15:30 NLT
Dear brothers and sisters, I urge you in the name of our Lord Jesus Christ to join in my struggle by praying to God for me. Do this because of your love for me, given to you by the Holy Spirit.

2 Corinthians 1:11 ESV
You also must help us by prayer, so that many will give thanks on our behalf for the blessing granted us through the prayers of many.

1 Timothy 2:1-2 NLT
I urge you, first of all, to pray for all people. Ask God to help them; intercede on their behalf, and give thanks for them. Pray this way for kings and all who are in authority so that we can live peaceful and quiet lives marked by godliness and dignity.

James 5:13-14 NIV
Is anyone among you in trouble? Let them pray. Is anyone happy? Let them sing songs of praise. Is anyone among you sick? Let them call the elders of the church to pray over them and anoint them with oil in the name of the Lord.

James 5:16 ESV
Therefore, confess your sins to one another and pray for one another, that you may be healed. The prayer of a righteous person has great power as it is working.

Excellent site for additional Bible translations
http://www.biblegateway.com/resources/commentaries/
Excellent resource for additional Bible study:
(Be sure to read the instructions on their page)
http://www.blueletterbible.org/commentaries/

Prayer- Christian Quotes

"Beware in your prayers, above everything else, of limiting God, not only by unbelief, but by fancying that you know what He can do. Expect unexpected things, 'above all that we ask or think'. Each time, before you intercede, be quiet first, and worship God in His glory. Think of what He can do, and how He delights to hear the prayers of His redeemed people. Think of your place and privilege in Christ, and expect great things!"
Andrew Murray

"Those persons who know the deep peace of God, the unfathomable peace that passeth all understanding, are always men and women of much prayer."
R. A. Torrey

"Don't pray when you feel like it. Have an appointment with the Lord and keep it. A man is powerful on his knees."
Corrie ten Boom

"You may as soon find a living man that does not breath, as a living Christian that does not pray."
Matthew Henry

"Prayer will make a man cease from sin, or sin will entice a man to cease from prayer."
John Bunyan

"We have to pray with our eyes on God, not on the difficulties."
Oswald Chambers

"It is the burning lava of the soul that has a furnace within- a very volcano of grief and sorrow- it is that burning lava of prayer that finds its way to God. No prayer ever reaches God's heart which does not come from our hearts."
C.H. Spurgeon

"Prayer cannot truly be taught by principles and seminars and symposiums. It has to be born out of a whole environment of felt need. If I say, "I ought

to pray," I will soon run out of motivation and quit; the flesh is too strong. I have to be driven to pray."
Jim Cymbala

"Believers do not pray with the view of informing God about things unknown to Him, or of exciting Him to do His duty, or of urging Him as though He were reluctant. On the contrary, they pray in order that they may arouse to seek Him, that they may exercise their faith in meditating on His promises, that they may relieve themselves from their anxieties by pouring them into His bosom; in a word, that they may declare that from Him alone they hope and expect, both for themselves and for others, all good things."
John Calvin

"Prayer girds human weakness with divine strength, turns human folly into heavenly wisdom, and gives to troubled mortals the peace of God. We know not what prayer can do."
C.H. Spurgeon

"If God sees that my spiritual life will be furthered by giving the things for which I ask, then He will give them, but that is not the end of prayer. The end of prayer is that I come to know God Himself."
Oswald Chambers

"Prayer does not equip us for greater works – prayer is the greater work."
Oswald Chambers

Promises of God

Promises of God - Bible Verses

2 Peter 1:4 NLT
And because of his glory and excellence, he has given us great and precious promises. These are the promises that enable you to share his divine nature and escape the world's corruption caused by human desires.

Jeremiah 29:11 NIV
For I know the plans I have for you," declares the Lord, "plans to prosper you and not to harm you, plans to give you hope and a future.

Matthew 11:28-29 NIV
"Come to me, all you who are weary and burdened, and I will give you rest. Take my yoke upon you and learn from me, for I am gentle and humble in heart, and you will find rest for your souls.

Isaiah 40:29-31 NIV
He gives strength to the weary
   and increases the power of the weak.
Even youths grow tired and weary,
   and young men stumble and fall;
but those who hope in the Lord
   will renew their strength.
They will soar on wings like eagles;
   they will run and not grow weary,
   they will walk and not be faint.

Philippians 4:19 NLT
And this same God who takes care of me will supply all your needs from his glorious riches, which have been given to us in Christ Jesus.

Romans 8:37-39 NIV
No, in all these things we are more than conquerors through him who loved us. For I am convinced that neither death nor life, neither angels nor demons, neither the present nor the future, nor any powers, neither height nor depth, nor anything else in all creation, will be able to separate us from the love of God that is in Christ Jesus our Lord.

Proverbs 1:33 NLT
But all who listen to me will live in peace,
untroubled by fear of harm."

John 14:27 NASB
Peace I leave with you; My peace I give to you; not as the world gives do I give to you. Do not let your heart be troubled, nor let it be fearful.

Romans 10:9 NASB
that if you confess with your mouth Jesus as Lord, and believe in your heart that God raised Him from the dead, you will be saved;

Romans 6:23 NASB
For the wages of sin is death, but the free gift of God is eternal life in Christ Jesus our Lord.

The promises of God are powerful and awesome to grasp. I pray that these scriptures about God's promises were helpful to you today.

Excellent site for additional Bible translations:
http://www.biblegateway.com/resources/commentaries/
Excellent resource for additional Bible study:
(Be sure to read the instructions on their page)
http://www.blueletterbible.org/commentaries/

Promises of God- Christian Quotes

"When you look at the Cross, what do you see? You see God's awesome faithfulness. Nothing – not even the instinct to spare His own Son – will turn him back from keeping His word."
Sinclair Ferguson

"The primary ground of assurance is rooted in the promises of God, but those promises must become increasingly real to the believer through the subjective evidences of grace and the internal witness of the Holy Spirit."
Joel R. Beeke

"There are more than 14,000 promises in the Bible – God has not broken one of them."
 Unknown

"The permanence of God's character guarantees the fulfillment of his promises."
A.W. Pink

"What greater rebellion against God, what greater wickedness, what greater contempt of God is there than not believing His promise? For what is this but to make God a liar or to doubt that He is truthful."
Martin Luther

"Satan promises the best, but pays with the worst; he promises honor, and pays with disgrace; he promises pleasure, and pays with pain; he promises profit, and pays with loss; he promises life, and pays with death. But God pays as He promises; all His payments are made in pure gold."
Thomas Brooks

"Prayer helps us cling to the altar of God's promises by which we lay hold of God Himself."
Joel R. Beeke

"Faith is always tied to a promise of God."
Unknown

"All God's promises depend upon Christ alone. This is a notable assertion and one of the main articles of our faith. It depends in turn upon another principle – that it is only in Christ that God the Father is graciously inclined towards us. His promises are the testimonies of His fatherly goodwill towards us. Thus it follows that they are fulfilled only in Christ... Secondly, we are incapable of possessing God's promises till we have received the remission of our sins and that comes to us through Christ."
John Calvin

Respect

Respect - Bible Verses

Deuteronomy 6:4-5 ESV
"Hear, O Israel: The LORD our God, the LORD is one. You shall love the LORD your God with all your heart and with all your soul and with all your might.

Romans 1:20-22 NIV
For since the creation of the world His invisible attributes, His eternal power and divine nature, have been clearly seen, being understood through what has been made, so that they are without excuse. For even though they knew God, they did not honor Him as God or give thanks, but they became futile in their speculations, and their foolish heart was darkened. Professing to be wise, they became fools,

1 Peter 3:14-6 NASB
But even if you should suffer for the sake of righteousness, you are blessed. And do not fear their intimidation, and do not be troubled, but sanctify Christ as Lord in your hearts, always being ready to make a defense to everyone who asks you to give an account for the hope that is in you, yet with gentleness and reverence; and keep a good conscience so that in the thing in which you are slandered, those who revile your good behavior in Christ will be put to shame.

Revelation 4:11 ESV
"Worthy are you, our Lord and God, to receive glory and honor and power, for you created all things, and by your will they existed and were created."

Revelation 5:11-12 NASB
Then I looked, and I heard the voice of many angels around the throne and the living creatures and the elders; and the number of them was myriads of myriads, and thousands of thousands, saying with a loud voice,

"Worthy is the Lamb that was slain to receive power and riches and wisdom and might and honor and glory and blessing."

Leviticus 19:32 ESV
"You shall stand up before the gray head and honor the face of an old man, and you shall fear your God: I am the LORD."

Romans 13:2 ESV
Therefore whoever resists the authorities resists what God has appointed, and those who resist will incur judgment.

Romans 13:7 ESV
Pay to all what is owed to them: taxes to whom taxes are owed, revenue to whom revenue is owed, respect to whom respect is owed, honor to whom honor is owed.

1 Timothy 6:1-2 KJV
Let as many servants as are under the yoke count their own masters worthy of all honour, that the name of God and his doctrine be not blasphemed. And they that have believing masters, let them not despise them, because they are brethren; but rather do them service, because they are faithful and beloved, partakers of the benefit. These things teach and exhort.

1 Thessalonians 5:12-13 NLT
Dear brothers and sisters, honor those who are your leaders in the Lord's work. They work hard among you and give you spiritual guidance. Show them great respect and wholehearted love because of their work. And live peacefully with each other.

Hebrews 13:17 NLT
Obey your spiritual leaders, and do what they say. Their work is to watch over your souls, and they are accountable to God. Give them reason to do this with joy and not with sorrow. That would certainly not be for your benefit.

Exodus 20:12 ESV
"Honor your father and your mother, that your days may be long in the land that the LORD your God is giving you.

Matthew 15:4 NLT
For instance, God says, 'Honor your father and mother,' and 'Anyone who speaks disrespectfully of father or mother must be put to death.'

Colossians 3:21 ESV
Fathers, do not provoke your children, lest they become discouraged.

Ephesians 5:33 NLT
So again I say, each man must love his wife as he loves himself, and the wife must respect her husband.

Ephesians 6:2 NLT
"Honor your father and mother." This is the first commandment with a promise:

Hebrews 12:9 ESV
Besides this, we have had earthly fathers who disciplined us and we respected them. Shall we not much more be subject to the Father of spirits and live?

1 Peter 3:7 ESV
Likewise, husbands, live with your wives in an understanding way, showing honor to the woman as the weaker vessel, since they are heirs with you of the grace of life, so that your prayers may not be hindered.

Philippians 2:3 KJV
Let nothing be done through strife or vainglory; but in lowliness of mind let each esteem other better than themselves.

1 Peter 2:17 KJV
Honour all men. Love the brotherhood. Fear God. Honour the king.

Deuteronomy 6:6-9 KJV

And these words, which I command thee this day, shall be in thine heart: And thou shalt teach them diligently unto thy children, and shalt talk of them when thou sittest in thine house, and when thou walkest by the way, and when thou liest down, and when thou risest up.

And thou shalt bind them for a sign upon thine hand, and they shall be as frontlets between thine eyes.

And thou shalt write them upon the posts of thy house, and on thy gates.

Excellent site for additional Bible translations:
http://www.biblegateway.com/resources/commentaries/
Excellent resource for additional Bible study:
(Be sure to read the instructions on their page)
http://www.blueletterbible.org/commentaries/

Respect - Christian Quotes

"To be sure, reputations are not always accurate. Yet, in the long run we usually get a reputation that is close to what we deserve. The inner man shows himself often enough that our reputation at least roughly matches our character."
Dan Doriani

"It is not the being seen of men that is wrong, but doing these things for the purpose of being seen of men. The problem with the hypocrite is his motivation. He does not want to be holy; he only wants to seem to be holy. He is more concerned with his reputation for righteousness than about actually becoming righteous. The approbation of men matters more to him than the approval of God."
Augustine

"Your reputation is what people say about you. Your character is what God and your wife know about you."
Bill Sunday

"If I take care of my character, my reputation will take care of me."
D. L. Moody

"Be careful, dear friends, that you do not misrepresent God yourselves. You who murmur; you who say that God deals hardly with you, you give God an ill character; when you look so melancholy, worldlings say, "The religion of Jesus is intolerable;" and so you stain the honor of God."
Charles Spurgeon

"It is more to the honor of a Christian by faith to overcome the world, than by monastical vows to retreat from it; more for the honor of Christ to serve him in the city, than to serve him in the cell."
Matthew Henry

"Naturally, men are prone to spin themselves a web of opinions out of their own brain, and to have a religion that may be called their own. They are far

readier to make themselves a faith, than to receive that which God hath formed to their hands; are far readier to receive a doctrine that tends to their carnal commodity, or honor, or delight, than one that tends to self-denial."
Richard Baxter

Rest

Rest - Bible Verses

Genesis 2:2-3 NASB
By the seventh day God completed His work which He had done, and He rested on the seventh day from all His work which He had done. Then God blessed the seventh day and sanctified it, because in it He rested from all His work which God had created and made.

Exodus 20:8-10 NASB
"Remember the sabbath day, to keep it holy. Six days you shall labor and do all your work, but the seventh day is a sabbath of the Lord your God; in it you shall not do any work, you or your son or your daughter, your male or your female servant or your cattle or your sojourner who stays with you.

Exodus 23:12 KJV
Six days thou shalt do thy work, and on the seventh day thou shalt rest: that thine ox and thine ass may rest, and the son of thy handmaid, and the stranger, may be refreshed.

Genesis 8:4 KJV
And the ark rested in the seventh month, on the seventeenth day of the month, upon the mountains of Ararat.

Song of Solomon 1:7 NASB
"Tell me, O you whom my soul loves,
Where do you pasture your flock,
Where do you make it lie down at noon?
For why should I be like one who veils herself
Beside the flocks of your companions?"

Jeremiah 33:12 ESV
"Thus says the LORD of hosts: In this place that is waste, without man or beast, and in all of its cities, there shall again be habitations of shepherds resting their flocks…"

Psalm 37:7 ESV
Be still before the LORD and wait patiently for him; fret not yourself over the one who prospers in his way, over the man who carries out evil devices!

Psalm 55:6 ESV
And I say, "Oh, that I had wings like a dove! I would fly away and be at rest

Isaiah 14:3-4 NASB
And it will be in the day when the Lord gives you rest from your pain and turmoil and harsh service in which you have been enslaved, that you will take up this taunt against the king of Babylon, and say,
"How the oppressor has ceased,
And how fury has ceased!

Ecclesiastes 2:24-25 NIV
A person can do nothing better than to eat and drink and find satisfaction in their own toil. This too, I see, is from the hand of God, for without him, who can eat or find enjoyment?

2 Corinthians 2:13-14 NIV
I still had no peace of mind, because I did not find my brother Titus there. So I said goodbye to them and went on to Macedonia.
But thanks be to God, who always leads us as captives in Christ's triumphal procession and uses us to spread the aroma of the knowledge of him everywhere.

Philippians 4:6-7 NLT
Don't worry about anything; instead, pray about everything. Tell God what you need, and thank him for all he has done. Then you will experience God's peace, which exceeds anything we can understand. His peace will guard your hearts and minds as you live in Christ Jesus.

Mark 6:31 ESV
And he said to them, "Come away by yourselves to a desolate place and rest a while." For many were coming and going, and they had no leisure even to eat.

Matthew 8:24 ESV
And behold, there arose a great storm on the sea, so that the boat was being swamped by the waves; but he was asleep.

Matthew 26:45 ESV
Then he came to the disciples and said to them, "Sleep and take your rest later on. See, the hour is at hand, and the Son of Man is betrayed into the hands of sinners.

Jeremiah 6:16 ESV
Thus says the LORD:"Stand by the roads, and look, and ask for the ancient paths, where the good way is; and walk in it, and find rest for your souls. But they said, 'We will not walk in it.'

Matthew 11:28-29 NLT
Then Jesus said, "Come to me, all of you who are weary and carry heavy burdens, and I will give you rest. Take my yoke upon you. Let me teach you, because I am humble and gentle at heart, and you will find rest for your souls.

Hebrews 4:9-10 NLT
So there is a special rest still waiting for the people of God. For all who have entered into God's rest have rested from their labors, just as God did after creating the world.

Revelation 6:11 ESV
Then they were each given a white robe and told to rest a little longer, until the number of their fellow servants and their brothers should be complete, who were to be killed as they themselves had been.

Revelation 14:13 ESV

And I heard a voice from heaven saying, "Write this: Blessed are the dead who die in the Lord from now on." "Blessed indeed," says the Spirit, "that they may rest from their labors, for their deeds follow them!"

Excellent site for additional Bible translations:
http://www.biblegateway.com/resources/commentaries/
Excellent resource for additional Bible study:
(Be sure to read the instructions on their page)
http://www.blueletterbible.org/commentaries/

Rest - Christian Quotes

"The bow cannot be always bent without fear of breaking. Repose is as needful to the mind as sleep to the body... Rest time is not waste time. It is economy to gather fresh strength."
Charles Spurgeon

"Someone may ask, "But why should I rise early?" To remain too long in bed is a waste of time. Wasting time is unbecoming of a saint who is bought by the precious blood of Jesus. His time and all he has is to be used for the Lord. If we sleep more than is necessary for the refreshment of the body, it is wasting time the Lord has entrusted us to be used for His glory, for our own benefit, and for the benefit of the saints and unbelievers around us."
George Muller

"Measure the time of your sleep appropriately so that you do not waste your precious morning hours sluggishly in your bed. Let the time of your sleep be matched to your health and labor, and not to slothful pleasure."
Richard Baxter

"So long as we are occupied with any other object than God Himself, there will be neither rest for the heart nor peace for the mind. But when we receive all that enters our lives as from His hand, then, no matter what may be our circumstances or surroundings--whether in a hovel or prison-dungeon, or at a martyr's stake--we shall be enabled to say, " The lines are fallen unto me in pleasant places" (Ps. 16:6). But that is the language of faith, not of sight nor of sense."
A. W. Pink

"Rest time is not waste time. It is economy to gather fresh strength... It is wisdom to take occasional furlough. In the long run, we shall do more by sometimes doing less.}
Charles Spurgeon

"The sovereign God wants to be loved for Himself and honored for Himself, but that is only part of what He wants. The other part is that He wants us to know that when we have Him we have everything - we have all the rest."
A. W. Tozer

"Riches have never yet given anybody either peace or rest."
Billy Sunday

"It is only in proportion as the Christian manifests the fruit of a genuine conversion that he is entitled to regard himself and be regarded by others as one of the called and elect of God. It is just in proportion as we add to our faith the other Christian graces that we have solid ground on which to rest in the assurance we belong to the family of Christ. It is not those who are governed by self-will, but "as many as are led by the Spirit of God, they are the sons of God" (Rom. 8:14)."
A. W. Pink

"Genuine faith that saves the soul has for its main element - trust - absolute rest of the whole soul - on the Lord Jesus Christ to save me, whether He died in particular or in special to save me or not, and relying, as I am, wholly and alone on Him, I am saved."
Charles Spurgeon

"Jesus is hungry but feeds others; He grows weary but offers others rest; He is the King Messiah but pays tribute; He is called the devil but casts out demons; He dies the death of a sinner but comes to save His people from their sins; He is sold for thirty pieces of silver but gives His life a ransom for many; He will not turn stones to bread for Himself but gives His own body as bread for people."
D. A. Carson

"In these times, God's people must trust him for rest of body and soul."
David Wilkerson

Serving

Serving - Bible Verses

Malachi 3:17-18 NLT
"They will be my people," says the Lord of Heaven's Armies. "On the day when I act in judgment, they will be my own special treasure. I will spare them as a father spares an obedient child. Then you will again see the difference between the righteous and the wicked, between those who serve God and those who do not."

John 12:26 NIV
Whoever serves me must follow me; and where I am, my servant also will be. My Father will honor the one who serves me.

1 Thessalonians 1:8-10 NIV
The Lord's message rang out from you not only in Macedonia and Achaia—your faith in God has become known everywhere. Therefore we do not need to say anything about it, for they themselves report what kind of reception you gave us. They tell how you turned to God from idols to serve the living and true God, and to wait for his Son from heaven, whom he raised from the dead—Jesus, who rescues us from the coming wrath.

Hebrews 6:10 ESV
For God is not unjust so as to overlook your work and the love that you have shown for his name in serving the saints, as you still do.

Hebrews 9:13-14 NIV
The blood of goats and bulls and the ashes of a heifer sprinkled on those who are ceremonially unclean sanctify them so that they are outwardly clean. How much more, then, will the blood of Christ, who through the eternal Spirit offered himself unblemished to God, cleanse our consciences from acts that lead to death, so that we may serve the living God!

Revelation 7:14-15 ESV

I said to him, "My lord, you know." And he said to me, "These are the ones who come out of the great tribulation, and they have washed their robes and made them white in the blood of the Lamb. For this reason, they are before the throne of God; and they serve Him day and night in His temple; and He who sits on the throne will spread His tabernacle over them.

Matthew 6:24 ESV

No one can serve two masters, for either he will hate the one and love the other, or he will be devoted to the one and despise the other. You cannot serve God and money.

Luke 22:27 ESV

For who is the greater, one who reclines at table or one who serves? Is it not the one who reclines at table? But I am among you as the one who serves.

Romans 12:1 KJV

I beseech you therefore, brethren, by the mercies of God, that ye present your bodies a living sacrifice, holy, acceptable unto God, which is your reasonable service.

Romans 12:10-11 ESV

Love one another with brotherly affection. Outdo one another in showing honor. Do not be slothful in zeal, be fervent in spirit, serve the Lord.

Ephesians 6:6-8 NIV

Obey them not only to win their favor when their eye is on you, but as slaves of Christ, doing the will of God from your heart. 7 Serve wholeheartedly, as if you were serving the Lord, not people, 8 because you know that the Lord will reward each one for whatever good they do, whether they are slave or free.

Romans 12:4-7 NLT

Just as our bodies have many parts and each part has a special function, so it is with Christ's body. We are many parts of one body, and we all belong to each other.

In his grace, God has given us different gifts for doing certain things well. So if God has given you the ability to prophesy, speak out with as much faith as God has given you. If your gift is serving others, serve them well. If you are a teacher, teach well.

Romans 15:15-16 NLT
Even so, I have been bold enough to write about some of these points, knowing that all you need is this reminder. For by God's grace, I am a special messenger from Christ Jesus to you Gentiles. I bring you the Good News so that I might present you as an acceptable offering to God, made holy by the Holy Spirit.

1 Corinthians 9:13 ESV
Do you not know that those who are employed in the temple service get their food from the temple, and those who serve at the altar share in the sacrificial offerings?

Acts 20:18-21 NLT
When they arrived he declared, "You know that from the day I set foot in the province of Asia until now I have done the Lord's work humbly and with many tears. I have endured the trials that came to me from the plots of the Jews. I never shrank back from telling you what you needed to hear, either publicly or in your homes. I have had one message for Jews and Greeks alike —the necessity of repenting from sin and turning to God, and of having faith in our Lord Jesus.

Acts 26:6-7 ESV
And now I stand and am judged for the hope of the promise made of God, unto our fathers: Unto which promise our twelve tribes, instantly serving God day and night, hope to come.

Galatians 5:13 ESV
For you were called to freedom, brothers. Only do not use your freedom as an opportunity for the flesh, but through love serve one another.

Colossians 3:23-24 NLT

Work willingly at whatever you do, as though you were working for the Lord rather than for people. Remember that the Lord will give you an inheritance as your reward, and that the Master you are serving is Christ.

1 Peter 1:12 ESV

It was revealed to them that they were serving not themselves but you, in the things that have now been announced to you through those who preached the good news to you by the Holy Spirit sent from heaven, things into which angels long to look.

Excellent site for additional Bible translations:
http://www.biblegateway.com/resources/commentaries/
Excellent resource for additional Bible study:
(Be sure to read the instructions on their page)
http://www.blueletterbible.org/commentaries/

Serving - Christian Quotes

"Work! Walk through every open door; be ready in season and out of season as if everything depended on your labor. This is one of the great secrets in connection with successful service for the Lord – work as if everything depended on your diligence, and trust in the blessing of the Lord to bring success."
George Muller

"We are prepared to serve the Lord only by sacrifice. We are fit for the work of God only when we have wept over it, prayed about it, and then we are enabled by Him to tackle the job that needs to be done. May God give to us hearts that bleed, eyes that are wide open to see, minds that are clear to interpret God's purposes, wills that are obedient, and a determination that is utterly unflinching as we set about the tasks He would have us do."
Alan Redpath

"Are you still diligently living for God and serving Him, even in these last days? Now is not the time to ease up, but to charge forward and continue living for the Lord."
Paul Chappell

"God's people cannot be shamed into serving God; they need to be challenged."
Jack Hyles

"In the Kingdom of God, service is not a stepping-stone to nobility: it is nobility, the only kind of nobility that is recognized."
T.W. Manson

"I am tired in the Lord's work, but not tired of it."
George Whitfield

"Expect great things from God; attempt great things for God."
William Carey

"If you have no opposition in the place you serve, you're serving in the wrong place."
G. Campbell Morgan

"Good duties must not be pressed and beaten out of us, as the waters came out of a rock when Moses smote it with his rod; but must freely drop from us, as myrrh from the tree, or honey from the comb."
Thomas Watson

The supreme test of service is this: For whom am I doing this? Much that we call service to Christ is not such at all....If we are doing this for Christ, we shall not care for human reward or even recognition.
A. T. Pierson

"If any occupation or association is found to hinder our communion with God or our enjoyment of spiritual things, then it must be abandoned. Anything in my habits or ways which mars happy fellowship with the brethren or robs me of power in service, is to be unsparingly judged and made an end of-- 'burned.' Whatever I cannot do for God's glory must be avoided."
A. W. Pink

Sick

Sick - Bible Verses

Deuteronomy 7:15 NIV
The Lord will keep you free from every disease. He will not inflict on you the horrible diseases you knew in Egypt, but he will inflict them on all who hate you.

Exodus 23:25 ESV
You shall serve the Lord your God, and he will bless your bread and your water, and I will take sickness away from among you.

Psalm 34:19 ESV
Many are the afflictions of the righteous, but the Lord delivers him out of them all.

Psalm 105:37 NIV
He brought them forth also with silver and gold: and there was not one feeble person among their tribes.

Psalm 107:20 ESV
He sent out his word and healed them, and delivered them from their destruction.

Jeremiah 30:17 NASB
'For I will restore you to health
And I will heal you of your wounds,' declares the Lord,
'Because they have called you an outcast, saying:
"It is Zion; no one cares for her."'

Matthew 12:15 ESV
Jesus, aware of this, withdrew from there. And many followed him, and he healed them all

Matthew 14:14 ESV
When he went ashore he saw a great crowd, and he had compassion on them and healed their sick.

Acts 10:37-38 NIV
you yourselves know the thing which took place throughout all Judea, starting from Galilee, after the baptism which John proclaimed. You know of Jesus of Nazareth, how God anointed Him with the Holy Spirit and with power, and how He went about doing good and healing all who were oppressed by the devil, for God was with Him..

John 11:41-45 NASB
So they removed the stone. Then Jesus raised His eyes, and said, "Father, I thank You that You have heard Me. I knew that You always hear Me; but because of the people standing around I said it, so that they may believe that You sent Me." When He had said these things, He cried out with a loud voice, "Lazarus, come forth." The man who had died came forth, bound hand and foot with wrappings, and his face was wrapped around with a cloth. Jesus *said to them, "Unbind him, and let him go."
Therefore many of the Jews who came to Mary, and saw what He had done, believed in Him.

Acts 9:1-9 NIV
Meanwhile, Saul was still breathing out murderous threats against the Lord's disciples. He went to the high priest and asked him for letters to the synagogues in Damascus, so that if he found any there who belonged to the Way, whether men or women, he might take them as prisoners to Jerusalem. As he neared Damascus on his journey, suddenly a light from heaven flashed around him. He fell to the ground and heard a voice say to him, "Saul, Saul, why do you persecute me?"
"Who are you, Lord?" Saul asked.
"I am Jesus, whom you are persecuting," he replied. "Now get up and go into the city, and you will be told what you must do."
The men traveling with Saul stood there speechless; they heard the sound but did not see anyone. Saul got up from the ground, but when he opened

his eyes he could see nothing. So they led him by the hand into Damascus. For three days he was blind, and did not eat or drink anything.

2 Corinthians 1:8-11 NLT
We think you ought to know, dear brothers and sisters, about the trouble we went through in the province of Asia. We were crushed and overwhelmed beyond our ability to endure, and we thought we would never live through it. In fact, we expected to die. But as a result, we stopped relying on ourselves and learned to rely only on God, who raises the dead. And he did rescue us from mortal danger, and he will rescue us again. We have placed our confidence in him, and he will continue to rescue us. And you are helping us by praying for us. Then many people will give thanks because God has graciously answered so many prayers for our safety.

Matthew 10:1 KJV
And when he had called unto him his twelve disciples, he gave them power against unclean spirits, to cast them out, and to heal all manner of sickness and all manner of disease.

Luke 9:1 KJV
Then he called his twelve disciples together, and gave them power and authority over all devils, and to cure diseases.

Acts 14:3 KJV
Long time therefore abode they speaking boldly in the Lord, which gave testimony unto the word of his grace, and granted signs and wonders to be done by their hands.

Acts 28:8 NASB
And it happened that the father of Publius was lying in bed afflicted with recurrent fever and dysentery; and Paul went in to see him and after he had prayed, he laid his hands on him and healed him.

Hebrews 4:16 KJV
Let us therefore come boldly unto the throne of grace, that we may obtain mercy, and find grace to help in time of need.

James 5:15-16 NLT

Such a prayer offered in faith will heal the sick, and the Lord will make you well. And if you have committed any sins, you will be forgiven.

Confess your sins to each other and pray for each other so that you may be healed. The earnest prayer of a righteous person has great power and produces wonderful results.

Excellent site for additional Bible translations:
http://www.biblegateway.com/resources/commentaries/
Excellent resource for additional Bible study:
(Be sure to read the instructions on their page)
http://www.blueletterbible.org/commentaries/

Sick - Christian Quotes

"I venture to say that the greatest earthly blessing that God can give to any of us is health, with the exception of sickness. Sickness has frequently been of more use to the saints of God than health has."
C.H. Spurgeon

"The storms of winter often bring out the defects in a man's dwelling, and sickness often exposes the gracelessness of a man's soul. Surely anything that makes us find out the real character of our faith is a good."
J.C. Ryle

"I wish you could convince yourself that GOD is often (in some sense) nearer to us, and more effectually present with us, in sickness than in health."
Brother Lawrence

"I venture to say that the greatest earthly blessing that God can give to any of us is health, with the exception of sickness. Sickness has frequently been of more use to the saints of God than health has."
Charles Spurgeon

"Health is a good thing; but sickness is far better, if it leads us to God."
J.C. Ryle

"I will trust Him. Whatever, wherever I am, I can never be thrown away. If I am in sickness, my sickness may serve Him; in perplexity, my perplexity may serve Him; if I am in sorrow, my sorrow may serve Him. My sickness, or perplexity, or sorrow may be necessary causes of some great end, which is quite beyond us. He does nothing in vain."
John Henry Newman

Sin

Sin - Bible Verses

Romans 3:23 NLT
For everyone has sinned; we all fall short of God's glorious standard.

Isaiah 64:6 NLT
We are all infected and impure with sin.
　　When we display our righteous deeds,
　　they are nothing but filthy rags.
Like autumn leaves, we wither and fall,
　　and our sins sweep us away like the wind.

Proverbs 28:13 NLT
People who conceal their sins will not prosper, but if they confess and turn from them, they will receive mercy.

Hosea 5:15 NLT
Then I will return to my place
　　until they admit their guilt and turn to me.
For as soon as trouble comes,
　　they will earnestly search for me."

1 John 1:7-9 ESV
But if we walk in the light, as he is in the light, we have fellowship with one another, and the blood of Jesus, his Son, purifies us from all sin.
If we claim to be without sin, we deceive ourselves and the truth is not in us.
If we confess our sins, he is faithful and just and will forgive us our sins and purify us from all unrighteousness.

Luke 17:3-4 NLT
So watch yourselves.

"If your brother or sister sins against you, rebuke them; and if they repent, forgive them. Even if they sin against you seven times in a day and seven times come back to you saying 'I repent,' you must forgive them."

Colossians 3:5-6 NIV
Put to death, therefore, whatever belongs to your earthly nature: sexual immorality, impurity, lust, evil desires and greed, which is idolatry. Because of these, the wrath of God is coming.

Galatians 5:19-21 NASB
Now the deeds of the flesh are evident, which are: immorality, impurity, sensuality, idolatry, sorcery, enmities, strife, jealousy, outbursts of anger, disputes, dissensions, factions, envying, drunkenness, carousing, and things like these, of which I forewarn you, just as I have forewarned you, that those who practice such things will not inherit the kingdom of God.

1 Corinthians 15:57 NLT
But thank God! He gives us victory over sin and death through our Lord Jesus Christ.

Romans 8:1 NLT
So now there is no condemnation for those who belong to Christ Jesus.

Excellent site for additional Bible translations:
http://www.biblegateway.com/resources/commentaries/
Excellent resource for additional Bible study:
(Be sure to read the instructions on their page)
http://www.blueletterbible.org/commentaries/

Sin - Christian Quotes

"And indeed, there is no little sin, because there is no little God to sin against. In general, what to (humans) seems a small offense, to Him who knows the heart may appear a heinous crime."
John Wesley

"Sin is believing the lie that you are self-created, self-dependent and self-sustained."
Augustine

"What is sin? Sin is a species of rebellion against God. It is self-pleasing: it is the utter ignoring of God's claims: being completely indifferent whether my conduct pleases or displeases Him."
A.W. Pink

"If Christ has died for me – ungodly as I am, without strength as I am – then I can no longer live in sin, but must arouse myself to love and serve Him who has redeemed me. I cannot trifle with the evil that killed my best Friend. I must be holy for his sake. How can I live in sin when He has died to save me from it?"
C.H. Spurgeon

"Look to the cross, and hate your sin, for sin nailed your Well Beloved to the tree. Look up to the cross, and you will kill sin, for the strength of Jesus' love will make you strong to put down your tendencies to sin."
C.H. Spurgeon

"It does not spoil your happiness to confess your sin. The unhappiness is in not making the confession."
C.H. Spurgeon

"When a man has judged himself, Satan is put out of office. When he lays anything to a saint's charge, he is able to retort and say, "It is true, Satan, I am guilty of these sins, but I have judged myself already for them; and

having condemned myself in the lower court of conscience, God will acquit me in the upper court of heaven."
Thomas Watson

"The Bible teaches that all sin, past, present, and future, is forgiven through faith in the atoning death and resurrection of Jesus Christ. Eternal destiny is sealed and set at the moment of justifying faith. Our depth of intimacy, fellowship and joy is certainly affected adversely when we fail to confess and repent of daily sin. But our eternal destiny has already and forever been determined. We must recognize the distinction between the eternal forgiveness of the guilt of sin that is ours the moment we embrace Jesus in faith, and that temporal forgiveness of sin we receive on a daily basis that enables us to experience the happiness of intimacy with the Father [when we confess our sin]."
Sam Storms

Strength

Strength - Bible Verses

Isaiah 40:28-31 NLT
Have you never heard?
   Have you never understood?
The Lord is the everlasting God,
   the Creator of all the earth.
He never grows weak or weary.
   No one can measure the depths of his understanding.
He gives power to the weak
   and strength to the powerless.
Even youths will become weak and tired,
   and young men will fall in exhaustion.
But those who trust in the Lord will find new strength.
   They will soar high on wings like eagles.
They will run and not grow weary.
   They will walk and not faint.

Isaiah 41:10 ESV
fear not, for I am with you;   be not dismayed, for I am your God; I will strengthen you, I will help you, I will uphold you with my righteous right hand.

1 Chronicles 16:11 NLT
Search for the Lord and for his strength;
   continually seek him.

Exodus 15:2 ESV
The LORD is my strength and my song, and he has become my salvation; this is my God, and I will praise him, my father's God, and I will exalt him.

Philippians 4:13
I can do all things through him who strengthens me.

Psalm 18:32-34 ESV
the God who equipped me with strength and made my way blameless. He made my feet like the feet of a deer and set me secure on the heights. He trains my hands for war, so that my arms can bend a bow of bronze.

1 Corinthians 10:13 NLT
The temptations in your life are no different from what others experience. And God is faithful. He will not allow the temptation to be more than you can stand. When you are tempted, he will show you a way out so that you can endure.

Psalm 119:23 ESV
Even though princes sit plotting against me, your servant will meditate on your statutes.

1 Samuel 30:6 ESV
And David was greatly distressed, for the people spoke of stoning him, because all the people were bitter in soul, each for his sons and daughters. But David strengthened himself in the LORD his God.

2 Timothy 4:17 ESV
But the Lord stood by me and strengthened me, so that through me the message might be fully proclaimed and all the Gentiles might hear it. So I was rescued from the lion's mouth.

1 Peter 4:11 ESV
whoever speaks, as one who speaks oracles of God; whoever serves, as one who serves by the strength that God supplies—in order that in everything God may be glorified through Jesus Christ. To him belong glory and dominion forever and ever. Amen.

Genesis 22:1-3 NLT
Some time later God tested Abraham. He said to him, "Abraham!"
"Here I am," he replied.

Then God said, "Take your son, your only son, whom you love—Isaac—and go to the region of Moriah. Sacrifice him there as a burnt offering on a mountain I will show you."

Early the next morning Abraham got up and loaded his donkey. He took with him two of his servants and his son Isaac. When he had cut enough wood for the burnt offering, he set out for the place God had told him about.

Psalm 27:1 NASB
The Lord is my light and my salvation;
Whom shall I fear?
The Lord is the defense of my life;
Whom shall I dread?

Matthew 17:20 SEV
He said to them, "Because of your little faith. For truly, I say to you, if you have faith like a grain of mustard seed, you will say to this mountain, 'Move from here to there,' and it will move, and nothing will be impossible for you."

Mark 10:52 ESV
And Jesus said to him, "Go your way; your faith has made you well." And immediately he recovered his sight and followed him on the way.

Matthew 21:21 ESV
And Jesus answered them, "Truly, I say to you, if you have faith anddo not doubt, you will not only do what has been done to the fig tree, but even if you say to this mountain, 'Be taken up and thrown into the sea,' it will happen.

Deuteronomy 31:6 NIV
Be strong and courageous. Do not be afraid or terrified because of them, for the Lord your God goes with you; he will never leave you nor forsake you."

John 16:33 ESV
I have said these things to you, that in me you may have peace. In the world you will have tribulation. But take heart; I have overcome the world."

Psalm 23:4 NIV
Even though I walk through the valley of the shadow of death, I will fear no evil, for you are with me; your rod and your staff, they comfort me.

Zephaniah 3:17 NIV
The Lord your God is with you,
   the Mighty Warrior who saves.
He will take great delight in you;
   in his love he will no longer rebuke you,
   but will rejoice over you with singing."

2 Corinthians 4:16-18 NIV
Therefore we do not lose heart, but though our outer man is decaying, yet our inner man is being renewed day by day. For momentary, light affliction is producing for us an eternal weight of glory far beyond all comparison, while we look not at the things which are seen, but at the things which are not seen; for the things which are seen are temporal, but the things which are not seen are eternal.

2 Timothy 1:7 NASB
For God has not given us a spirit of timidity, but of power and love and discipline.

Job 13:15 ESV
Though he slay me, I will hope in him; yet I will argue my ways to his face.

Romans 5:5 NASB
and hope does not disappoint, because the love of God has been poured out within our hearts through the Holy Spirit who was given to us.

Excellent site for additional Bible translations:
http://www.biblegateway.com/resources/commentaries/
Excellent resource for additional Bible study:
(Be sure to read the instructions on their page)
http://www.blueletterbible.org/commentaries/

Strength - Christian Quotes

If we are whimpering, and sniveling, and begging to be spared the discipline of life that is sent to knock some smatterings of manhood into us, the answer to that prayer may never come at all. Thank God! If you are not bleating to get off, but asking to be given grace and strength to see this through with honour, "The very day" you pray that prayer, the answer always comes.
A. J. Gossip

Before He furnishes the abundant supply, we must first be made conscious of our emptiness. Before he gives strength, we must be made to feel our weakness. Slow, painfully slow, are we to learn this lesson; and slower still to own our nothingness and take the place of helplessness before the Mighty One.
A. W. Pink

"Those who serve God must serve Him in His own way, and in His strength, or He will never accept their service. That which man doth, unaided by divine strength, God can never own. The mere fruits of the earth He casteth away; He will only reap that corn, the seed of which was sown from heaven, watered by grace, and ripened by the sun of divine love. God will empty out all that thou hast before He will put His own into thee; He will first clean out thy granaries before He will fill them with the finest of the wheat. The river of God is full of water; but not one drop of it flows from earthly springs. God will have no strength used in His battles but the strength which He Himself imparts. Are you mourning over your own weakness? Take courage, for there must be a consciousness of weakness before the Lord will give thee victory. Your emptiness is but the preparation for your being filled, and your casting down is but the making ready for your lifting up."
Charles Spurgeon

"The danger may exceed thy resistance, but not God's assistance; the enemies' power may surpass thy strength, their subtlety outwit thy prudence, but neither can excel the wisdom and might of God that is with thee."

Abraham Wright

"Trying to do the Lord's work in your own strength is the most confusing, exhausting, and tedious of all work. But when you are filled with the Holy Spirit, then the ministry of Jesus just flows out of you."
Corrie Ten Boom

"If you partner with God, Make your plans big!" I encourage you today to make God your partner. Whatever your burden is that caused you to search for strength, give it up to him now. Do not let another minute go by without completely surrendering your burdens to Him. God wants to be your strength. Surrender to Him in your weakness and let Him show Himself strong. Remember if God brings you to it, He will bring you through it!"
D. L. Moody

"Before He furnishes the abundant supply, we must first be made conscious of our emptiness. before he gives strength, we must be made to feel our weakness. Slow, painfully slow, are we to learn this lesson; and slower still to own our nothingness and take the place of helplessness before the Mighty One."
Arthur W. Pink

Stress

Stress - Bible Verses

John 14:27 ESV
Peace I leave with you; my peace I give to you. Not as the world gives do I give to you. Let not your hearts be troubled, neither let them be afraid.

Isaiah 40:30-31 NASB
Though youths grow weary and tired,
And vigorous young men stumble badly,
Yet those who wait for the Lord
Will gain new strength;
They will mount up with wings like eagles,
They will run and not get tired,
They will walk and not become weary.

Malachi 4:2 ESV
But for you who fear my name, the sun of righteousness shall rise with healing in its wings. You shall go out leaping like calves from the stall.

Romans 8:6 NASB
For the mind set on the flesh is death, but the mind set on the Spirit is life and peace,

Romans 16:20 NASB
The God of peace will soon crush Satan under your feet.
The grace of our Lord Jesus be with you.

Philippians 4:6-7 NASB
Be anxious for nothing, but in everything by prayer and supplication with thanksgiving let your requests be made known to God. And the peace of God, which surpasses all comprehension, will guard your hearts and your minds in Christ Jesus.

1 Peter 5:6-7 NIV
Humble yourselves, therefore, under God's mighty hand, that he may lift you up in due time. Cast all your anxiety on him because he cares for you.

Psalm 37:5 ESV
Commit your way to the LORD; trust in him, and he will act.

Psalm 55:22 ESV
Cast your burden on the LORD, and he will sustain you; he will never permit the righteous to be moved.

Psalm 103:1-5 NIV
Praise the Lord, my soul;
   all my inmost being, praise his holy name.
Praise the Lord, my soul,
   and forget not all his benefits—
who forgives all your sins
   and heals all your diseases,
who redeems your life from the pit
   and crowns you with love and compassion,
who satisfies your desires with good things
   so that your youth is renewed like the eagle's.

Proverbs 16:3 ESV
Commit your work to the LORD, and your plans will be established.

Jeremiah 17:7-8 NIV
"But blessed is the one who trusts in the Lord,
   whose confidence is in him.
They will be like a tree planted by the water
   that sends out its roots by the stream.
It does not fear when heat comes;
   its leaves are always green.
It has no worries in a year of drought
   and never fails to bear fruit."

Romans 12:2 ESV

Do not be conformed to this world, but be transformed by the renewal of your mind, that by testing you may discern what is the will of God, what is good and acceptable and perfect.

James 1:2-4 NLT

Dear brothers and sisters, when troubles come your way, consider it an opportunity for great joy. For you know that when your faith is tested, your endurance has a chance to grow. So let it grow, for when your endurance is fully developed, you will be perfect and complete, needing nothing.

Isaiah 55:1-3 NLT

"Is anyone thirsty?
  Come and drink—
  even if you have no money!
Come, take your choice of wine or milk—
  it's all free!
Why spend your money on food that does not give you strength?
  Why pay for food that does you no good?
Listen to me, and you will eat what is good.
  You will enjoy the finest food.
"Come to me with your ears wide open.
  Listen, and you will find life.
I will make an everlasting covenant with you.
  I will give you all the unfailing love I promised to David.

Habakkuk 3:17-19 NIV

Though the fig tree does not bud
  and there are no grapes on the vines,
though the olive crop fails
  and the fields produce no food,
though there are no sheep in the pen
  and no cattle in the stalls,
yet I will rejoice in the Lord,
  I will be joyful in God my Savior.

The Sovereign Lord is my strength;
> he makes my feet like the feet of a deer,
> he enables me to tread on the heights.

For the director of music. On my stringed instruments.

Matthew 11:28-30 NASB
"Come to Me, all who are weary and heavy-laden, and I will give you rest. Take My yoke upon you and learn from Me, for I am gentle and humble in heart, and you will find rest for your souls. For My yoke is easy and My burden is light."

Luke 10:41-42 NASB
But the Lord answered and said to her, "Martha, Martha, you are worried and bothered about so many things; but only one thing is necessary, for Mary has chosen the good part, which shall not be taken away from her."

John 12:32 KJV
And I, if I be lifted up from the earth, will draw all men unto me.

1 Corinthians 3:11 NIV
For no one can lay any foundation other than the one already laid, which is Jesus Christ.

Excellent site for additional Bible translations:
http://www.biblegateway.com/resources/commentaries/

Excellent resource for additional Bible study:
(Be sure to read the instructions on their page)
http://www.blueletterbible.org/commentaries/

Stress - Christian Quotes

"In almost everything that touches our everyday life on earth, God is pleased when we're pleased. He wills that we be as free as birds to soar and sing our maker's praise without anxiety [stress]."
A.W. Tozer

"True leadership is tested and proved in crises. The real leader is the one who can handle the stress. He is the one who can solve the problems, bear the burdens, find the solutions, and win the victories when everyone else is merely flustered, confounded, and perplexed."
John MacArthur

"Many of those who once were so passionately in love with Christ now run about pursuing their own interests. They're burdened down with stress and problems, chasing after riches and the things of this world."
David Wilkerson

"An unpeaceful mind cannot operate normally. Hence the Apostle teaches us to "have no anxiety [stress] about anything" (Phil. 4:6). Deliver all anxious thoughts to God as soon as they arise. Let the peace of God maintain your heart and mind (v. 7)."
Watchman Nee

Temptation

Temptation - Bible Verses

Matthew 6:13 ESV
And lead us not into temptation, but deliver us from evil.

Matthew 26:41 ESV
Watch and pray that you may not enter into temptation. The spirit indeed is willing, but the flesh is weak."

Luke 4:13 ESV
And when the devil had ended every temptation, he departed from him until an opportune time.

Luke 11:4 ESV
and forgive us our sins, for we ourselves forgive everyone who is indebted to us. And lead us not into temptation."

Luke 22:40 ESV
And when he came to the place, he said to them, "Pray that you may not enter into temptation."

1 Corinthians 7:2 NIV
But since sexual immorality is occurring, each man should have sexual relations with his own wife, and each woman with her own husband.

1 Corinthians 10:13 NIV
No temptation has overtaken you except what is common to mankind. And God is faithful; he will not let you be tempted beyond what you can bear. But when you are tempted, he will also provide a way out so that you can endure it.

1 Timothy 6:9 NIV
Those who want to get rich fall into temptation and a trap and into many foolish and harmful desires that plunge people into ruin and destruction.

Exodus 17:2 NIV
So they quarreled with Moses and said, "Give us water to drink."
Moses replied, "Why do you quarrel with me? Why do you put the Lord to the test?"

Exodus 20:20 NIV
"Don't be afraid," Moses answered them, "for God has come in this way to test you, and so that your fear of him will keep you from sinning!"

Deuteronomy 6:16 NLT
You must not test the Lord your God as you did when you complained at Massah.

1 Chronicles 29:17 NLT
I know, my God, that you examine our hearts and rejoice when you find integrity there. You know I have done all this with good motives, and I have watched your people offer their gifts willingly and joyously.

2 Chronicles 32:31 NLT
However, when ambassadors arrived from Babylon to ask about the remarkable events that had taken place in the land, God withdrew from Hezekiah in order to test him and to see what was really in his heart.

Psalm 26:2 ESV
Prove me, O LORD, and try me; test my heart and my mind

Jeremiah 9:7 ESV
Therefore thus says the LORD of hosts: "Behold, I will refine them and test them, for what else can I do, because of my people?

Jeremiah 17:10 NLT
But I, the Lord, search all hearts
   and examine secret motives.
I give all people their due rewards,
   according to what their actions deserve."

Malachi 3:10 NASB
Bring the whole tithe into the storehouse, so that there may be food in My house, and test Me now in this," says the Lord of hosts, "if I will not open for you the windows of heaven and pour out for you a blessing until it overflows.

Matthew 4:7 NASB
Jesus said to him, "On the other hand, it is written, 'You shall not put the Lord your God to the test.'"

Matthew 22:18 NASB
But Jesus perceived their malice, and said, "Why are you testing Me, you hypocrites?

Mark 8:11 ESV
The Pharisees came and began to argue with him, seeking from him a sign from heaven to test him.

Mark 12:15 ESV
But, knowing their hypocrisy, he said to them, "Why put me to the test? Bring me a denarius and let me look at it."

John 8:6 ESV
This they said to test him, that they might have some charge to bring against him. Jesus bent down and wrote with his finger on the ground.

Excellent site for additional Bible translations:
http://www.biblegateway.com/resources/commentaries/
Excellent resource for additional Bible study:
(Be sure to read the instructions on their page)

http://www.blueletterbible.org/commentaries/

Temptation - Christian Quotes

"No man knows how bad he is till he has tried very hard to be good. A silly idea is current that good people do not know what temptation means. This is an obvious lie. Only those who try to resist temptation know how strong it is. After all, you find out the strength of the German army by fighting it, not by giving in. A man who gives in to temptation after five minutes simply does not know what it would have been like an hour later. That is why bad people, in one sense, know very little about badness. They have lived a sheltered life by always giving in. We never find out the strength of the evil impulse inside us until we try to fight it."
C.S. Lewis

"Christ, because He was the only Man who never yielded to temptation, is also the only Man who knows to the full what temptation means."
C.S. Lewis

"When Christians find themselves exposed to temptation they should pray to God to uphold them, and when they are tempted they should not be discouraged. It is not a sin to be tempted; the sin is to fall into temptation."
D.L. Moody

"The first degree (of temptation) relates to the mind – it is dragged away from its duties by the deceit of sin. The second aims at the affections – they are enticed and entangled. The third overcomes the will – the consent of the will is the conception of actual sin. The fourth degree disrupts our way of life as sin is born into it. The fifth is the flesh's goal, a hardened life of sin, which leads to eternal death (James 1:14-15)."
Kris Lundgaard

"Let no man think himself to be holy because he is not tempted, for the holiest and highest in life have the most temptations. How much higher the hill is, so much is the wind there greater; so, how much higher the life is, so much the stronger is the temptation of the enemy."
John Wycliffe

"There is no point in praying for victory over temptation if we are not willing to make a commitment to say no to it."
Jerry Bridges
"God delights in our temptations and yet hates them. He delights in them when they drive us to prayer; He hates them when they drive us to despair."
Martin Luther

"Temptations, of course, cannot be avoided, but because we cannot prevent the birds from flying over our heads, there is no need that we should let them nest in our hair."
Martin Luther

Trials

Trials - Bible Verses

James 1:2-4 ESV
Count it all joy, my brothers, when you meet trials of various kinds, for you know that the testing of your faith produces steadfastness. And let steadfastness have its full effect, that you may be perfect and complete, lacking in nothing.

Romans 5:3-5 NASB
And not only this, but we also exult in our tribulations, knowing that tribulation brings about perseverance; and perseverance, proven character; and proven character, hope; and hope does not disappoint, because the love of God has been poured out within our hearts through the Holy Spirit who was given to us.

James 1:1-2 NIV
James, a servant of God and of the Lord Jesus Christ,
To the twelve tribes scattered among the nations:
Greetings.
Consider it pure joy, my brothers and sisters, whenever you face trials of many kinds,

Psalm 13:1-6 NIV
How long, Lord? Will you forget me forever?
　How long will you hide your face from me?
How long must I wrestle with my thoughts
　and day after day have sorrow in my heart?
　How long will my enemy triumph over me?
Look on me and answer, Lord my God.
　Give light to my eyes, or I will sleep in death,
and my enemy will say, "I have overcome him,"
　and my foes will rejoice when I fall.

But I trust in your unfailing love;
>   my heart rejoices in your salvation.
I will sing the Lord's praise,
>   for he has been good to me.

1 Peter 1:3-7 ESV

Blessed be the God and Father of our Lord Jesus Christ! According to his great mercy, he has caused us to be born again to a living hope through the resurrection of Jesus Christ from the dead, to an inheritance that is imperishable, undefiled, and unfading, kept in heaven for you, who by God's power are being guarded through faith for a salvation ready to be revealed in the last time. In this you rejoice, though now for a little while, if necessary, you have been grieved by various trials, so that the tested genuineness of your faith—more precious than gold that perishes though it is tested by fire—may be found to result in praise and glory and honor at the revelation of Jesus Christ.

2 Corinthians 12:7-10 NLT

even though I have received such wonderful revelations from God. So to keep me from becoming proud, I was given a thorn in my flesh, a messenger from Satan to torment me and keep me from becoming proud.
8 Three different times I begged the Lord to take it away. 9 Each time he said, "My grace is all you need. My power works best in weakness." So now I am glad to boast about my weaknesses, so that the power of Christ can work through me. 10 That's why I take pleasure in my weaknesses, and in the insults, hardships, persecutions, and troubles that I suffer for Christ. For when I am weak, then I am strong.

Genesis 22:1-14 NASB

Now it came about after these things, that God tested Abraham, and said to him, "Abraham!" And he said, "Here I am." He said, "Take now your son, your only son, whom you love, Isaac, and go to the land of Moriah, and offer him there as a burnt offering on one of the mountains of which I will tell you." So Abraham rose early in the morning and saddled his donkey, and took two of his young men with him and Isaac his son; and he split wood for the burnt offering, and arose and went to the place of which God had told him. On the third day Abraham raised his eyes and saw the place from a distance. Abraham said to his young men, "Stay here with the donkey, and I and the lad will go over there; and we will worship and return to you." Abraham took the wood of the burnt offering and laid it on Isaac his son, and he took in his hand the fire and the knife. So the two of them walked on together. Isaac spoke to Abraham his father and said, "My father!" And he said, "Here I am, my son." And he said, "Behold, the fire and the wood, but where is the lamb for the burnt offering?" Abraham said, "God will provide for Himself the lamb for the burnt offering, my son." So the two of them walked on together.

Then they came to the place of which God had told him; and Abraham built the altar there and arranged the wood, and bound his son Isaac and laid him on the altar, on top of the wood. Abraham stretched out his hand and took the knife to slay his son. But the angel of the Lord called to him from heaven and said, "Abraham, Abraham!" And he said, "Here I am." He said, "Do not stretch out your hand against the lad, and do nothing to him; for now I know that you fear God, since you have not withheld your son, your only son, from Me." Then Abraham raised his eyes and looked, and behold, behind him a ram caught in the thicket by his horns; and Abraham went and took the ram and offered him up for a burnt offering in the place of his son. Abraham called the name of that place The Lord Will Provide, as it is said to this day, "In the mount of the Lord it will be provided."

Job 1:1-22 NLT

There once was a man named Job who lived in the land of Uz. He was blameless—a man of complete integrity. He feared God and stayed away from evil. He had seven sons and three daughters. He owned 7,000 sheep, 3,000 camels, 500 teams of oxen, and 500 female donkeys. He also had many servants. He was, in fact, the richest person in that entire area.

Job's sons would take turns preparing feasts in their homes, and they would also invite their three sisters to celebrate with them. When these celebrations ended—sometimes after several days—Job would purify his children. He would get up early in the morning and offer a burnt offering for each of them. For Job said to himself, "Perhaps my children have sinned and have cursed God in their hearts." This was Job's regular practice.

Job's First Test

One day the members of the heavenly court came to present themselves before the Lord, and the Accuser, Satan, came with them. "Where have you come from?" the Lord asked Satan.

Satan answered the Lord, "I have been patrolling the earth, watching everything that's going on."

Then the Lord asked Satan, "Have you noticed my servant Job? He is the finest man in all the earth. He is blameless—a man of complete integrity. He fears God and stays away from evil."

Satan replied to the Lord, "Yes, but Job has good reason to fear God. You have always put a wall of protection around him and his home and his property. You have made him prosper in everything he does. Look how rich he is! But reach out and take away everything he has, and he will surely curse you to your face!"

"All right, you may test him," the Lord said to Satan. "Do whatever you want with everything he possesses, but don't harm him physically." So Satan left the Lord's presence.

One day when Job's sons and daughters were feasting at the oldest brother's house, a messenger arrived at Job's home with this news: "Your oxen were plowing, with the donkeys feeding beside them, when the Sabeans raided us. They stole all the animals and killed all the farmhands. I am the only one who escaped to tell you."

While he was still speaking, another messenger arrived with this news: "The fire of God has fallen from heaven and burned up your sheep and all the shepherds. I am the only one who escaped to tell you. While he was still speaking, a third messenger arrived with this news: "Three bands of Chaldean raiders have stolen your camels and killed your servants. I am the only one who escaped to tell you."

While he was still speaking, another messenger arrived with this news: "Your sons and daughters were feasting in their oldest brother's home. Suddenly, a powerful wind swept in from the wilderness and hit the house on all sides. The house collapsed, and all your children are dead. I am the only one who escaped to tell you."

Job stood up and tore his robe in grief. Then he shaved his head and fell to the ground to worship. He said,

"I came naked from my mother's womb,
   and I will be naked when I leave.

The Lord gave me what I had,
   and the Lord has taken it away.
Praise the name of the Lord!"
In all of this, Job did not sin by blaming God.

Excellent site for additional Bible translations:
http://www.biblegateway.com/resources/commentaries/
Excellent resource for additional Bible study:
(Be sure to read the instructions on their page)
http://www.blueletterbible.org/commentaries/

Trials - Christian Quotes

You will have no test of faith that will not fit you to be a blessing if you are obedient to the Lord. I never had a trial but when I got out of the deep river I found some poor pilgrim on the bank that I was able to help by that very experience.
A.B. Simpson

The devil tempts, that he may deceive; but God suffers us to be tempted, to try us. Temptation is a trial of our sincerity.
Thomas Watson

Of course one must take "sent to try us" the right way. God has not been trying an experiment on my faith or love in order to find out their quality. He knew it already. It was I who didn't.
C.S. Lewis

Trials come to prove and improve us.
Augustine

Whomever the Lord has adopted and deemed worthy of His fellowship ought to prepare themselves for a hard, toilsome, and unquiet life, crammed with very many and various kinds of evil. It is the Heavenly Father's will thus to exercise them so as to put His own children to a definite test. Beginning with Christ, His first-born, He follows this plan with all His children.
John Calvin

Faith upholds a Christian under all trials, by assuring him that every painful dispensation is under the direction of his Lord; that chastisements are a token of His love; that the season, measure, and continuance of his sufferings, are appointed by Infinite Wisdom, and designed to work for his everlasting good; and that grace and strength shall be afforded him, according to his need.
John Newton

Trials always change our relationship with God. Either they drive us to Him, or they drive us away from Him. The extent of our fear of Him and our awareness of His love for us determine in which direction we will move.
Jerry Bridges
The Practice of Godliness, NavPress, 1996, p. 179

In trial and weakness and trouble, He seeks to bring us low, until we learn that His grace is all, and to take pleasure in the very thing that brings us and keeps us low. His strength is made perfect in our weakness. His presence filling and satisfying our emptiness, becomes the secret of humility that need never fail. The humble man has learned the secret of abiding gladness. The weaker he feels, the lower he sinks, and the greater his humiliations appear, the more power and the presence of Christ are his portion.
Andrew Murray

For God to explain a trial would be to destroy its purpose, calling forth simple faith and implicit obedience.
Alfred Edersheim

You may readily judge whether you are a child of God or a hypocrite by seeing in what direction your soul turns in seasons of severe trial. The hypocrite flies to the world and finds a sort of comfort there. But the child of God runs to his Father and expects consolation only from the Lord's hand.
C.H. Spurgeon

There are two ways of getting out of a trial. One is simply to try to get rid of the trial, and be thankful when it is over. The other is to recognize the trial as a challenge from God to claim a larger blessing than we have ever had, and to hail it with delight as an opportunity of obtaining a larger measure of divine grace.
A.B. Simpson

The only way to learn strong faith is to endure great trials. I have learned my faith by standing firm amid severe testings.
George Muller

Truth

Truth - Bible Verses

Psalm 119:160 ESV
The sum of your word is truth, and every one of your righteous rules endures forever.

Daniel 10:21 ESV
But I will tell you what is inscribed in the book of truth: there is none who contends by my side against these except Michael, your prince.

John 17:17 ESV
Sanctify them in the truth; your word is truth.

Ephesians 1:13-14 NASB
In Him, you also, after listening to the message of truth, the gospel of your salvation—having also believed, you were sealed in Him with the Holy Spirit of promise, who is given as a pledge of our inheritance, with a view to the redemption of God's own possession, to the praise of His glory.

James 1:18 ESV
Of his own will he brought us forth by the word of truth, that we should be a kind of first fruits of his creatures.

Job 34:12 ESV
Of a truth, God will not do wickedly, and the Almighty will not pervert justice.

Psalm 25:5 ESV
Lead me in your truth and teach me, for you are the God of my salvation; for you I wait all the day long.

Psalm 43:3 ESV

Send out your light and your truth; let them lead me; let them bring me to your holy hill and to your dwelling!

Psalm 86:11 KJV

Teach me thy way, O Lord; I will walk in thy truth: unite my heart to fear thy name.

James 1:18 NLT

He chose to give birth to us by giving us his true word. And we, out of all creation, became his prized possession.

Matthew 22:16 NASB

And they sent their disciples to Him, along with the Herodians, saying, "Teacher, we know that You are truthful and teach the way of God in truth, and defer to no one; for You are not partial to any.

John 1:14 ESV

And the Word became flesh and dwelt among us, and we have seen his glory, glory as of the only Son from the Father, full of grace and truth.

John 8:31-32 NASB

So Jesus was saying to those Jews who had believed Him, "If you continue in My word, then you are truly disciples of Mine; and you will know the truth, and the truth will make you free."

John 17:8 NASB

for the words which You gave Me I have given to them; and they received them and truly understood that I came forth from You, and they believed that You sent Me.

Psalm 15:1-2 KJV

Lord, who shall abide in thy tabernacle? who shall dwell in thy holy hill?
He that walketh uprightly, and worketh righteousness, and speaketh the truth in his heart.

Zechariah 8:16 ESV
These are the things that you shall do: Speak the truth to one another; render in your gates judgments that are true and make for peace;

Ephesians 4:25 NIV
Therefore each of you must put off falsehood and speak truthfully to your neighbor, for we are all members of one body.

1 John 1:8 NIV
If we claim to be without sin, we deceive ourselves and the truth is not in us.

1 John 3:18 NLT
Dear children, let's not merely say that we love each other; let us show the truth by our actions.

Excellent site for additional Bible translations:
http://www.biblegateway.com/resources/commentaries/
Excellent resource for additional Bible study:
(Be sure to read the instructions on their page)
http://www.blueletterbible.org/commentaries/

Truth - Christian Quotes

"Today not only in philosophy but in politics, government, and individual morality, our generation sees solutions in terms of synthesis and not absolutes. When this happens, truth, as people have always thought of truth, has died."
Francis Schaeffer

"One never errs more safely than when one errs by too much loving the truth."
Augustine

"Nothing makes a man so virtuous as belief of the truth. A lying doctrine will soon beget a lying practice. A man cannot have an erroneous belief without by-and-by having an erroneous life. I believe the one thing naturally begets the other."
C.H. Spurgeon

"When regard for truth has been broken down or even slightly weakened, all things will remain doubtful."
Augustine

"I believe that in the end the truth will conquer."
John Wycliffe

"Let us rejoice in the truth, wherever we find its lamp burning." ~ Albert Schweitzer
"Never let us be guilty of sacrificing any portion of truth on the altar of peace."
J. C. Ryle

"As a matter of honor, one man owes it to another to manifest the truth."
Thomas Aquinas

"Do not burn false fire upon God's altar; do not pose and pretend, either to Him or to yourself, in your religious exercises; do not say more than you

mean, or use exaggerated language that goes beyond the facts, when speaking to Him whose word is truth."
A. J. Gossip

Trust

Trust - Bible Verses

Psalm 18:2 ESV
The Lord is my rock, my fortress and my deliverer;
    my God is my rock, in whom I take refuge,
    my shield and the horn of my salvation, my stronghold.

Psalm 91:2 NIV
I will say of the Lord, "He is my refuge and my fortress,
    my God, in whom I trust."

Nahum 1:7 NASB
The Lord is good,
A stronghold in the day of trouble,
And He knows those who take refuge in Him.

2 Samuel 22:31 NIV
"As for God, his way is perfect:
    The Lord's word is flawless;
    he shields all who take refuge in him.

Job 13:15 KJV
"Though he slay me, yet will I trust in him: but I will maintain mine own ways before him."

Psalm 7:1 NIV
Lord my God, I take refuge in you;
    save and deliver me from all who pursue me,

Psalm 25:1-2 NASB
To You, O Lord, I lift up my soul.

O my God, in You I trust,
Do not let me be ashamed;
Do not let my enemies exult over me.

Proverbs 30:5 KJV
"Every word of God is pure: he is a shield unto them that put their trust in him."

Psalm 9:10 NASB
And those who know Your name will put their trust in You,
For You, O Lord, have not forsaken those who seek You.

Psalm 22:4 NLT
Our ancestors trusted in you,
   and you rescued them.

Psalm 37:5 KJV
"Commit thy way unto the LORD; trust also in him; and he shall bring it to pass."

Psalm 56:3-4 NIV
When I am afraid, I put my trust in you.
   In God, whose word I praise—
in God I trust and am not afraid.
   What can mere mortals do to me?

Psalm 71:5 KJV
"For thou art my hope, O Lord GOD: thou art my trust from my youth."

Isaiah 26:3 KJV
"Thou wilt keep him in perfect peace, whose mind is stayed on thee: because he trusteth in thee."

1 Timothy 4:10 NIV
That is why we labor and strive, because we have put our hope in the living God, who is the Savior of all people, and especially of those who believe.

Psalm 20:7 KJV
Some trust in chariots, and some in horses: but we will remember the name of the Lord our God.

Psalm 32:10 ESV
Many are the sorrows of the wicked,
　　but steadfast love surrounds the one who trusts in the Lord.

Psalm 118:8 NASB
It is better to trust in the Lord than to put confidence in man.

Proverbs 3:5 NIV
Trust in the Lord with all your heart
　　and lean not on your own understanding;

Excellent site for additional Bible translations:
http://www.biblegateway.com/resources/commentaries/
Excellent resource for additional Bible study:
(Be sure to read the instructions on their page)
http://www.blueletterbible.org/commentaries/

Trust - Christian Quotes

"I will trust Him. Whatever, wherever I am, I can never be thrown away. If I am in sickness, my sickness may serve Him; in perplexity, my perplexity may serve Him; if I am in sorrow, my sorrow may serve Him. My sickness, or perplexity, or sorrow may be necessary causes of some great end, which is quite beyond us. He does nothing in vain."
John Henry Newman

"A person who wholly follows the Lord is one who believes that the promises of God are trustworthy, that He is with His people, and that they are well able to overcome."
Watchman Nee

"You have trusted Him in a few things, and He has not failed you. Trust Him now for everything, and see if He does not do for you exceeding abundantly above all that you could ever have asked or thought, not according to your power or capacity, but according to His own mighty power, that will work in you all the good pleasure of His most blessed will. You find no difficulty in trusting the Lord with the management of the universe and all the outward creation, and can your case be any more complex or difficult than these, that you need to be anxious or troubled about His management of it?"
Hannah Whitall Smith

"Satan is ever seeking to inject that poison into our hearts to distrust God's goodness - especially in connection with his commandments. That is what really lies behind all evil, lusting and disobedience. A discontent with our position and portion, a craving from something which God has wisely held from us. Reject any suggestion that God is unduly severe with you. Resist with the utmost abhorrence anything that causes you to doubt God's love and his lovingkindness toward you. Allow nothing to make you question the Father's love for his child."
Arthur W. Pink

"To trust Him means, of course, trying to do all that He says. There would be no sense in saying you trusted a person if you would not take his advice.

Thus if you have really handed yourself over to Him, it must follow that you are trying to obey Him. But trying in a new way, a less worried way. "
C. S. Lewis

"Fear is born of Satan, and if we would only take time to think a moment we would see that everything Satan says is founded upon a falsehood. He is the father of lies. Even his fears are falsehoods and his terrors ought to serve as encouragements. When Satan tells you, therefore, that some ill is going to come, you may quietly look in his face and tell him he is a liar. Instead of ill, goodness and mercy shall follow you all the days of your life. And then turn to your blessed Lord and say, What time I am afraid, I will trust in thee (Psalm 56:3). Every fear is distrust, and trust is the remedy for fear."
A. B. Simpson

"God will never, never, never let us down if we have faith and put our trust in Him. He will always look after us. So we must cleave to Jesus. Our whole life must simply be woven into Jesus."
Mother Teresa

Wisdom

Wisdom - Bible Verses

Job 12:12 NIV
Is not wisdom found among the aged?
   Does not long life bring understanding?

Job 28:28 NASB
"And to man He said, 'Behold, the fear of the Lord, that is wisdom;
And to depart from evil is understanding.'"

Psalm 111:10 NASB
The fear of the Lord is the beginning of wisdom;
A good understanding have all those who do His commandments;
His praise endures forever.

Proverbs 1:7 ESV
The fear of the LORD is the beginning of knowledge: but fools despise wisdom and instruction.

Proverbs 3:7 ESV
Be not wise in thine own eyes: fear the LORD, and depart from evil.

Proverbs 4:5-7 NASB
Acquire wisdom! Acquire understanding!
Do not forget nor turn away from the words of my mouth.
"Do not forsake her, and she will guard you;
Love her, and she will watch over you.
"The beginning of wisdom is: Acquire wisdom;
And with all your acquiring, get understanding.

Proverbs 9:10 NASB
The fear of the Lord is the beginning of wisdom,
And the knowledge of the Holy One is understanding.

Proverbs 11:2 NIV
When pride comes, then comes disgrace,
   but with humility comes wisdom.

Proverbs 11:30 NASB
The fruit of the righteous is a tree of life,
And he who is wise wins souls.

Proverbs 14:8 NASB
The wisdom of the sensible is to understand his way,
But the foolishness of fools is deceit.

Proverbs 16:16 NIV
How much better to get wisdom than gold,
   to get insight rather than silver!

Proverbs 29:15 NASB
The rod and reproof give wisdom,
But a child who gets his own way brings shame to his mother.

Ecclesiastes 7:12 ESV
For the protection of wisdom is like the protection of money,
   and the advantage of knowledge is that wisdom preserves the life of him who has it.

James 1:5-6 NIV
If any of you lacks wisdom, you should ask God, who gives generously to all without finding fault, and it will be given to you. But when you ask, you must believe and not doubt, because the one who doubts is like a wave of the sea, blown and tossed by the wind.

James 3:17 NLT
But the wisdom from above is first of all pure. It is also peace loving, gentle at all times, and willing to yield to others. It is full of mercy and good deeds. It shows no favoritism and is always sincere..

Excellent site for additional Bible translations:
http://www.biblegateway.com/resources/commentaries/
Excellent resource for additional Bible study:
(Be sure to read the instructions on their page)
http://www.blueletterbible.org/commentaries/

Wisdom - Christian Quotes

The simplicity of the gospel gives what the complexity of human wisdom promises but never delivers."
John MacArthur

"I need not despair because the living God is my partner. I do not have sufficient wisdom to meet these difficulties, but He is able to direct me. I can pour out my heart to God and ask Him to guide and direct me and to supply me with wisdom. Then I have to believe that He will do so. I can go with good courage to my business and expect help from Him in the next difficulty that may come before me."
George Muller

"To do anything less than commit ourselves completely to our Lord in simple trust during the troubling times in our lives is to insult His wisdom. To resist Him, question Him, doubt Him, or criticize what He allows in our lives is to deny that He is the only wise God, and claim that we are wiser than He."
Richard L. Strauss

"Wisdom is the right use of knowledge. To know is not to be wise. Many men know a great deal, and are all the greater fools for it. There is no fool so great a fool as a knowing fool. But to know how to use knowledge is to have wisdom."
Charles Spurgeon

"Every person in the world, including yourself, will encounter various trials throughout life. Satan seeks to defeat you by tempting you to trust your own wisdom, to live according to your self-centered feelings, and to gratify the desires of your flesh. In contrast, God's will is for you to be an overwhelming conqueror in all of these tests for His honor and glory."
John C. Broger

"Prayer girds human weakness with divine strength, turns human folly into heavenly wisdom, and gives to troubled mortals the peace of God. We know not what prayer can do."
Charles Spurgeon

"Not until we have become humble and teachable, standing in awe of God's holiness and sovereignty. acknowledging our own littleness, distrusting our own thoughts, and willing to have our minds turned upside down, can divine wisdom become ours."
J. I. Packer

"The word "philosophy" simply means "a pursuit of wisdom, the purpose of life, and a search for Truth." However, this quest, because it originates with man, can never find the answers. In fact, man cannot reach God or know God by intellectual pursuit."
Jimmy Swaggart

"Man, in his own wisdom, has developed a vast number of philosophies and theories seeking to explain one's thoughts, words, and actions. In doing so, man has pridefully sought to deny his own sinfulness and has confused any clear definition of God's standards of right and wrong."
John C. Broger

"The fear of the Lord helps us recognize our accountability to God for the stewardship of leadership. It motivates us to seek the Lord's wisdom and understanding in difficult situations. And it challenges us to give our all to the Lord by serving those we lead with love and humility."
Paul Chappell

Storms can bring fear, cloud judgment, and create confusion. Yet God promises that as you seek Him through prayer, He will give you wisdom to know how to proceed. The only way you will survive the storm will be on your knees.
Paul Chappell

Women

Women - Bible Verses

Titus 2:2-5 NLT
Teach the older men to be temperate, worthy of respect, self-controlled, and sound in faith, in love and in endurance.

Likewise, teach the older women to be reverent in the way they live, not to be slanderers or addicted to much wine, but to teach what is good. Then they can urge the younger women to love their husbands and children, to be self-controlled and pure, to be busy at home, to be kind, and to be subject to their husbands, so that no one will malign the word of God.

Proverbs 31 10-31 ESV
An excellent wife who can find?
   She is far more precious than jewels.
The heart of her husband trusts in her,
   and he will have no lack of gain.
She does him good, and not harm,
   all the days of her life.
She seeks wool and flax,
   and works with willing hands.
She is like the ships of the merchant;
   she brings her food from afar.
She rises while it is yet night
   and provides food for her household
   and portions for her maidens.
She considers a field and buys it;
   with the fruit of her hands she plants a vineyard.
She dresses herself with strength
   and makes her arms strong.
She perceives that her merchandise is profitable.
   Her lamp does not go out at night.
She puts her hands to the distaff,
   and her hands hold the spindle.

She opens her hand to the poor
   and reaches out her hands to the needy.
She is not afraid of snow for her household,
   for all her household are clothed in scarlet.
She makes bed coverings for herself;
   her clothing is fine linen and purple.
Her husband is known in the gates
   when he sits among the elders of the land.
She makes linen garments and sells them;
   she delivers sashes to the merchant.
Strength and dignity are her clothing,
   and she laughs at the time to come.
She opens her mouth with wisdom,
   and the teaching of kindness is on her tongue.
She looks well to the ways of her household
   and does not eat the bread of idleness.
Her children rise up and call her blessed;
   her husband also, and he praises her:
"Many women have done excellently,
   but you surpass them all."
Charm is deceitful, and beauty is vain,
   but a woman who fears the Lord is to be praised.
Give her of the fruit of her hands,
   and let her works praise her in the gates.

Proverbs 11:16 NLT
A gracious woman gains respect,
   but ruthless men gain only wealth.

Genesis 2:18 NLT
Then the Lord God said, "It is not good for the man to be alone. I will make a helper who is just right for him."

Genesis 2:21-24 NLT
So the Lord God caused the man to fall into a deep sleep. While the man slept, the Lord God took out one of the man's ribs and closed up the

opening. Then the Lord God made a woman from the rib, and he brought her to the man.

"At last!" the man exclaimed.
"This one is bone from my bone,
   and flesh from my flesh!
She will be called 'woman,'
   because she was taken from 'man.'"
This explains why a man leaves his father and mother and is joined to his wife, and the two are united into one.

1 Corinthians 11:3 KJV
But I would have you know, that the head of every man is Christ; and the head of the woman is the man; and the head of Christ is God.

Ephesians 5:22-23 KJV
Wives, submit yourselves to your own husbands as you do to the Lord. For the husband is the head of the wife as Christ is the head of the church, his body, of which he is the Savior.

1 Peter 3:1-2 NIV
Wives, in the same way submit yourselves to your own husbands so that, if any of them do not believe the word, they may be won over without words by the behavior of their wives, 2 when they see the purity and reverence of your lives.

Excellent site for additional Bible translations:
http://www.biblegateway.com/resources/commentaries/
Excellent resource for additional Bible study:
(Be sure to read the instructions on their page)
http://www.blueletterbible.org/commentaries/

Women - Christian Quotes

I cannot tell you how much I owe to the solemn word of my good mother.
Charles Spurgeon

I remember my mother's prayers and they have always followed me. They have clung to me all my life.
Abraham Lincoln

All places where women are excluded tend downward to barbarism; but the moment she is introduced, there come in with her courtesy, cleanliness, sobriety, and order.
Harriet Beecher Stowe

God is looking for imperfect men and women who have learned to walk in moment-by-moment dependence on the Holy Spirit. Christians who have come to terms with their inadequacies, fears, and failures. Believers who have become discontent with 'surviving' and have taken the time to investigate everything God has to offer in this life.
Charles Stanley

Earth has nothing more tender than a woman's heart when it is the abode of piety.
Martin Luther

I learned more about Christianity from my mother than from all the theologians in England.
John Wesley

She has a more influential and powerful role than any political, military, religious or educational figure. Her words are never fully forgotten. If you were blessed with a good mother, you will enjoy the advantages for the rest of your days. If your mother neglected you and her responsibilities, unfortunately the impact is almost certainly still felt today. Whether it's good or whether it's evil, a mother's impact is permanent. A child's mother

is arguably the most influential figure in their life, giving credence to the old adage: the hand that rocks the cradle rules the world.
Unknown

Worry

Worry - Bible Verses

Matthew 6:25-27 ESV
"Therefore I tell you, do not be anxious about your life, what you will eat or what you will drink, nor about your body, what you will put on. Is not life more than food, and the body more than clothing? Look at the birds of the air: they neither sow nor reap nor gather into barns, and yet your heavenly Father feeds them. Are you not of more value than they? And which of you by being anxious can add a single hour to his span of life?

Matthew 6:34 NIV
Therefore do not worry about tomorrow, for tomorrow will worry about itself. Each day has enough trouble of its own.

Matthew 11:28-30 ESV
Come to me, all who labor and are heavy laden, and I will give you rest. 29 Take my yoke upon you, and learn from me, for I am gentle and lowly in heart, and you will find rest for your souls. 30 For my yoke is easy, and my burden is light."

Luke 12:25 ESV
And which of you by being anxious can add a single hour to his span of life?

John 14:27 ESV
Peace I leave with you; my peace I give to you. Not as the world gives do I give to you. Let not your hearts be troubled, neither let them be afraid.

Colossians 3:15 ESV
And let the peace of Christ rule in your hearts, to which indeed you were called in one body. And be thankful.

2 Thessalonians 3:16 ESV
Now may the Lord of peace himself give you peace at all times in every way. The Lord be with you all.

Psalm 55:22 ESV
Cast your burden on the LORD, and he will sustain you; he will never permit the righteous to be moved

Philippians 4:6-7 NASB
Be anxious for nothing, but in everything by prayer and supplication with thanksgiving let your requests be made known to God. And the peace of God, which surpasses all comprehension, will guard your hearts and your minds in Christ Jesus.

1 Peter 5:7 ESV
casting all your anxieties on him, because he cares for you.

Psalm 23:4 ESV
Even though I walk through the valley of the shadow of death, I will fear no evil, for you are with me; your rod and your staff, they comfort me.

Isaiah 43:1-3 NASB
But now, thus says the Lord, your Creator, O Jacob,
And He who formed you, O Israel,
"Do not fear, for I have redeemed you;
I have called you by name; you are Mine!
"When you pass through the waters, I will be with you;
And through the rivers, they will not overflow you.
When you walk through the fire, you will not be scorched,
Nor will the flame burn you.
"For I am the Lord your God,
The Holy One of Israel, your Savior;
I have given Egypt as your ransom,
Cush and Seba in your place.

Hebrews 13:6 NASB
so that we confidently say,
"The Lord is my helper, I will not be afraid.
What will man do to me?"

Psalm 46:10 KJV
Be still, and know that I am God: I will be exalted among the heathen, I will be exalted in the earth.

Psalm 121:1-2 KJV
I will lift up mine eyes unto the hills, from whence cometh my help.
My help cometh from the Lord, which made heaven and earth.

Proverbs 3:5-6 NIV
Trust in the Lord with all your heart
   and lean not on your own understanding;
in all your ways submit to him,
   and he will make your paths straight

1 Corinthians 10:13 ESV
No temptation has overtaken you that is not common to man. God is faithful, and he will not let you be tempted beyond your ability, but with the temptation he will also provide the way of escape, that you may be able to endure it.

Romans 8:31 NIV
What, then, shall we say in response to these things? If God is for us, who can be against us?

Excellent site for additional Bible translations:
http://www.biblegateway.com/resources/commentaries/
Excellent resource for additional Bible study:
(Be sure to read the instructions on their page)
http://www.blueletterbible.org/commentaries/

Worry - Christian Quotes

"We imagine that a little anxiety and worry are an indication of how really wise we are; it is much more an indication of how really wicked we are. Fretting springs from a determination to get our own way. Our Lord never worried and He was never anxious, because He was not "out" to realize His own ideas; He was "out" to realize God's ideas. Fretting is wicked if you are a child of God. Have you been bolstering up that stupid soul of yours with the idea that your circumstances are too much for God? Put all "supposing" on one side and dwell in the shadow of the Almighty. Deliberately tell God that you will not fret about that thing. All our fret and worry is caused by calculating without God."
Oswald Chambers

"Worry does not empty tomorrow of its sorrow. It empties today of its strength."
Corrie Ten Boom

"I'll give you some symptoms of a sign that your faith is deteriorating—whenever you face all of your problems and you trust only your plans to get you out—it is a sign that your faith is deteriorating."
T.D. Jakes

"Knowing that God is faithful, it really helps me to not be captivated by worry. But knowing that He will do what He has said, He will cause it to happen, whatever He has promised, and then it causes me to be less involved in worrying about a situation."
Josh McDowell

"Worry is the sin of distrusting the promise and providence of God, and yet it is a sin that Christians commit perhaps more frequently than any other."
John MacArthur

"Our yesterdays present irreparable things to us; it is true that we have lost opportunities which will never return, but God can transform this destructive anxiety into a constructive thoughtfulness for the future. Let the

past sleep, but let it sleep on the bosom of Christ. Leave the Irreparable Past in His hands, and step out into the Irresistible Future with Him."
Oswald Chambers

Printed in Great Britain
by Amazon.co.uk, Ltd.,
Marston Gate.